FLY-FISHING
for
SMALLMOUTH

FLY-FISHING *for* SMALLMOUTH

Bob Clouser

with Jay Nichols

STACKPOLE
BOOKS

Published by
STACKPOLE BOOKS
5067 Ritter Road
Mechanicsburg, PA 17055
www.stackpolebooks.com

Printed in China

First edition

10 9 8 7 6 5 4 3 2

Illustrations by Dave Hall

Library of Congress Cataloging-in-Publication Data

Clouser, Bob.
    Fly-fishing for smallmouth / Bob Clouser with Jay Nichols. — 1st ed.
      p. cm.
    Includes index.
    ISBN-13: 978-0-8117-0173-0
    ISBN-10: 0-8117-0173-5
  1. Smallmouth bass fishing. I. Nichols, Jay. II. Title.

SH681.C63 2007
799.17'7388—dc22

                                 2006016356

DEDICATION

Michael Clouser, to whom this book is dedicated, loves fishing for smallmouth bass.

I dedicate this book to my family for putting up with my addiction to fishing and tying flies: my wife, Joan; my sons Michael, Bob Jr., and David; and my two wonderful daughters, Sherry and Robin. They missed a lot of Sunday drives and trips to amusement parks because of it.

I'd like to single out one son and thank him for the love he has given our family and friends. Because of his condition, my son Michael is unable to cast a fly rod. He has counted on me to take him out on the river in the jet boat, cast the fly, and hook a bass so he could then take the rod and fight and land the fish. Michael is my special buddy, and to him I dedicate this book.

CONTENTS

Acknowledgments ix

Introduction xi

CHAPTER 1   Smallmouth Bass 1

CHAPTER 2   Seasons of Smallmouth 13

CHAPTER 3   Finding Fish 29

CHAPTER 4   What They Eat 55

CHAPTER 5   My Fly Box 77

CHAPTER 6   Casting Tips 105

CHAPTER 7   Presentations 119

CHAPTER 8   Ten Tips to Catch a Trophy 151

CHAPTER 9   Equipment 169

CHAPTER 10   Bass Waters 191

Index 223

ACKNOWLEDGMENTS

I would like to thank my family and friends for all of their support and Jay Nichols for helping me complete my second book. Thanks also to Lefty Kreh for reviewing the entire manuscript and Andrew Shiels at the Pennsylvania Fish and Game Commission for reviewing chapters 1 and 2; all the great anglers who contributed their knowledge of other smallmouth waters in chapter 10—Lefty Kreh, John Randolph, Steve May and Ken Collins, Dave Duffy, Anthony Hipps, James Buice, Chuck Kraft, Mike O'Brien, Brian Shumaker, Roger Lapentor, and Tony Buzolich; and the following fine photographers for sharing their pictures of smallmouth bass and the environs in which they live—Jack Hanrahan, King Montgomery, Steve May and Ken Collins, Ross Purnell, Jay Nichols and John Randolph at *Fly Fisherman* magazine, Lefty Kreh, Mike O'Brien, John Sherman, Ralph Cutter, and Kevin McKay at www.maineflyfish.com.

INTRODUCTION

My first encounter with smallmouth bass was with my father. He would take me fishing on Swatara Creek, a tributary to the Susquehanna River near my home. My father fished with spinning, casting, and fly rods. Like many anglers of that time, you weren't *only* a fly fisherman or *just* a spin fisherman. You were simply a fisherman who wanted to catch fish.

I caught my first smallmouth when I was ten years old on a casting rod using a wooden broken-back lure, similar to a modern Rapala. I was casting the lure across the bottom side of a rock ledge on Swatara Creek when

I hooked that eleven-inch bass. I caught my first smallmouth on the fly a year and a half later along a brush pile on the same creek using my dad's bamboo fly rod and a size 8 fly made from a black chenille body with black hackle wound around the front of the body, and a red feather tail. In my younger days, this fly, along with the black fly attached to the rear of a small spinner, accounted for many enjoyable days on the creek.

One of my most vivid memories of fishing with my dad was going to a local farm and catching mice, putting them in a small wire box, and using them to catch big bass. My dad would take me out on the creek in his

Smallmouth bass are gaining in popularity as great sportfish. With relatively clean water, good habitat, and an abundance of food, smallmouth can thrive—even in urban areas. BARRY BECK

wooden boat. We would anchor the boat above a brush pile or fallen tree where he knew a few big bass were holding. He would use rubber bands to secure the hook to the mouse, then set the mouse on a piece of bark (which he would collect from fallen trees before the trip), put the bark and mouse on the water's surface, and let it drift to within six or eight inches from the front of the brush pile and then jerk the mouse off onto the water. The mouse would try to swim to the brush but was held back by the tension of the line. This commotion attracted big bass, which would attack the mouse. This technique taught me to cast poppers or other floating flies to the front or outside edges of brush jams.

Like my dad took me, I have taken all my children and my wife smallmouth fishing and have seen the smiles on their faces every time one of them would catch a fish. I remember watching my oldest son Bob Jr. catch his first bass from the Susquehanna River on a worm under a bobber when he was five years old. I watched my second son David catch his first smallmouth along with my daughters Sherry and Robin. I also have a third son Michael who is not able to master fly fishing but loves to go along, and he uses a spincast rod to catch his smallmouth. I remember all my friends—it would take a whole book just to mention their first names. And I remember my clients, who I also regard as friends, and the smiles they wore when fighting a bass.

In many ways, I think all this watching and sharing special moments with family and clients in my twenty-plus years as a fly-fishing guide for smallmouth has helped me understand the fish better. I also think by being a guide you learn more about fishing than if you just fished, because you get the chance to observe all the surroundings and activities prior to catching the bass. You also learn from other anglers by watching their techniques and methods; you build up a memory bank that tells you the right or wrong ways—the ways that are successful and the ones that aren't. The many days on the water have given me the insight into many of the questions and challenges anglers face when they first encounter a smallmouth river, and I hope this book answers some of those questions.

Over the years, I have developed a series of flies just for smallmouth. Many of my ideas for patterns come from observing smallmouth and their eating habits throughout the various months and seasons. Today some of these patterns are highly effective for many saltwater species. This is because saltwater species share many of the aggressive feeding traits of smallmouth. Like the smallmouth, they eat many sizes of baitfish and will attack a school of bait in the same voracious manner.

Smallmouth bass are gaining in popularity as great sportfish. With relatively clean water, good habitat, and an abundance of food, smallmouth can thrive—even in urban areas. They eat all types of food ranging from small insects to large baitfish and take flies aggressively and fight strongly. Best of all, smallmouth can add months of pleasure to the fly rodder's year. When trout fishing slows down as many waters reach 70 degrees, smallmouth fishing begins to really pick up since smallmouth readily chase surface flies while most trout species become sluggish in the warm water. They will feed actively in water temperatures from 55 degrees upward.

In the warmer reaches of a coldwater stream, smallmouth live side by side with trout, but they also live in the same waters as other undiscovered fly-fishing opportunities such as carp, pike, musky, pickerel, catfish, and a variety of panfish species. A day spent angling for bass can bring you many surprises! I touch on some of these other species in this book, and many smallmouth patterns will also work for them.

Because of the smallmouth's growing popularity, many books have been written on them. I hope that my book contributes to the growing body of work dedicated to this great gamefish. If you are a trout or saltwater angler, the transition to smallmouth angling is easy. I hope that this book will show you how. There are other books on smallmouth bass in general, but much of my experience is with rivers and streams, and that is what I focus on here. Once you understand some of the basic requirements of bass, which I talk about in the book, you can also use many of the flies and techniques to catch them in still waters.

When you sit down to write a book, you can't include everything, so you need to make a decision about what you want to include and what you have to leave for another book. I don't intend for this book to be a complete, comprehensive text on all aspects of fishing for smallmouth. You should also buy some good basic fly-fishing books on tackle, knots, and casting. I chose to focus on a range of techniques and tackle that are specific to bass and bass fishing, and in many instances I discuss more intermediate and advanced methods. You will find that in the casting chapter I focus on casting weighted flies and lines instead of basic casting techniques to describe the methods, flies, and techniques I use when fly-fishing for smallmouth. In the section on flies, I thought the best thing for readers interested in how Bob

Right: The Clouser Deep Minnow and all of its variations revolutionized the way I fished for smallmouth bass.
JACK HANRAHAN

The larger, weighted flies that are most effective for smallmouth require special casting and fishing techniques. JACK HANRAHAN

Clouser catches smallmouth would be to include only the flies that I use and design and carry in my fly box. Because I like to design flies to imitate local baits, most of these patterns are mine, but that does not mean that there aren't a lot of other effective bass flies out there. It's just that I feel most confident in writing only about what I use and have experience with.

Because I know that other people have different perspectives on smallmouth, and because I wanted to show that there is good bass fishing across North America, I asked some of my friends to write about their favorite smallmouth rivers. There are good bass waters in just about every state, and though I could not include them all, I hope some of these waters will attract readers' interest. These contributions are valuable not only for the waters the writers describe, but also because they provide insight on how some of the top anglers or bass guides in the country fish for this great species. And that is one of the greatest things about smallmouth—they are the most accessible and abundant gamefish in the country.

I hope readers will enjoy this book and that it, along with *Clouser's Flies* (Stackpole Books, 2006)—a collection of my patterns and how to tie them—represents my lifelong love affair with smallmouth bass. If any readers want to contact me, they can do so via my website at www.clouserflyfishing.com. I will be eager to talk with you about bass fishing, and I am also eager to hear about new bass spots.

CHAPTER 1

Smallmouth Bass

STEVE MAY

Understanding some basics about the small-mouth's natural history is an important first step in improving your ability to catch them. Such things as range, spawning behavior, and general traits of the species can provide important clues to help you become a better angler.

WHAT'S IN A NAME?

The classification of smallmouth bass has caused a lot of confusion over the years. To begin with, smallmouth bass are not really bass at all; they are members of the sunfish family, which includes pumpkinseeds, bluegills, crappies, and rock bass. Smallmouth bass belong to a genus that scientists collectively call black bass, with six species in North America: largemouth, smallmouth, spotted, Guadalupe, Suwannee, and redeye bass. The term *black bass* comes from the black coloration of the juvenile fish of these species.

To make matters even more complicated, the Latin name, *Micropterus dolomieu,* doesn't tell us much about the nature of this gamefish and, in fact, seems to be based on a damaged specimen. Dr. J. A. Henshall writes in his

Smallmouth bass have prominent red eyes with black bars radiating from them like war paint. Overlooked for many years by fly fishers more interested in trout, smallmouth bass today are recognized as strong-fighting gamefish that aggressively take flies.

1

classic 1881 *Book of the Black Bass* that in 1802, the French ichthyologist Lacepede received a fish from someone in America. A few dorsal fin rays were broken off, and it looked as if the fish had a separate small fin next to its dorsal fin. Lacepede thought this was a distinguishing feature of the species and named it *Micropterus,* which means "small fin." The species name, *dolomieu,* honors Lacepede's friend M. Dolomieu, the French mineralogist who also has a mineral—dolomite—named after him. Henshall, referring to the poorly named smallmouth, writes: "This representative American fish was first brought to the light of science in a foreign land, and under the most unfavorable auspices. Its scientific birth was . . . untimely; it was, unhappily, born a monstrosity; its baptismal names were, consequently, incongruous, and its sponsors were, most unfortunately, foreign naturalists." It seems that Henshall was upset not only that the smallmouth bass was wrongly named, but that this fish, native to the United States, was named by scientists who were not as familiar or passionate about the species as he was.

The common name bronzeback is a little more descriptive, though even this isn't entirely accurate, because the color of smallmouth bass varies with their environment and may be light to deep bronze, green, or brownish green, depending on habitat, water color, and season. When found in cool, clear waters, they can range from light yellow to a deep bronze and green. In cloudy or heavily discolored water, they take on a pale whitish green to yellow shade. Smallmouth color also varies with the habitat in which they live. Some take on a blackish green color when they are over a dark, rocky bottom, and the ones that live around grass tend to have a greenish cast. The variations in color can change throughout the year as well.

Bass from Pennsylvania's Susquehanna River. BOB CLOUSER

Bass from Ontario's Maitland River. JAY NICHOLS

Bass from Oregon's John Day River. JOHN RANDOLPH

Bass from small stream in Pennsylvania. JAY NICHOLS

Unlike their cousins the largemouth bass, smallmouth prefer rivers with higher levels of dissolved oxygen and swifter currents. Instead of slow-moving water with silty bottoms, they favor cleaner water with rocky bottoms and often share the same waters with trout, becoming more prominent as water temperatures become too warm for trout. STEVE MAY

DISTINGUISHING FEATURES

Smallmouth have a few important features that distinguish them from their cousins the largemouth bass (*Micropterus salmoides*). Generally, smallmouth prefer cooler, cleaner, and more oxygenated water than largemouth. Smallmouth are generally slimmer and do not get as big as largemouth, though pound for pound, they typically fight harder. They also often have broken dark bars running vertically down their bodies, whereas largemouth usually have a series of black or green blotches centered along the lateral line. Smallmouth also have black bands that radiate from their brilliant red eyes like war paint.

Another way to tell the difference between smallmouth and largemouth bass is the size of the mouth. When the mouth is closed, the smallmouth has a maxillary, a large flap at the end of the upper jaw, that extends to the middle of the eye, whereas the largemouth has a maxillary that extends behind the eye. In reality, a smallmouth's mouth is proportionately sized, allowing it to consume large prey items. It is the largemouth bass's mouth that is disproportionately large, which led to the use of *small* and *large* in the naming of these closely related species.

All black bass are cold-blooded, which means that their metabolism varies and their body temperature is determined by the temperature of the water surrounding them. This is an extremely important consideration when fishing for smallmouth bass, because the water temperature affects most everything they do. As the water warms, the smallmouth's metabolism increases. As it cools, it decreases. Smallmouth are most active in temperature ranges from 55 to 85 degrees Fahrenheit. Below about 50 degrees, their metabolism slows, and they don't eat as often. When the water reaches 80 degrees and above, the higher temperatures demand more frequent eating in order to supply the energy needed to survive. Some of my most productive periods for catching large bass are during midday in the month of August, when the stream feels like bathwater.

Smallmouth require relatively high levels of dissolved oxygen in the water. Studies have shown that dissolved oxygen levels below 1.5 parts per million (ppm) are lethal to smallmouth bass. For optimum health and growth, however, smallmouth need dissolved oxygen levels of around 5 to 7 ppm, particularly at summertime water temperatures. Dissolved oxygen level requirements are reduced in colder water conditions, because the fish's metabolic rate and therefore oxygen needs decrease accordingly. Because cold water holds more dissolved oxygen, bass in cold, flowing waters are rarely confronted by low-oxygen conditions. Low dissolved-oxygen levels stress smallmouth bass, and they will die if they can't find water with more oxygen. In some instances, smallmouth seek out faster-moving water, riffles, rapids, spring holes, tributaries, or turbulent water at the base of dams to find water with higher oxygen levels. In most healthy smallmouth streams, dissolved oxygen levels usually exceed these minimums, though certain events, such as algae blooms caused by pollution or extreme low water, can cause unnaturally low dissolved-oxygen levels, thereby stressing the fish and leading to fish kills.

Bass are a schooling fish, which means that where you catch one bass, you are likely to catch more. Once you locate bass, fish the area thoroughly. Bass are cannibals and the largest will always eat the smallest, so fish of similar sizes tend to school together. In many areas where bass are concentrated because of suitable habitat, anglers will encounter smallmouth from one to three years old, in some cases lots of them.

RANGE

Smallmouth bass originally lived in rivers and lakes west of the Appalachian Mountains, in a range extending from southern Quebec to northern Minnesota in the north, and from northern Georgia to eastern Oklahoma in the south. Smallmouth were widely stocked and are now found in every state except Florida, Louisiana, and Alaska. They also have been stocked in most Canadian provinces, as well as in Asia, Africa, Europe, and South America.

As with many introduced species, the distribution of smallmouth coincides with the expansion of the railroads in the late 1800s. "Fish cars," railroad cars outfitted with water tanks, carried bass and other species of fish across the country. For instance, the original brood that is now in the Potomac River basin in Maryland and the Susquehanna River in Pennsylvania came from the Ohio River via the Baltimore and Ohio railroad system. Cali-

fornia's population of smallmouth came from Lake Ontario via New York.

SIZE

Smallmouth growth rates depend on the abundance and availability of food and the length of their growing season. In some relatively infertile northern waters where food is scarce and the growing seasons are short, it can take up to four years to produce a nine-inch smallmouth; in rivers in more moderate climates with longer growing seasons, bass can grow nine inches in two years. In Pennsylvania, a sixteen-inch bass is approximately two pounds and a little over seven years old; a twenty-inch bass weighs more than four pounds and is about twelve years old. Steve May, a guide in Ontario, says that an eighteen-inch bass in the rivers up there can be over twenty years old.

The International Game Fish Association (IGFA) trophy smallmouth is eleven pounds, fifteen ounces. Smallmouth can potentially reach a maximum weight of about twelve pounds, but these fish are caught in lakes and reservoirs. River fish are smaller, and any fish from three to six pounds caught in a stream or river is a trophy. The largest fish I have seen was a twenty-three-and-a-half-inch behemoth that weighed approximately six pounds. I didn't catch it, but I knew where it lived and was proud to have guided a client to the catch. As of 2005, fly-rod world records for bass, all of them from lakes, do not exceed six pounds.

HABITAT

Bass live in a variety of habitats, including lakes and reservoirs, small streams, and large rivers. Though this book is about fly-fishing for smallmouth bass in rivers, great smallmouth fishing can be had in lakes and reservoirs across the country, and many of the tactics that I discuss in this book can be applied to those fisheries.

River smallmouth prefer water flowing over gravel, boulders, and broken bedrock. In rivers, water temperature usually determines where bass are found. At water

Railroad cars outfitted with water tanks, called "fish cars," transported many species of fish across the country, including smallmouth bass.
PENNSYLVANIA FISH AND BOAT
COMMISSION

FOR THE RECORD

On July 8, 1955, David Hayes, from Litchfield, Kentucky, caught a behemoth bass in Dale Hollow Lake on the Tennessee-Kentucky border and took his catch to a marina, where it weighed in at eleven pounds, fifteen ounces, and measured twenty-seven inches long. The fish had a twenty-one-and-two-thirds-inch girth. Hayes entered the fish with *Field & Stream* magazine, which, at the time, kept the freshwater records. *Field & Stream* awarded Hayes's fish a record for the heaviest smallmouth bass ever taken on rod and reel, and in 1978, when the IGFA took over freshwater record keeping from *Field & Stream,* it was then granted a world all-tackle record.

But on August 17, 1955, unknown to *Field & Stream* or the IGFA, Raymond Barlow submitted an affidavit to the U.S. Army Corps of Engineers stating that Hayes's fish had weighed only eight pounds, fifteen ounces, and that Hayes had stuffed three pounds of metal in the fish's mouth and stomach to make it a record. It wasn't until forty years later, when the affidavit was uncovered, that the IGFA was contacted and informed about the sworn statement.

After reviewing the affidavit in 1996, the IGFA rescinded Hayes's record, and a ten-pound, fourteen-ounce smallmouth caught by John Gorman in 1969, also on Dale Hollow Lake, was recognized as the new all-tackle record. However, recent documentation, including polygraph results, was supplied to the IGFA indicating that David Hayes's fish was never tampered with. Further investigation also found that the dimensions of Hayes's fish would make it very

David Hayes holds the IGFA all-tackle record smallmouth bass he caught in Dale Hollow Lake on the Tennessee-Kentucky line on July 8, 1955.
INTERNATIONAL GAME FISH ASSOCIATION

unlikely to have weighed just eight pounds, fifteen ounces when compared with Gorman's all-tackle fish, which was twenty-six and a quarter inches in length and twenty-one and a half inches in girth. Based on this information, the IGFA decided to reinstate David Hayes's catch as the all-tackle smallmouth bass record, returning him to his rightful place in the IGFA world records.

temperatures below 55 degrees, smallmouth are found in depths of four feet or more, usually around structure that blocks the flow of water. At water temperatures above 55 degrees, smallmouth prefer shallow areas over gravel bars, along shorelines, in grass beds, and in other habitat with structure. One foot of water is sufficient at summer temperatures if the habitat is suitable for bass.

Many small streams hold resident populations of bass as well as migratory populations of spawning bass that enter small streams that are tributaries of larger rivers. Small streams are often less crowded by anglers than lakes and reservoirs and even larger rivers. They hold less

fish but nonetheless offer good angling possibilities in relative solitude. Look for bass holding below tributaries, in deep pools, and sometimes even in the shallower riffle sections, especially during low-light conditions. Small streams can be hot spots in the spring for prespawn and spawning bass. Also, small streams typically warm more quickly than larger streams, allowing anglers to find active bass earlier in the season.

SPAWNING BEHAVIOR

In the spring, increasing daylight hours and water temperatures in the high fifties and low sixties cause sexually

Oregon's John Day River flows through colorful canyons, broad valleys, and dramatic scenery. Bass, introduced here in the 1970s, have flourished and grow large on the river's abundant food. JOHN RANDOLPH

Pennsylvania's Susquehanna River is one of the best rivers in the East for smallmouth bass. PHILIP HANYOK

Left: Ontario's Maitland River provides the chance to sight-fish for trophy bass in clear water. ROSS PURNELL

Below: Floating some bass rivers in the East, such as the Potomac River, provides opportunities to get away from crowds and, when the fishing is on, catch fish on almost every cast. KING MONTGOMERY

Below: The farther south you travel, the longer the bass growing season. A state like Virginia is blessed with many fine big-bass waters, including the New and the James. BOB CLOUSER

mature smallmouth to move into the tributaries of large rivers and lakes to spawn. If the habitat is suitable, some smallmouth spawn in the same river in which they spend the rest of the year. Throughout the country, smallmouth bass spawn from early spring through mid-summer, depending on when water temperatures reach the magic range of 58 to 72 degrees. In the Susquehanna River near Harrisburg, Pennsylvania, spawning activity begins in mid-April, peaks in May, and continues through June. To the north, bass tend to spawn later, and to the south, they spawn earlier. Even though broad generalizations can be made regarding spawning periods related to latitude, water temperature plays a prominent role and ultimately determines when spawning occurs, regardless of geography.

Because spawning is dependent on water temperatures, not all smallmouth spawn at the same time in a given area. Water temperatures can vary widely within the same river, and bass may be at different stages of the spawn in different sections of the river only a mile or so apart. A variety of factors influence water temperatures, such as warmer or cooler flows from tributary streams, water depth, shade, wind, and orientation to the sun. Also, spawning can occur at different times from year to year. If the spring is warmer or the water is lower than average, spawning can occur earlier than if the weather were colder than is typical. Therefore, it is difficult to predict a precise time when spawning will occur each year. My best advice is to familiarize yourself with the waters you fish by observing fish behavior and water temperatures, keep good notes, and carefully observe weather trends.

Bass seek protected areas, such as behind rocks or downstream of gravel bars, to spawn. To prepare the spawning bed, the male bass fans out silt to clear the rocks. You can easily spot these nests in clear water. JAY NICHOLS

Smallmouth prefer to spawn near structure that shelters their nests from strong currents and provides protection from predators that try to feed on the fry, such as in or at the lower end of an underwater grass bed. The grass blocks much of the current's flow but allows enough to provide the oxygen necessary to keep the eggs alive. The grass also creates a place for newly hatched fry to hide from predators. Other good spawning sites are downstream from or under sunken trees or logs or behind rocks or rock ledges. I have also seen nesting smallmouth along shorelines in slow-moving pockets and eddies and in side channels.

Smallmouth usually build their nests, or redds, on sand, gravel, or fine rubble in one- to three-foot-deep water, though they will nest in deeper water. I have seen smallmouth on nests in clear-water lakes in depths of ten feet or more. Nest depth is often related to water clarity. In general, the clearer the water, the deeper the fish can nest. Bass tend to avoid mud and silty conditions, because such areas do not have strong enough current flow, but they have been known to spawn in these areas when optimum conditions are not available.

Rock bass and sunfish build similar nests and spawn in the same way by depositing eggs over clean gravel. An adult of the species protects the nest from predators. The size of the nest depends on the size of the fish building it. Smallmouth generally build nests away from other nesting smallmouth, but panfish are more communal and sometimes build nests so close together that the outer ring of one nest touches the outer ring of another.

As soon as water temperatures stabilize in the spring between 55 and 60 degrees, male smallmouth begin building nests. The male uses his tail to fan out a large, circular depression about twice his body length (nest diameters vary from fifteen to more than twenty inches) and from two to four inches deep. A male nests in the same area each year as long as conditions remain the same, and he sometimes uses the same nest. He fans out the fine gravel with his tail and roots out any small rocks with his nose. When he is done, the clean rocks in the center of the nest are ready for the female's eggs, which will adhere to them after being fertilized.

Females approach the nesting areas a few days later. When the male spots a female, he attempts to drive her to the nest, and if she is ready, she comes to the nest. When the fish spawn—when the water is between approximately 60 and 70 degrees—they lay side by side, both facing the same direction. When the female tips on her side to lay her eggs, the male releases his milt. The female deposits only a portion of her eggs at one time. She may return to deposit more eggs in the same nest or move to another nest and another male and repeat the

In low, clear water, large bass are harder to fool than small ones. You must learn to cast long distances and approach fish without spooking them. Wearing drab clothing helps you blend into your environment. JAY NICHOLS

procedure. As many as three different females may spawn in the same nest.

The female leaves the nest after spawning, but the male remains, fanning the eggs to prevent silt from depositing on them, remove metabolic wastes, and increase the levels of dissolved oxygen. He also guards the nest against any predators, such as suckers, sunfish, rock bass, yellow perch, catfish, carp, turtles, or crayfish. He is aggressive and will attack fish larger than himself. The time it takes for the eggs to hatch depends on water temperature, ranging from a few days to more than a week.

The male guards the hatched eggs, called fry, on the nest for about a week. The fry are jet black for several weeks, then turn green, bronze, or brown. At this early stage, all species of bass are black, hence the term "black bass." The young have tail fins with a yellowish orange base, black center, and white tip.

Fry face many challenges and survival is generally low. Not only do smallmouth eat their own offspring, but baby bass are also consumed by other fish species, birds, frogs, snakes, and land animals that frequent the water for food.

Young-of-the-year and yearling smallmouth often hug the shorelines for safety and food. Shallow, near-shore areas typically have higher water temperatures, greater light penetration, and consequently more plankton than deeper areas. Also, submerged and emergent aquatic vegetation found along shorelines provides cover where young bass can escape and hide from predators. Smallmouth bass fry at the earliest ages consume various aquatic insect larvae, rotifers, and zooplankton such as daphnia, copepods, and other microscopic items. As they grow to fingerling size, two to six inches, the bulk of their diet consists of juvenile crayfish, mayflies, caddisflies, other aquatic invertebrates, and young-of-the-year baitfish. Simply put, anything smaller than the baby bass is fair game. I have often seen schools of similar-size fingerling bass herding small schools of juvenile baitfish in the shallows.

After the bass spawn and the fry leave the nest, the adult bass spend up to a week or two recovering from their spawning activities. At this time, fishing is often subpar, but because bass begin and end spawning at different times, you can always find fish that are past this recovery stage.

SENSES

Bass have lateral lines that run from head to tail. These lines, each of which is actually a series of pores, can transmit vibrations or waves from the water to the bass's

HANDLING FISH

Catch-and-release fishing is an important part of fly fishing. Though smallmouth caught in clean lakes and rivers can be excellent table fare, large fish should be released to be caught another day. Fish over sixteen inches have survived a lot to have grown to that size, and they are worth saving to be caught again.

Fortunately, many bass fly fishers have already learned how to properly handle trout. Though small-mouth are hardier than trout, you should still exercise similar care when handling bass. With barbless hooks, it is usually fairly simple to release the bass without taking the fish from the water by grabbing the hook and twisting it out. If you hook a bass deeply, it is often better to cut the tippet and leave the hook in the fish than it is to try to remove the hook with pliers. Avoid excessive contact with the bass's skin, because you can wipe

Take a picture, not a fish, to preserve memories of your catch. Lefty Kreh takes a quick shot of Bob Clouser with a nice bass.
JACK HANRAHAN

Often it's not necessary to take the fish out of the water to release it or for a photo. When releasing a fish, take the time to revive it by holding it in the water until it starts to swim away on its own. JAY NICHOLS

off the outer layer of mucus that protects the bass from waterborne bacteria and fungus. I have found, especially when landing large bass, that aggressive handling only encourages aggressive struggling from the bass. I prefer to slide my hand under the bass and slowly lift it so it lies on its side on the palm of my hand. The large bass will lie there without struggling.

Many anglers now prefer to take pictures of their catches instead of taking the fish home, but it's important to take care of the bass when you are posing with it. When picking up the bass for a picture, it's okay to hold it by the lip, but keep the fish vertical, or if lifting it into a horizontal position, support the rest of the fish so you don't damage the bass's mouth. Many times, it's better just to take the picture with the fish half out of the water. If you are alone and you want a

picture of the bass you just caught, don't drag it up on the rocks for a photograph; leave it in the water. Likewise, when bringing a bass to the boat, don't let it flop around on the bottom of the boat; leave it in the water or a net in the water for your picture. Nets constructed of rubber or soft knitted mesh are less harmful to fish than hard nylon, knotted strand nets.

When releasing the bass, take the time to revive it. Give it extra time if you played it for a long time or it appears injured. Cradling its body, hold the bass facing into a slow or moderate current so oxygenated water can flow over its gills. Keep the fish out of fast current until it is strong enough to swim away on its own accord. As water temperatures increase, the longer you take to play the fish, and the more you stress it. Use tackle stout enough to land a fish quickly.

brain. No one knows exactly how much information bass receive from their lateral lines, but they are sensitive to vibrations in the water—everything from waves created by a carelessly wading angler to the movements of a small baitfish—and can use that information to discern whether those vibrations are coming from a prey item or something else. The ability of bass to detect subtle vibrations in the water is one of the primary reasons that fishing at night with surface lures is so effective.

Though I don't know about fish intelligence, or even if there is such a thing, I do know that bass learn. In my experience, older bass are typically more wary. In my home waters, the big bass are the first to move to the spawning grounds and take charge of prime spawning spots. They also know the location of the prime holding spots in the river and take over these areas.

Large bass are much harder to catch in clear water than their smaller counterparts. I have watched big bass scurry for cover long before smaller bass in the same area took flight. I have also noticed that big bass are much harder to catch on the same fly the second time I fish over their territory. I am most successful when I change the color, size, and shape of a fly pattern.

I can remember each of the smallmouth over five pounds I caught on a fly. One in particular stands out. This bass selected a long, deep trench with two large, submerged boulders in it. When water conditions were clear enough to see the tops of the boulders, which were four feet under the surface, the bass would hold and feed on top of the first boulder. The first time I caught him was on a size 4 chartreuse-and-white Clouser Minnow. I waited for a week and then went back to see if I could catch him again. From seventy feet away, I could see his black form on top of the same rock. As the boat drifted into casting position, I cast a Clouser Minnow at him, but he refused to hit it. I thought it would be worth another try, so I repeated the same drift and presentation. This time the big smallmouth just slid off the rock and disappeared to the bottom.

I knew he was feeding because of where he was holding. I tried this area for two more days, and the same thing always happened. The bass would just disappear into the depths. I knew I had to do something different to entice him to eat one of my flies. I rested the area for another week and then tried a size 1/0 white Lefty's Bug tied to a 10-pound-test tippet. I also changed my approach by drifting the boat past the holding area from the opposite side of the boulder.

I could see the big smallmouth holding on top of the same rock as I approached. As the boat drifted into position, I cast the big Lefty's Bug. It settled on the water four feet in front of the fish, and I watched with excitement as the bass slowly and deliberately rose to inhale the bug without caution. I remember feeling guilty but happy to have fooled that big rascal a second time. I never saw the bass again and always thought that he left the area to find a new hideout because of my intrusions. That is the kind of intelligence I think bass have.

CHAPTER 2

Seasons of Smallmouth

Smallmouth behavior is controlled by water temperature, food, protection, and the urge to spawn. Understanding these things and how they are interconnected will help you be more successful when fishing for bass throughout the seasons.

In search of preferred water temperatures, safety, food, or good spawning sites, smallmouth move throughout a stream during the year and head to fairly dependable places. During the summer and early fall, bass, especially large ones, like to stay in one place. During their fall migration to winter holding areas and their spring migration to suitable spawning sites, bass tagged by biologists have been recorded swimming more than fifty miles. Smallmouth also move to adapt to streamflow and to short-term condition changes such as flooding or murky water. For example, smallmouth move from backwaters during high-volume water flows to riffles as the currents decrease. Though no two streams are the same—or no two bass, for that matter—following are some generalizations about bass behavior through the seasons.

On many streams across the country, smallmouth bass and trout rise to the same spring hatches.

One of the best times to target large bass is in the spring before they spawn. ROSS PURNELL

SPRING

Spring is a time of growth on streams across the country, and smallmouth that have hunkered down through the winter are awakening with the warmer water temperatures and beginning to feed and preparing to spawn. Smallmouth, lying low in their winter holding areas—deep water, eddies with slower currents, spring holes, warmwater inflows—prepare to spawn by feeding to store up energy for the rigors of nest building and defense that are to come. By the time water temperatures reach the upper forties, bass begin actively feeding. In central Pennsylvania, this happens in late March through mid-April. Though the main river current may not be in this temperature range, certain areas may be warmer. Good places to find warm water in the winter and early spring are warmwater inflows from power plants, tributaries, and springs; dark bottoms that absorb light and heat up the water; and shallow areas that warm quicker than other deeper areas.

Trout anglers have long had a rule that the best time of day to fish is the time of day that is most comfortable for them to do so, and this is partly true for smallmouth anglers, especially at this time of the year. In the early spring, there is generally no need to start fishing until the afternoon, after the sun has had a chance to warm up the water a bit. Even an increase of water temperature by a few degrees can trigger more feeding activity—and better fishing. As a general rule, the warmest parts of the day will be the most productive—and the most pleasurable—for you.

Before spawning, bass feed heavily and are likely to take your fly if it is presented properly. Though the increasing water temperatures are enough to trigger the fish to feed, they are still below the bass's optimal temperature range, so the fish may not be super aggressive. Once you find the fish, try to swim your fly as close as possible to them. At this time of year, sluggish fish may not chase a streamer. One of the most effective methods is to slowly dead drift a Clouser Deep Minnow or other heavily weighted streamer along the bottom of the river. Experiment to see whether the fish prefer a dead drift or a more active, stripped presentation.

The light-colored Silver Shiner, Gizzard Shad, all-white, and River Shiner Clouser Deep Minnows work best for me at this time of year, because minnows provide the bulk of the bass's food. I use minnows with a 1/24-ounce metallic eye for fast currents. Most often when dead drifting the fly, I use a floating line, but sinking-tip lines can be effective at times. Whatever tackle you use, it is important that you are fishing your fly in front of the fish. If they are holding in deep water or are right on the bottom, you must find a way to get your fly down. It is because of this that during the early spring, before the bass begin to spawn and the water temperatures reach about 60 degrees, anglers fishing with spinning and casting rods have an advantage. You can catch fish with a fly rod and flies, but do not expect a lot of them.

Dead-drifted nymphs also catch bass in the spring. Many anglers have success with dark Woolly Buggers and other buggy patterns, especially where there are good populations of hellgrammites or stoneflies. Because bass sometimes won't move far to take a dead-drifted fly, you may have to make many presentations in order to get the right drift that will catch a bass. Fish slower-moving, deep pools thoroughly and methodically, focusing on any visible current seams or foam lines.

Early-spring conditions can also coincide with run-off and high, muddy water. Though I often take advantage of this time to prepare my flies and get all my gear in order, you can be successful this time of the year fishing sinking-tip lines and large, dark-colored flies that have a strong profile even in muddy water or bright Cactus Chenille or Estaz-type flies like Lefty Kreh's Cactus Minnow, or chartreuse-and-yellow Clouser Minnows. Other tactics for high water include fishing close to shore where the current is slower or in riffles.

One of the best tactics for high water is to fish smaller, clearer tributaries. Feeder creeks and streams are usually the first to clear in a watershed, and some clear

Right: Just before spawning, bass feed heavily to prepare for the rigors of nest building, protecting the young, and laying eggs. This time can provide an excellent opportunity to catch large bass during bluebird days. KEN COLLINS

The best time to fish in the spring is after the sun has had a chance to warm the water up. Even a change of a few degrees can get the bass moving. In this shot, the sun on the rocks heated the extremely shallow water above the ledge, and the water in the pool below the ledge—chock full of bass—warmed dramatically throughout the day, turning on the fishing. JAY NICHOLS

In the early season, water levels are often high, and you may need to use lead-core or other sinking lines, split shot, and weighted flies to get down to the bottom. JAY NICHOLS

more quickly than others. Look for spring-fed waters or streams in forested terrain or with rocky bottoms and shorelines to clear faster than streams with muddy bottoms. It's nice to know which tributaries clear the quickest so you can always have a backup plan. Also, sometimes the water in the main river downstream from the tributary is clearer than other water in the river and becomes a magnet for feeding bass. These tactics apply when there is high and off-colored water at any time of the year.

As soon as the water temperatures stabilize in the mid-fifties, bass begin building their nests to prepare for spawning. Ideal spawning sites are areas with reduced current flow at the downstream end of rocks, submerged grass beds, or any other structure that meets these criteria. I have seen smallmouth nesting inside grass beds

covered with water. They clean off all the silt from the river bottom, exposing a clean, circular depression one to two times as long as their bodies. These depressions are visible in clear water.

Spawning bass are easy targets in clear water—in more ways than one. Though they do not eat while they are on the nest, they become extremely protective and act aggressively toward anything that comes near it, including flies on and below the surface. While on the nest, they will pick up a fly or anything else that settles on the bottom of the nest, carry it away, and spit it out. Many anglers think that fishing for bass at this time is unethical, but if you choose to fish for them, leave your fly on the nest—in or on top of the water—until the bass grabs it. It is not necessary to impart action to the fly. The fact that it is there is enough to suggest to the bass that something is threatening its territory or young. Because a bass will spit out something that it picks up on its nest, you should set the hook as soon as the fish grabs the fly.

Though bass will return to their nests after being hooked, I don't think fishing for them at this time is a good idea, as it is a stressful period for them to begin with. Catching a smallmouth on a nest and removing it leaves the nest open to predation from nest raiders such as rock bass, sunfish, and crayfish. Research in Canada has shown that nest predation is directly related to the amount of time the guarding male is away from the nest, and once nest predators see that he is absent, they rush in to consume eggs or fry.

The male bass protect their nests at all costs. In many cases, they are so physically stressed after the eggs hatch into fry and leave the nest that they will sulk for a week or two until they gain their strength back. I have seen postspawn bass that were so beat up from nest protection that their mouths and parts of their body showed visible sores, tears, and other skin mutilation. Recovering bass generally do not strike flies.

Spawning is tough on bass—both the adults and the young, which are susceptible not only to predation, but also to abrupt changes in weather. Water temperatures changing abruptly from warm to cold can kill fry. Likewise, when a severe cold front moves through while adult bass are spawning in the shallows, additional stress caused by rapidly changing water temperatures can lead to fish kills usually resulting from secondary fungal

Males protecting their nests are easy targets. Though many anglers catch their largest fish at this time, I prefer not to fish for spawning bass. It is not much of a challenge, and the bass are already stressed.

infections. Also, rising water levels that increase the amount of water flowing over the nest make the bass work harder to remove silt from the nest.

Because of these forces, some years are better than others for spawning. Research shows that smallmouth bass reproductive success is greatest during years with lower-than-average flows and stable, higher-than-average water temperatures during the spawning period. Conversely, high-flow years with persistent high river levels decrease smallmouth spawning success.

Smallmouth often spawn in two to five feet of water behind rocks, stumps, or other obstructions. In the spring, males fan silt and debris from the stream bottom, forming saucer-shaped nests about twice the length of their bodies.

SUMMER

I usually begin my guiding season for bass immediately after the postspawn doldrums, which often coincides with July 1 on the rivers I fish. Generally, by this time of the year, the water has dropped and cleared, exposing the structure and making the water easier to read. Water temperatures are in the mid-sixties to high seventies, and the fish are aggressive and looking for food. Because their metabolism is regulated by water temperatures, large bass need to feed frequently in the summer, making it my favorite time to catch bass.

A July 1 start date also happens to coincide with the unofficial end of trout season on eastern freestone streams. By this time, most of the great early-season hatches are over, and the water is getting a little too warm to fish for trout without stressing them. Smallmouth bass, however, are in their prime at this time of the year.

Though bass can tolerate warm water—even thrive in it—most of the prey they feed on prefer cooler temperatures. To find feeding bass, locate cooler water spots such as springs, riffles, shaded areas, and where tributaries enter the main river. Tributary mouths often provide cooler water temperatures, increased oxygen, and food, though some can become almost dry in the summer, especially during drought periods, and thus will not attract smallmouth.

In the spring, you can wait until the water warms up after lunch to begin fishing, but during the warm days of

Many feel that bass fishing is at its best in the summer. Warm water temperatures mean wet wading and aggressive fish.
KING MONTGOMERY

Early mornings are often ideal times to fish in the summer, because bass are less wary in low light. Being on the water before other anglers also gives you a shot at fish that have been rested. JACK HANRAHAN

summer, it's wiser to be on the water early or plan to stay late. One of the great things about bass is that you can catch them all day long under all but the most extreme summer conditions, but many of the summer insects hatch at or near dark. Being on the water early, before boats and other anglers disturb fish, is an advantage. Not only are there strategic reasons for getting on the water early, it's also one of the most pleasant parts of the day for fishing in the summer heat.

As the water clears and drops, far-and-fine techniques become critical. You must make long casts to skittish fish that can be alerted to your presence a long way off by shadows, waves, noise, and sloppy casts. See chapter 7 for more information on stealth and sight-fishing techniques, which become critical in the low, clear water of late summer and fall. Low water usually concentrates smallmouth in the deep areas surrounded by shallows.

Left: The warmer water temperatures in the summer mean that big bass have to feed more frequently, even on bright, sunny days. KEN COLLINS

Although smallmouth will feed in the deeper pools, they prowl the shallows in the early morning and evening, on cloudy days, and after nightfall.

Though I still fish subsurface patterns for large bass during the summer, it is an excellent time to use top-water lures such as poppers, Floating Minnows, and other, similar patterns. I like to take advantage of the fact that in the summer, lots of food is found on the surface, ranging from dragonflies and damselflies to small minnows feeding on the many aquatic insect hatches. The whitefly hatch on many eastern rivers often brings out rising fish in good numbers, and you can follow the progression of the hatch upstream to get first-rate dry-fly fishing for the host of species that frequently live in smallmouth rivers. On my home river, we have good populations of catfish and carp that feed on the surface during these dense hatches.

Summer is a time when the fishing is so good that it can be hard to leave the river once it gets dark, because you can still hear fish rising around you late into the night. When you fish the surface at night, large deer-hair bugs or mice that move a lot of water work well as long as you can produce a continuous wake. Fishing a popping bug at night works best if you keep popping the fly steadily during the retrieve. The pop-and-stop method I describe in chapter 7 is not very productive at night unless a bright moon is illuminating the surface. The moonlight silhouettes the fly against the sky, allowing the fish to see their potential prey. On dark nights, you must keep the bug constantly popping so the bass can hunt the sounds and vibration. I have caught large bass

after dark by fishing over shallow water that flows over gravel beds. Cast across current and allow the fly to drag or swing with the current. When the fly gets below you, make a steady, slow retrieve forming a V-wake off each side of the fly. This V-wake disturbs the surface of the water and suggests life.

Even through the dog days, bass continue to bite. In August on many streams in the country, rivers can feel like bathwater, but large fish will feed. In fact, I have found that the large fish feed more through the day in August than they do at night, but smaller bass typically feed more during the evenings. I'm not exactly sure why this is, but I suspect it has something to do with a big bass's metabolism.

Look for rock formations, islands, and weed beds surrounded by or near water depths of three feet or more. Smallmouth use the deeper water for protection from the glaring rays of the sun, and as the need to eat increases, they move to areas of heavy structure, usually in shallow water, where they can feed on minnows, crayfish, and other food items necessary for their survival.

Smallmouth bass have no eyelids, nor do their pupils dilate for protection from indirect or direct rays of the sun. Alert anglers use this trait and adjust their fishing

In the summer, the water drops and clears. While this makes finding fish easier, it also makes it easier for them to spot you. Lefty Kreh stays low sight-casting to shallow-water smallmouth in July. BOB CLOUSER

During summer, the fishing can be so good it's hard to leave the river once it gets dark, because you can still hear fish rising around you late into the night. If boating after dark, be familiar with the water and follow all safety precautions. If wading, you should also know the water and carry a light. LEFTY KREH

Right: To help fish find the fly as the light gets low, I switch to poppers that make commotion on the water's surface or use large, dark streamers that have a good silhouette underwater.
JAY NICHOLS

Left: Because of the heat, many insects hatch at or near dark during the summer. Under the cover of night, bass feed on these insects with reckless abandon. Lefty Kreh holds a ball of whitefly spinners during a dense hatch. BOB CLOUSER

In the low, clear water of summer, look for fish around islands, gravel beds, and rocks. JAY NICHOLS

techniques accordingly on bright, sunny days. The sun's position during August, especially at high noon, does not cause any glare on the water surface if a river flows from west to east. I often wonder why bass will feed during certain time periods at one depth and other times at another. It might be possible that the sun glaring in their eyes at certain times can affect their ability to see or focus on objects at different levels in the water. Bass will feed most of the time while in shade-covered areas, but in sunlit areas they will not feed at times.

For a longer productive evening of fishing, select a bend of the river with the shoreline or a mountainside protecting the western shore. This location will have shade over the water early, while the eastern shore is still exposed to the glaring light conditions. Selecting an area with these conditions and using the outward-moving shade line should give you more productive fish-catching time than fishing a brightly lit area.

In summer, I also like to sight-fish for carp on the flats or along muddy shorelines and shallow gravel bars. When I get a client who can cast well and wants to try to catch a carp, we look for fish rooting in the mud in the shallows and wait until the fish is feeding head-down before casting the fly. We observe the fish to get a sense of the direction in which it is feeding, and then try to cast in front of the fish so that it sees the fly. To know when to strike, watch the carp. When you see its yellow-ish orange mouth open, it looks like somebody turned on a lightbulb. When that light goes out, tighten up your line. Some of my most effective carp flies are Clouser Swimming Nymphs, Clouser Crayfish, Foxee Redd Minnows, and dark, weighted Woolly Buggers.

Right: Carp eat a variety of foods, including crayfish, minnows, and aquatic insects. My best carp flies are (from bottom to top) the Clouser Crayfish, Foxee Redd Minnow, and Swimming Nymph.

Weather fronts and runoff from thunderstorms can also affect late-summer angling. If you are on the water during an approaching storm, you should leave the water and seek shelter. After a storm has passed, smallmouth typically go on a feeding frenzy. Large, wide rivers with ever-changing currents are not usually affected by short-term storm runoff. Some areas below tributaries or sections of main current flow may get muddy, but you can fish the edges where the dirty and clear water mix.

Algae is another summer problem on many smallmouth streams across the country. Algae forms with the right combination of water temperatures, sunlight, and nutrients present in the water. As summer temperatures warm the water to above the mid-seventies, the combination of warm water and nutrients cause the algae to bloom. A lot of algae can decrease the amount of oxygen available to bass, causing stress and affecting their feeding schedules and activity. It also reduces water clarity. Algae can be so thick that you can't see the bottom in ten inches of water. When this occurs, look for faster water, such as riffles or structure that water flows over, increasing its speed and turbulence. Usually these areas have better water clarity and higher levels of dissolved oxygen. I have found that smallmouth there are more active than those that inhabit the slower water. Anglers that fish these faster flows usually catch more fish, as the bass not only are more active, but also less wary in the broken water.

Sight-casting to carp in low, clear water demands accuracy, good casting skills, and patience. MIKE O'BRIEN

JAY NICHOLS

In fall, the forests are alive with color, the bass are on the bite, and generally fewer anglers are around. JAY NICHOLS

FALL

If I had a choice of two months that would make a year, I would choose September and October. These are the months of beauty—the colors of a forest, the cooler air and water temperatures, and a strong smallmouth that pushes holes in the water's surface the size of a five-gallon bucket as it attempts to shake a fly from its jaw.

In the fall, big smallmouth are at peak strength. Bass must eat a lot of food at this time of year to maintain their strength and store enough energy to last through winter. Fortunately for the bass, most young fish species born in the spring of that year, including baby small-mouth, have grown larger and reached lengths of three to six inches. These hungry bass find large flies like Lefty's Deceivers and Clouser Half and Halfs hard to resist.

Large Half and Halfs and Clouser Deep Minnows are my flies of choice for large autumn bass. JACK HANRAHAN

Though I love summer's exciting topwater action and the challenge of long casts to fish I've spotted, it's the fall fishing that I consider the best, partly because of the pleasant temperatures and scenery, but also because the bass are more aggressive as they feed heavily to prepare for winter. As summer temperatures slowly give way to the coolness of September, changes occur that affect the habits of the smallmouth bass, such as the position of the sun and the slowly falling temperatures of the water.

The rays of the sun now become less direct on the water's surface, giving smallmouth longer periods during the daylight hours to spot their prey. Another factor that combines with the lessening effects of glaring light is the first noticeable drop in the water temperature, which affects the bass's metabolism. As water temperatures fall between 65 and 52 degrees, smallmouth become aggressive and eager to chase a fast-moving streamer fly. Also at this time, they will come a long distance to strike a noisy, rapidly moving surface bug.

In early fall, mayflies still hatch throughout the day on many streams, drawing the smaller species of all types of fish to feed on the surface. Also in fall, ants migrate in the eastern United States and sometimes fall into the water on this long journey, causing a feeding frenzy. Using flies that imitate the many smaller species of fish feeding on the ants improves your chances of catching bigger smallmouth.

September can have many changes in its weather. Don't miss the opportunity to be on the water when an approaching weather front brings cloudy and light drizzly conditions. This type of weather usually makes for a calm, windless day, ideal conditions for fishing. With no bright sunlight affecting their sight and no shadows to warn them of you, smallmouth usually take well-presented flies with abandon.

When water temperatures fall into the mid-sixties and mid-fifties, smallmouth are in shallow water, and they become active and feed for long periods. Bass fishing at this time usually offers the best chance to catch large, three- to five-pounders. Bass now prowl the locations that attract their prey, which are also affected by the falling water temperatures. Minnows and crayfish seek out shallow areas such as sun-warmed water near rocky gravel bars, edges of willow grass beds, and fast-flowing riffles. Smallmouth actively chase bait and will sometimes move ten feet to grab a lure. Cast lures to the edges of shallow bars using a steady to fast retrieve with long, steady strips, about two and a half to three feet per pull. Concentrations of food and smallmouth in the shallows are an exciting combination. Through fall,

Fall bass feed heavily to prepare for winter and take large streamers and poppers. Because fall fishing can coincide with hunting season, take precautions such as wearing orange when you go fishing. BOB CLOUSER

bass continue to hit surface flies that represent crippled minnows and unfortunate insects fluttering on the surface.

Fall for many anglers is an exciting time to be on the river, but weather conditions can change quickly, so it's important to be prepared for the worst toward the end of the season, especially if planning a float trip or a long day on the river. Be sure to take clothing with you for both warm and cold weather conditions, as changing weather can cause a 25-degree temperature drop in less than a few hours. Along with falling air temperatures usually come heavy winds that can wreak havoc for small boats. Preplanning any trip with safety in mind usually results in an enjoyable experience.

LATE FALL AND WINTER

The feeding habits of bass change quickly as the water temperature falls to the lower fifties and forties. This drop causes the fish to move to water deeper than four feet with large, broken rock rubble and moderate current flow. As the fish's metabolism slows, so do its feeding methods. It doesn't have the energy to chase down fast-swimming minnows and instead opts for slower-moving prey.

Large bass, especially females, feed throughout the winter, even if the water temperatures are near freezing. It's possible that a reason for this coldwater feeding is to ensure that enough energy is stored for the growth of the egg mass the female will carry until the following spring. But because the metabolism of bass slows down so much in the cold water, they have to feed a lot less frequently in the winter than in the summer.

When fishing for bass in these low water temperatures, I like to use flies from 1 ¾ to 4 inches in length.

In the southern part of the bass's range, late-winter weather conditions can be very comfortable. You won't catch as many bass in the cold water, but it's a great way to cure cabin fever.
KING MONTGOMERY

Flies that match minnows or crayfish should be fished slow with a bottom-bouncing retrieve, slow swing, or strip retrieve. To get them down, use heavily weighted flies and sinking-tip lines if necessary with streamers, and use long leaders with strike indicators for crayfish fished dead drift. Because the fish are not as aggressive at this time of the year, their takes can be subtle and may go undetected if you are not paying attention. Watch your line where it enters the water, and set the hook at the slightest tap or movement. As with early-spring fishing, your chances of catching great numbers of bass now are slim, and if I had to catch bass at this time of year, using a fly rod would not be my first choice. It can be done, however, especially in the more southern part of their range.

Though smallmouth are sluggish in winter's cold water, certain areas of the stream may be warmer and provide prime places for bass to feed—even in the dead of winter—and changes in water temperature by even a few degrees can turn the fishing on. In addition to the deep pools, just as in the early spring, some good places to know about on your local water include warmwater inflows from power plants, bridge pilings, shallow water in the tailouts of pools, springs, dark-

When the weather cooperates, fishing in late fall, winter, or early spring can be a great way to find solitude—and hungry fish—on the water. At this time of year, it's important to slow your fly down, because the fish won't move far to take it. KING MONTGOMERY

bottomed stretches that warm quickly in the sun, even culverts draining surface water from the roads that has heated in the sun.

Once you become familiar with the winter environment on your stream, you may be surprised at how much activity takes place. In the area where I guide and fish, a warmwater outlet from a power plant enters the river. I have taken water temperatures at that location reading 110 degrees. Despite this hot water, all sizes of smallmouth feed on the bait that abound in it. Water downstream of the inflow is warmed to varying degrees and can be in the mid-sixties in the winter.

Fishing is a great way to break up a long winter, but it pays to have some common sense. If the weather is so cold that your guides are constantly freezing up, chances are that the water is too cold for decent fly fishing, and

in many instances spinning or conventional tackle would be a better choice. If you are a die-hard fly fisher, your time is probably better spent at home, maintaining and organizing your gear or tying flies.

If you do go, dress in layers with synthetic underwear (not cotton); carry an extra set of dry clothes in your vehicle; always tell someone where you are going; and limit your fishing to short periods, primarily during the warmest hours of the day—from noon to 4:00, for example. This is good advice at any time of year, but it's especially important in winter because of the risks of slipping on snow or ice or getting hypothermia from the cold water.

Before you know it, it'll be spring, and the seasonal cycle of the stream will begin again, with the bass on the move.

Find the largest fish in the river by learning where the largest fish live. Don't waste your time fishing in habitat that only supports small fish. BOB CLOUSER JR.

CHAPTER 3

Finding Fish

JAY NICHOLS

One of the challenges in all fishing is to first find the fish. This may sound simple, but many anglers waste a lot of time fishing in fishless water. Several critical factors in finding fish depend on their seasonal movements related to spawning and feeding. By understanding bass behavior, you will be able to increase your chances of success.

In addition to seasonal movements, other indicators will help you find fish, such as the presence of bait and birds; locating shade in warm, sunny weather; and understanding how to read the river or stream. Having an awareness of certain key spots that bass frequent will help you fish smarter and more productively. Fish hold in relatively predictable places throughout a stream, and understanding where these places are and why fish gather there—whether for food, protection, or both—can make you a better angler. You will spend more time casting your fly to fish rather than just blindly casting, and over time, that will mean an increase in your catch.

BREAKING THE RIVER INTO PARTS

One of the most daunting things for new fly fishers is determining where to begin fishing. This is especially true on large rivers. It's relatively easy to find smallmouth

One of the first steps to catching bass is learning where to find them. Big bass like water from two to four feet deep, with lots of structure where they can hide and ambush their prey.

in a river—if you cover the water with a surface fly, a bass will probably find your fly, whether you fish it through a deep or shallow riffle, in a pool, or behind rocks. But to catch bass larger than twelve to fourteen inches, it pays to have a plan.

A good place to begin is to break the river down into parts and learn to identify the best spots to find fish. Generally speaking, rivers are made up of fast, broken water of different depths, called riffles when they are shallow and runs or rapids when they are deeper, as well as slower-moving water of different depths called pools. Larger bass can be found throughout a river, but they prefer water from two to four feet deep with access to deeper water nearby. Bass also like to find structure, which not only provides an ambush spot, but also gives them a break from the flow of the current. At the same time, they look for spots that provide protection from predators and the sun. Once you begin to think about what a bass requires, you start thinking like a fish, and

thinking like a fish is one of the most important keys to becoming a good angler.

STRUCTURE

Changes in the water's direction and flow indicate the presence of some type of obstruction, which anglers call structure. Structure attracts smallmouth for safety from predators, food, and protection from the current, allowing fish to hold without expending much energy. Structure includes relatively permanent features of the stream bottom such as large rocks, islands, and gravel bars; other natural things like woody debris, flooded timber and brush, and overhanging trees; and man-made features such as boat docks, bridge pilings, old cars, and tires. Anything in the water that fish use for shelter or as part of their feeding areas is a good spot near which to try fishing a fly. Some of the most prominent forms of structure on most smallmouth streams are rocks and ledges, grass beds, islands, flats, and gravel bars.

Wood debris such as downed tree limbs or entire trees provide great cover for bass. To prevent snags, use weedless flies when fishing around this type of cover. JAY NICHOLS

Submerged rock provides excellent cover for bass and the food they prey on. JAY NICHOLS

In high water, bass hold behind the remnants of this eel weir and feed. In low water, they hold in front of the rocks and roam in the water pooled up between the rocks. JAY NICHOLS

Fish concentrate below dams because of the oxygenated water. This urban spot is particularly good, because the outflow from the treatment plant also attracts fish. JAY NICHOLS

EDDIES

Structure causes changes in currents called eddies. Eddies are places in the stream where obstructions divert water in many directions. Whether you see the obstruction or not, the water's surface reveals its presence through turbulence, waves, ripples, and other forms of disturbance. Bass love structure, so eddies are great targets for your flies. Eddies are most often formed when an object such as a rock, ledge, fallen tree, grass bed, gravel bar, bridge piling, or other obstruction, either submerged or protruding above the water's surface, diverts the water's flow. They can also form where tributaries enter a main river or at bends in the river.

Current speed frequently changes in a stream when water flows against an obstruction. That obstruction can be something obvious, like a large, exposed rock or a bridge piling, or it can be more subtle, such as an underwater gravel bar or change in stream depth. When currents of different speeds meet, seams are formed between them. For example, when flowing water hits a midstream rock, the water flowing around the rock moves a lot faster than the water behind the rock, and prominent seams form between the fast and slow water on both downstream sides of that rock.

Sometimes seams are formed when water flows in two different directions, such as in an eddy. One of the most obvious indicators of a seam is foam on the water's surface. Foam usually collects in the slower-moving current of a seam after it journeys through a run. Heavy concentrations of foam flowing downriver are easy to see and provide a clue to how these seams funnel and concentrate insects on the surface of the water. Anglers should find feeding smallmouth

continues on page 34

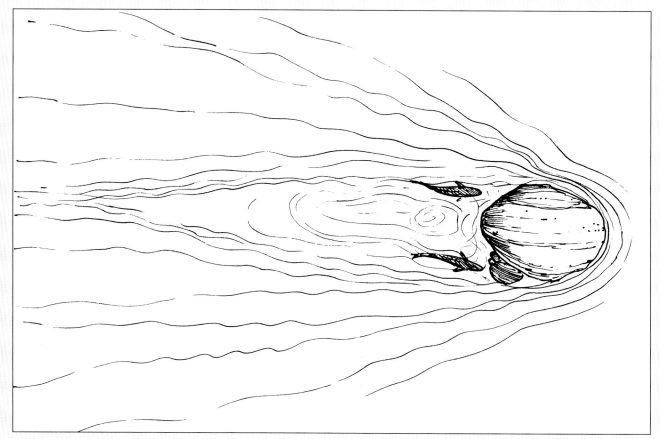

Smallmouth often hold in eddies behind large rocks, which block current and provide ideal resting spots for fish. Two seams form behind most rocks where the fast water meets the slower water. Fish the seam closest to you first so you don't spook as many bass.

An early riser fishes a popper along a seam formed where fast water meets slow. JACK HANRAHAN

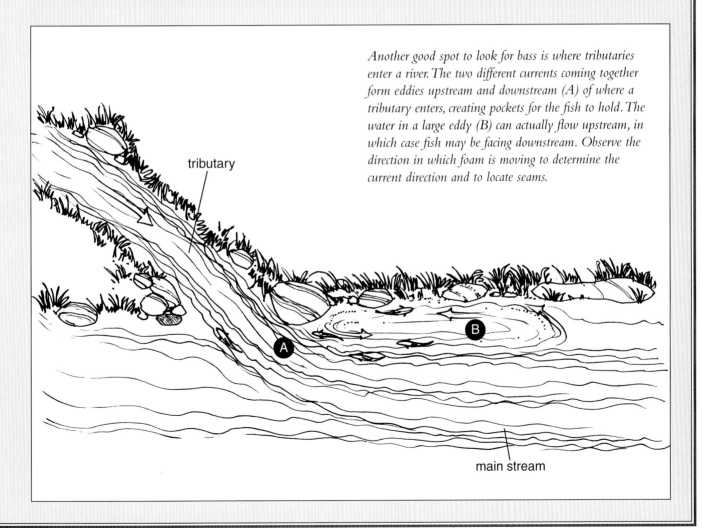

Another good spot to look for bass is where tributaries enter a river. The two different currents coming together form eddies upstream and downstream (A) of where a tributary enters, creating pockets for the fish to hold. The water in a large eddy (B) can actually flow upstream, in which case fish may be facing downstream. Observe the direction in which foam is moving to determine the current direction and to locate seams.

tributary

main stream

EDDIES *continued from page 32*

holding under the foam line along the seam. Smallmouth and the baitfish they prey on are attracted to these seams because floating or drifting food is moving along at a slower pace, making it easier for smallmouth and baitfish to feed without expending too much energy.

Sometimes the water in an eddy moves in a circular motion upstream, which can wreak havoc on a drifting fly. Because it's often hard, if not impossible, to beat the varying currents with a dry-fly, drag-free drift, I prefer to join them and strip weighted streamers through the currents, trying to entice bass on the lookout for baitfish caught off guard by the many currents. I like to stand across stream from the eddy and start at the lower end. I work my way upstream, casting my fly across both seams, and then stripping it back through the seams and the slower midsection with one cast.

If you want to fish dry flies or nymphs dead drift through an eddy, get almost directly below the obstruction and fish your way upstream. Focus on drifting your flies down each of the current seams. Because of the varying current speeds, you can't get a long dead drift presentation if you cast to the pocket behind the rock from across stream. Whether fishing with streamers or dry flies, I like to approach the fish from downstream of them so that they are less likely to be spooked by seeing me or sensing waves from my wading.

However, in some large eddies where water actually flows upstream, fish still feed facing into the current. This means they are facing downstream relative to the current flow in the main river, and they will be facing you if you approach from downstream. Keep this in mind when approaching an eddy and presenting your fly. In some situations, an approach from upstream would be stealthier.

Large eddies are easy to locate and generally hold several fish. Small eddies can be harder to find and often hold only one fish. These little microeddies usually are not much wider or longer than the smallmouth they harbor, but if you cast your fly into one, you will often get an instant hit.

To find these microeddies, look for subtle changes in water speed or slowly spinning circular currents around obstructions. Bass use many of these overlooked areas for protection from fast water currents during rising water. They also use these positions for ambushing prey. On one fishing trip, water levels were slowly rising and climbing up the trunks of small trees that lined the banks. We spotted a microeddy formed by the base of a tree in four feet of water. While I held the boat steady, the angler in the bow dropped his darter imitation within inches of the submerged tree. As the fly sank down along the bark of the tree, the leader tightened. He lifted the rod tip, and a four-pound-plus smallmouth came leaping out through the water's surface.

Rocks and Ledges

Different-size rocks strewn over the bottom of any river are an important part of prime smallmouth habitat. Gravel and small rocks are necessary for good spawning habitat. Small rocks are havens for a variety of foods, such as the crayfish, aquatic insects, and minnows that smallmouth thrive on, and larger rocks break the current flow and provide cushions, or comfort zones, that allow fish to hold in the water without expending much energy. Holding in the slack water provided by one of these rocks, fish can ambush bait and feed without exerting as much energy as if they held in unobstructed current. Sometimes these rocks break through the surface of the water and are easy to spot, but at other times they are completely submerged. Often variations in the water's surface are your first clue that something lies underneath.

Many anglers forget about drifting their flies in front of rocks and immediately cast behind them, but there is often a good spot for fish to hold in front of certain rocks. And where there is a spot for fish to hold, they will, because this spot allows them to see everything floating down toward them in the current. A rock's shape, both front and back, determines whether it slows or blocks water flowing against it and provides a comfort zone for fish. Rocks that are slanted in front and round or flat on the back have eddies only behind them, but round rocks and those with flat faces have eddies both in front of and behind them.

Right: Downstream of most rocks, there's a pocket of slower-moving water flanked by two current seams. This is a prime holding area for bass. JAY NICHOLS

When the water flowing downstream hits the face of the rock, it is deflected to both sides of the rock as well as upward and downward. The downward currents often carve out the stream bottom in front of the rock, and depending on the size of the rock, this can provide an area for the fish to hold where the water slows down. I like to cast my fly either upstream of the bulge, so that it drifts into the area where the bass is holding, or across the current above the bulge, allowing the fly to sink to the level where the fish is holding, and then stripping it across in front of the bass.

Downstream of every rock, there's a pocket of slow-moving water that has current seams on both sides of it that converge downstream. If you were to look at these currents from above, they would look like a V. This pocket is a prime spot for resting baitfish and provides an easy feeding area for bass. Bass will hold in the slower water behind the rock and feed on insects that collect in the seams on either side or ambush baitfish. The size of the eddy varies according to the speed and velocity of the water currents and the size of the obstruction.

When I fish areas like this, my strategy is to first cast to the outside seam of the pocket, then to the pocket, then to the far seam. I have found this sequence to be the best way to catch as many fish as possible out of these prime areas. Over the years, I discovered that if I first cast the fly into the slow-water pocket, I would get a quick strike from a fish, but the bass thrashed around and seemed to spook the other fish toward the seams. By

hooking and playing the bass in the closest seam first, I often catch more fish out of the pocket. Unless you have a particular fish in mind, it's generally best to fish the productive water closest to you first when searching the water.

This doesn't just apply to eddies. Many people charge into a stream without first considering the water along the banks or wade quickly to the prime lies without first fishing the water in front of them. This a good way to miss opportunities at catching fish you may have overlooked, and it is also a good way to spook the fish you have your sights set on. Hooking, playing, and landing a thrashing fish can scare off other fish in the pool. And small fish spooked in a pool can swim upstream and spook larger fish. It's better to approach each fishing spot, including eddies, with a plan instead of just using the chuck-and-chance-it method.

Ledges are large, long pieces of rock that sometimes stretch across the entire river. They often protrude above the water's surface, especially in low water, or change the flow of current. Ledges block the flow of water and force it upward and across their tops, creating visible flow lines on the surface. If ice, the force of the water's currents, or other floating debris has not broken a ledge up, it can reach from shore to shore.

This type of structure makes ideal habitat. It provides fast-flowing waters filled with oxygen, as well as cover and ambush opportunities for bass. I have found that with ledges with about a foot of water flowing

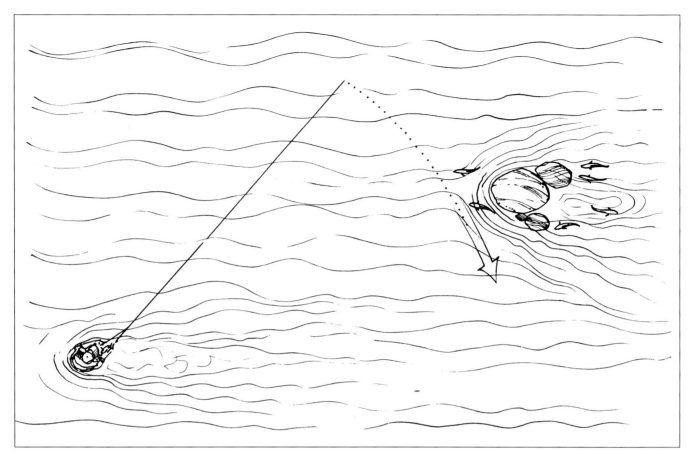

Water flowing downstream hits a rock face and is deflected up, down, and to each side. The downward currents often carve out the stream bottom in front of the rock, providing a depression and a pocket of slow water (depending on the size of the rock) where fish can hold. When fishing streamers, cast across the current above the bulge, allowing the fly to sink to the level the fish is holding, and then strip it across the current in front of the bass. Many anglers overlook this spot and only cast behind rocks.

Ledges mark a rapid change in water levels and are great spots to fish. They can run the width of the river or be broken, providing many different currents in which bass can hold.
JAY NICHOLS

Water turbulence creates foam, and downstream of its source, this foam settles into lanes that mark the prominent current seams. Fish your fly carefully through these seams to find bass.
JAY NICHOLS

across the top, smallmouth will lie on or just in front of them when feeding. During low or normal flows, I catch most fish upstream of the ledge. When there is a lot of water in the stream, the downstream side of a ledge is more productive. In high-water conditions, the speed of the current increases on the upriver side of the ledges, thereby decreasing the cushion of water smallmouth will lie in. This forces bass to take cover behind the ledge. Look for areas where sections of a ledge have been broken away. This type of structure provides many current seams and holding areas in which bass can hide and feed. Fish each seam and pocket carefully and methodically, rather than just blindly casting.

Water plunging over man-made dams or waterfalls creates a deep pool below. These areas always hold fish. Because the water turbulence can be heavy and the currents complicated, fishing surface flies dead drift is not the most effective technique. I prefer to fish a weighted minnow through the currents, pausing every once in a while so the fly gets caught by the currents and looks like a helpless baitfish. Not only do waterfalls create good holding water, but they also block the upstream migration of fish—another reason why fish are often concentrated under them.

Waterfalls and dams create turbulent water and deep plunge pools that hold fish, especially in the summer. STEVE MAY

Exposed grass beds provide shade and feeding areas for bass and are always worth a cast. BOB CLOUSER

This bass fell for a Clouser Minnow stripped just downstream of a submerged grass bed in high water. STEVE MAY

Right: Underwater grass beds can provide important spawning and rearing habitat for bass. BOB CLOUSER

Grass

Grass, whether visible above the water's surface or hidden below, is another smallmouth hot spot. Underwater grass ripples the water's surface, causing the currents to swirl in miniature runs and seams. Grass is a haven for insects, small fish, crayfish, and most other types of food that smallmouth eat. Smallmouth feed in front of, behind, on the edges of, or even in the midst of the grass. I have seen as many as half a dozen smallmouth at one time chasing baitfish over the entire width of the front of a grass bed.

In high water, smallmouth rest in the grass. In the spring, they spawn in the grass after clearing a nest. Grass beds are especially important rearing habitat for young bass, and they rely on these areas for cover and food such as plankton and insects, which are also attracted to the grass. For this reason, classes of bass lurk around these beds all year, waiting to capture young smallmouth that venture from their hideaway.

Bridges

Bridge abutments block the current's flow and make excellent ambush spots for bass. Also, water around bridge pylons is usually deeper than the surrounding water, and it often warms more quickly in cold weather because the pylons absorb the sun's rays and warm the water. The actual bridge provides shade and protection not only for bass from aerial predators, but also for the baitfish that bass feed on.

Bridges and bridge abutments are popular places to fish, and for good reason. Not only is there structure to block the current flow, but water around bridge pylons is usually deeper than surrounding water, and it often warms more quickly in cold weather because the pylons absorb the sun's rays and warm the water. Bridges provide shade and protection, both for bass from aerial predators and for the baitfish that bass feed on.
BOB CLOUSER

Because bridges are well-known fishing spots and access is often easy, the fish around bridges tend to be wary and used to human intruders. Sometimes, especially with bass that hold under small bridges, the fish lie in water outside of the bridge but retreat into the shadows at any sign of danger. These fish can be tough to catch.

Wood

Any type of wood in a river provides ideal cover for bass, and in rivers without a lot of rocks, wood may be the only structure available. Brush, tree limbs, and entire trees can pile up along shorelines where water currents are slow. Wooden boat docks and pilings, water-soaked lumber, railroad ties, logs, and tree stumps on the bottom are also good spots that provide the essentials of shade, protection, and available food for both predator and prey. It is not unusual to spot as many as a dozen bass of various sizes near a downed tree or sunken log.

I like to fish poppers around downed trees or mats of woody debris. I also cast minnow imitations across or to the edges and strip them back. With weedless EZ Poppers or Bendbacks, you can cast more aggressively than you would otherwise, because you have less fear of losing your pattern. I often cast my line right over the structure and retrieve my fly behind it.

Islands

Islands vary in size and shape. Some are wide, others long and narrow. Some have trees or other types of vegetation, which can fall into the water and create prime habitat, while others contain only rocks, rubble, boulders, mud, or sand. The shorelines of islands also differ in that some are steep and undercut by water currents, whereas the banks of others slope gently into the water.

Islands create prime wintering, feeding, spawning, safety, and resting areas for smallmouth. The head of an island breaks the flow of the main current into different current seams and eddies that attract fish. Fish will also hold and feed along the edges of an island, as well as in the slow water downstream. Islands are home to all sorts of terrestrial and aquatic insects, small birds and mam-

Downed trees in the water, whether along shore or in the middle of the river, provide a great resting spot for bass. BOB CLOUSER

Islands come in all shapes and sizes. Some are densely wooded, others rocky. All sides of an island can be productive. JAY NICHOLS

mals, and reptiles and amphibians such as frogs, turtles, snakes, and salamanders. Baitfish, crayfish, and hellgrammites are also abundant around islands.

Tree-lined shorelines can provide shade from the glaring sun. Anglers should fish the shady side of an island, around sunken logs or trees, or in rock- or boulder-strewn areas. I have found that in clear water on bright, sunny days, smallmouth and the bait they eat are most concentrated in the shaded areas along islands.

On one fishing trip, I was poling two anglers along a shaded shoreline. We came upon an opening with some sun peeking through the thinned-out trees. A large sunken log lay about three feet from the shoreline, creating a shadow along its lower side. I instructed my client to cast the fly just along the log at the edge of the shaded area. He complied and caught a four-pound smallmouth.

Learning from that episode that shade was important, I took advantage of another situation on a bright afternoon. I took a good fly caster to an area where a big smallmouth would hole up on a sunny day. The area was shallow and required a long cast so that we wouldn't spook the fish. A huge rock lay about four feet from the shoreline, and its top rose about a foot above the surface. The bass was between the shore and the rock in the shade. The angler hit his mark, which was seventy feet away. He twitched the Floating Minnow as it entered the shade, and the fish exploded on the fly.

The undercut banks of islands provide safe havens and great ambush areas. Undercut banks are formed by fast-moving currents forcing gravel and silt out from the sides of the banks and the outer edges of islands. This usually occurs when water levels rise, creating strong current flows, but this process of erosion happens any time the flow of water eats away at the side of a bank. I have seen areas where all the silt was washed away from tree roots, leaving only the roots and enough earth to hold the tree in place. Such washed-out undercut areas provide safe places for both baitfish and smallmouth, as well as food for the bass. Undercut banks also offer shade on bright days. I like to position my clients above these undercut areas and have them cast streamers below the undercut and retrieve them with the Susquehanna Strip. Another effective method is to position yourself directly across from the undercut and cast a streamer tight to the bank. Let the fly sink before beginning your retrieve. I have seen many smallmouth come out from under the bank and inhale the fly as it sank to the bottom.

ANATOMY OF A POOL

A pool is a section of water between two types of structure, one at the head and one at the rear, in which the current slows and deepens. Pools can be small or as long as half a mile or even longer. They are made up of various types of structure and often abound with fish. When waters warm during the summer, large smallmouth hold at the rear portions, or tailouts, of many pools. Pools can be surrounded by gravel bars or some type of shoreline that also contains shallow-water areas. On cloudy or overcast days or in the evening, smallmouth move to the edges of pools to feed. A pool can change with the varying heights of water, but the easiest and most effective time to fish is usually as the water recedes, making the pool's features more visible and concentrating the fish.

The head of a pool or run usually has fast currents and may be too fast and shallow to hold many bass, though there are frequently exceptions. The real sweet spot is where the current entering the pool just starts to flatten and slow down because the depth of the pool changes, often as a result of an underwater shelf. At the head of many pools are several current seams

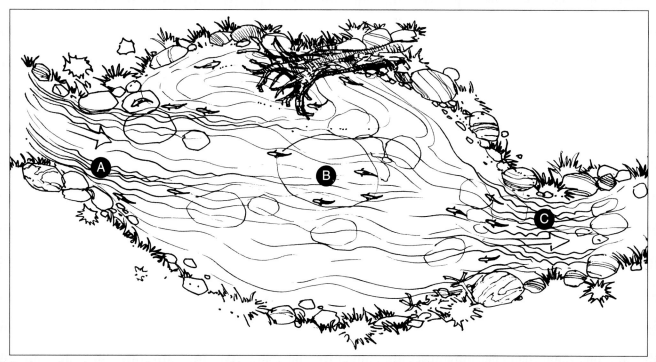

Pools are bass hot spots and come in many shapes and sizes. A pool is easier to fish when the water recedes, concentrating fish and making its features easier to read.

The best spot at the head of the pool (A) is where the current starts to flatten and slow down. This marks a change in depth, often because of an underwater shelf. The faster water at the head of the pool is highly oxygenated and a good bet in summer. Because the fast current masks both your approach and the splash of your fly when it hits the water, you can often get much closer to fish than in a smooth tailout.

The largest bass often live in the hole (B), the deepest area of the pool. Prime holes are dependable spots to catch big fish from year to year. A good place to start when fishing a hole is to look at where the current comes out of the head of the pool and how it funnels into the hole. You can look for clues such as small floating debris, insects, or foam to help you see how the currents are moving.

Water exits the pool at the tailout (C). The best tailouts for bass have various sizes of rocks or other types of structure or depressions in the stream bottom where fish can hold. Many tailouts are shallow and smooth, so fishing them requires a careful approach. An exciting and effective way to fish a tailout is to cast downstream and swing your fly (floating or subsurface) through the shallows, where you can often see wakes from a large bass chasing your fly.

This photo shows the relatively shallow run of water out of the tailout of the pool upstream, which forms the head of another pool. The sweet spot at the head of the pool (where the angler is casting) is right where the surface of the water starts to flatten out, signaling that it has gotten deeper. JAY NICHOLS

you should fish your fly through. On pools formed at a bend in the river, there is often a prominent eddy on the inside of the bend and faster water on the outside. It pays to concentrate on the seam between the run and the eddy.

This faster water at the head of the pool is highly oxygenated, and smallmouth bass do well here, especially in the higher temperatures of summer. More importantly, the water's surface is broken up, and it is easier to approach and cast to bass holding at the head of the pool. You can often get much closer to them than when fishing a smoother tailout.

Anglers sometimes describe the deepest area of a pool as a hole. Usually the largest smallmouth in the area will take over a hole, or at times, several large bass will share a spacious hole. Some holes contain the per-

fect combination of structure and food preferred by big smallmouth. If a big smallmouth is removed from a prime hole, another one will claim it. Because of this, prime holes are usually dependable spots to catch big fish year after year. A good place to start when fishing a hole is to observe where the current comes out of the head of the pool and how it funnels into the hole. You can look for clues such as small floating debris, insects, or foam to help you see how the currents are moving.

The tailout of a pool is where water exits. Not all tailouts are the same. Some don't have any structure that blocks the main speed of the current; others have rocks of different sizes or other types of structure, and the water leaves the pool in various places. The tailout *continues on page 44*
continues on page 44

ANATOMY OF A POOL *continued*

The tailout of a pool is shallower and provides a prime feeding location for fish, from which they can retreat to the deeper parts of a pool with any sign of danger. Currents in the tailout are often placid, and the shallow water makes accurate and delicate presentations imperative. In this photo, note where the water leaves the tailout and immediately begins another pool. JAY NICHOLS

with structure is the best one, because the structure gives bass places to hold.

Many tailouts are shallow and smooth, so fishing them requires a careful approach. Sometimes the bass are spooky, and you may need to fish a more subtle fly, such as a Floating Minnow, instead of a popper. Some tailouts have depressions with deeper water where the bass hold. They also hold in the deeper water right before the water shallows as it exits the pool.

Approaching the tailout of a pool from downstream can be tricky, because the currents below the tailout are moving much faster than the currents in it. If you are approaching from downstream, make your casts as short as possible, or hold your rod high to keep the line out of the faster water so it doesn't drag the fly. A good technique is to fish down on the tailout and swing your fly—floating or subsurface—through it. Tailouts are excellent places to try skating a dry fly. You can often see the wake from a large bass chasing your fly. When fishing a streamer, cast downstream toward the opposite bank, and let the fly swing through the tailout as you strip it.

Brush-lined banks, especially where the brush and grass extend into or onto the water, provide essential areas for bass to rest and feed. In rivers without a lot of midriver structure, smallmouth seek out the shorelines and hold under overhanging grass or brush. Big bass sometimes dwell in these areas, and anglers focusing their efforts on more prominent features in a river often overlook them. I have a few of these spots reserved for my clients. These areas usually don't have fast currents during summer's low flows, and you need to be careful not to spook the fish with boat waves. Approaching from downstream with the boat often proves most successful because, as when wading, the downstream current prevents your wakes from reaching the fish.

Smallmouth occupy the eddies below islands in early spring, fall, and winter during high-water conditions. These eddies are formed by the currents moving down along each side of the island and coming together again. The water height determines the size and length of the eddies. In some cases, there is a bar of silt at the bottom end, or foot, of the island, and below that a gravel bar just upstream of where the currents meet. Smallmouth hold in this slack water during high water flows and over the gravel just below the silt bar during low water. It pays to cast across the foot of the island and strip your flies across both areas. During low water, bass hold over the gravel just below the eddy if it contains a silt bottom and in the seams along both sides of the eddy. These areas typically are not silty. The foot of an island usually creates a mud bar or silt deposits. When vegetation grows on these silted bars, baitfish, crayfish, and nymphs abound.

One of my favorite spots is the head of an island, especially if there is a gravel bar just upstream. The head of an island deflects the flow of water, often forming a shallow bar extending upstream from the island's head. During overcast, cloudy, or low-light conditions, anglers can find smallmouth holding and feeding on these

The washed-out undercuts along the sides of islands provide safe places for baitfish and smallmouth and also provide the bass with food. You can float along the island, casting perpendicular to the bank and stripping your fly back, or cast straight downstream along the edge of the island and retrieve the fly straight upstream. PHILIP HANYOK

shallow bars all day long. I like to cast across the bar and quickly strip a minnow imitation back across the edges.

Sometimes water cuts into the islands, especially with larger ones, and in some cases it forms a stream that can cut an island in half. At certain times, especially during high water, the in- or outflows of the cut attract smallmouth. These areas offer protection from fast currents in high water. Look at both the entrance and exit of such a cut to determine whether there are slow currents or eddies where bass can hold.

Gravel Bars and Flats

Gravel bars are one of my favorite places to fish for bass. They come in many configurations, lengths, and widths and can be found at any water depth. In low water, they are often at least partially exposed.

A typical gravel bar has rocks from the size of marbles to baseballs or basketballs strewn over an area surrounded or separated by drop-offs or channels of deep water. The most common place to look for a gravel bar is upstream or downstream of any structure that diverts the flow of water, such as an island or grass bed. In fact, most grass beds are gravel bars that protrude above the water's surface in low water. In some areas, gravel bars can extend upstream of an island from one hundred feet to half a mile or more. You can also find gravel bars by observing current flow. Many rocks and other debris carried by these various currents during either flooding or ice movement are usually deposited at areas of the slowest water flow.

Gravel bars play an important part in the survival of smallmouth bass. The various sizes of rock and rubble provide cover and food for crayfish and aquatic insects, and the abundance of insects attracts minnows. The variety of foods attracts all sizes of smallmouth.

The shallow water of the bars often makes it easy for bass to feed. When mayflies are hatching, smallmouth frequently lie in small indentations on the bottom, covered by only inches of water. This allows the smallmouth to rise just a short distance to inhale its food. Smallmouth

In the summer, exposed gravel bars grow grass on them. These bars provide structure in low and high water. In rivers with a lot of water volume, new bars can appear each year. BOB CLOUSER

When fishing gravel bars from a boat, I like to anchor and fish the bar thoroughly. BOB CLOUSER

cruising these bars for food can stalk prey unnoticed by using the small piles of rocks as cover from which to ambush their food. And if threatened by a larger predator, smallmouth can react quickly and escape to the deeper water that surrounds many gravel bars. Small bass can easily escape and hide in the many crevices provided by the piles of rock and rubble on the bar.

Gravel bars and flats are prime places to search for bass in low light, but don't overlook them during the day. In some instances, my clients caught big smallmouth during midday on gravel bars with one or two feet of water over them, especially if there were depressions in the bar where larger bass could hold.

Whether fishing a bar while wading or floating, cover the water nearest to you first. Then you can float over the bar and fish the water you couldn't reach, if necessary. If I am fishing a bar from a boat, I often anchor up to cover certain areas thoroughly. During a hatch, smallmouth often feed in the shallowest water around the bar. Anchor the boat at the lower end of the bar so you can cast the fly up and across the flow of the water currents, allowing the fly to drift down to the feeding smallmouth. If you are wading, start at the downstream end of the gravel bar, and fish upstream by casting across and up along the edges of the bar, covering as much water as possible and casting to any bass you can

see feeding. To improve your success, wade quietly and don't cause excessive waves when wading shallow-water gravel bars. Shallow bars are especially productive during a hatch (usually in the evening in summer), in low light; or on drab, drizzly days, but they are worth fishing any time.

Like bars, flats mark a significant change in water depth in a river, and they are also favorite places for both fish and anglers. Flats are similar to gravel bars except that they don't have high centers like bars—they are flat all the way across. Under normal water flows, flats are shallow and have from one to three feet of water covering them. They vary in width and length and can be found in the middle of the river or along the banks. Productive flats also have some sort of structure, such as rocks and boulders, strewn across them. Some of my favorite flats have various sizes of gouges cut in the gravel bottom, and smallmouth love to hold and feed in them. Flats are some of my favorite spots to take clients to catch carp, because you can often see them tailing in the shallow water.

If the water is murky or low light prevents you from seeing the bottom of the river, you can still find a flat by observing the surface currents. In even a slight breeze, the shallow water over a flat shows very small pronounced ripples, while the deeper water looks smooth.

When they are on the flats, carp wave their tails in the air like redfish as they root out crayfish and other food. Sight-casting to these actively feeding fish is exhilarating. MIKE O'BRIEN

One of the best reasons to fish a flat is to sight-fish. The shallower water and lack of surface riffles allow you to see the bottom more effectively, making it easier to locate feeding fish. I will never forget an experience that my son Bob Jr. had while fishing a flat with Bob Popovics. In the clear water, they could see the dark form of a smallmouth holding over a boulder about seventy feet away. Bob Jr. positioned his boat for Bob Popovics to make the cast, while I held my boat still so my clients and I could watch. We were about 150 feet to the side of them when Bob let the cast go. We heard Bob Jr. exclaim, "He's on!" and saw a five-pound smallmouth arc into the air on the opposite side of his boat. I will never forget the big smile on Bob Popovics's face when he held that big bass up so we all could see it.

On another occasion, Lefty Kreh and I were drifting over a prime flat on my home river during late September. I told Lefty that the two rocks lying together out about sixty-five feet usually held a large smallmouth. Lefty immediately cast out his popper, and it landed on the water between the two rocks. Before I could say, "Great cast," the popper disappeared, and I watched another five-pound smallmouth do his surface dance.

I asked Lefty, "How come you always catch the biggest bass when we fish together?"

"I don't tell you everything," he replied.

SHADE

Shade is a feature provided by structure that attracts bass and the fish they feed on, and you should always be on the lookout for it in the summer and fall. Knowing the positions of the sun throughout the day helps you understand what parts of the river will be in the shade and what parts will be sunny. This information provides an important clue to finding shady, cool areas on hot, sunny days and warm, sunny spots in late winter and spring.

Shaded water can be a few degrees cooler than water in direct sunlight. In the summer, smallmouth are attracted to these shaded areas not only because they are great places for them to feed on the many baitfish that collect there, but also because they offer some relief from the bright sun. Smallmouth bass have no eyelids, and direct, glaring light rays penetrating the water's surface affect the distance, depth, and direction that bass can see. Fish facing the bright sun have a difficult time seeing their prey—and your flies. Shallow-water smallmouth will change their lies or ambush positions by relocating to a shadow-covered area.

In late fall, winter, and early spring, smallmouth may seek out water warmed by the sun. As water temperatures drop in the fall, bass in shaded areas may not feed as aggressively as those in areas warmed by the sun.

During the summer, bass feed in shade both because some of their prey prefer cooler temperatures and because they can see better out of the glaring sun. Bridges provide consistent sources of shade throughout the year. BOB CLOUSER

The position of the sun and direction of the river's flow determine when certain areas will be shaded. As a rule of thumb, during cold weather, fish sunny water; during hot weather, fish shade. BOB CLOUSER

The position of the sun and direction of the river's flow determine when certain areas will be shaded. On rivers flowing west to east, the largest amount of shade on the bottom from rocks, boulders, and other debris will be on the upstream side in the morning and the downstream side in the late afternoon. On rivers that flow north to south, the east side is in shade in the morning and the west side is shaded in the late afternoon and evening. This pattern applies to structure above the water's surface also. The longest shadows occur at first light in the morning and the last light of day. The location of shade on rivers changes according to the sun's summer migration. An area that is shaded at a certain time of day in June will not be shaded at the same time in September.

A direct overhead sun lights up the bottom and eliminates shadows, often making fishing less productive. As the sun moves west, shadows begin to form on the east side of rocks and other debris strewn over the river's bottom. Afternoon shadows fall opposite to the shadows created before noon. Anglers familiar with these changing shadows can select positions that will allow them to cast flies to these shaded areas.

TRIBUTARIES AND OTHER INFLOWS

Tributaries are smaller rivers entering a main river. They come in many sizes, from a few feet to a hundred or more across. Some have cold water and others warm, and the difference in temperature between the main river and the tributary can be an advantage to anglers at various times of the year. In the summer, cooler tributaries attract bass where they enter the main river. During the fall and winter, warmer tributaries such as spring creeks also attract feeding smallmouth.

In the spring, many tributaries provide important areas for spawning bass. Often tributaries have less silt and more clean gravel than the main river, and bass travel to use this habitat. Smallmouth bass from lakes seek out the clean, flowing water in tributary streams and sometimes hold over into summer when conditions are right. Tributaries to many large lakes, such as the Great Lakes, Lake Champlain in Vermont and New York, and the Finger Lakes in New York, can have terrific runs of lake smallmouth bass and give anglers the opportunity to catch large lake-bred bass in a small-stream setting.

In high water, smallmouth and the baitfish they eat find protection from the raging currents of the main

Cathy Beck releases a nice smallmouth from a tributary to the Susquehanna River. Some smallmouth from the Susquehanna swim up this tributary to spawn, but it also has a year-round population of fish. BOB CLOUSER

river in tributaries and their mouths. In some cases, the main river water may be dirty and murky, while the tributary water is clear enough for fish to find your fly.

In many places where a tributary enters the main water, the water can be deep. When it is more than four feet or so, I prefer a type 2 or 3 full-sinking fly line and a Clouser Minnow or similar weighted fly. I like my tippets to be no longer than 5 feet and no shorter than 4 attached to a sinking fly line. When the tributaries are rising, they may become cloudy or muddy, and the sinking line puts the fly down along the bottom where the fish can see it. Anglers should also note that eddies are usually formed downstream of where the tributary enters the main stem. This and the area in the mouth will hold most of the smallmouth.

Many tributaries deposit silt and sediment downstream of where they enter the main river, forming a shallow-water area that may or may not hold fish. These

Left: Tributary mouths are good places to fish. An angler casts downstream of where a tributary enters the main river.
JAY NICHOLS

areas are worth investigating, because at times the silted bottom will have some type of structure around it or growing from it. In some instances, I have found logs, limbs, and other debris hung up in these places.

During low flows when the water is clear, surface flies fish well near tributary mouths. You can either let them drift or give them some action on the retrieve. One six-foot-wide tributary that entered my home river always had shade on it during late afternoon. It had only two rocks in it for structure. I would ask my clients to cast a Floating Minnow into the mouth, and a nice-size smallmouth often would inhale the fly.

A word of caution about tributaries: Some of them may be polluted to the point where pH and oxygen levels have changed, making them unsuitable for smallmouth. Many times the water conditions below where a tributary flows into the main river are worse, because the tributary is muddy or carries a lot of agricultural or other pollution. They are not always clearer than the main river. The bottom line is that you should be familiar with all the tributaries of your home river, because they undoubtedly affect the main river—for better or for worse.

Always be on the lookout for pipes pouring water into a river; these can provide oxygen and a change of water temperature that attracts fish. Many anglers overlook this unobtrusive pipe, but a good bass always swims near it. JAY NICHOLS

Smallmouth bass fishing often takes place in an urban environment, which is one reason why it is so popular. Other inflows may include pipes or culverts running into the river or water from industrial operations or power plants. These places often provide turbulent water that differs in temperature from the river, which can attract fish.

Some warmwater discharges from power plants can be over 100 degrees. Sometimes warmwater inflows are from small pipes carrying heated water. Once the discharge mixes with the main river water, it can provide outstanding smallmouth fishing during the fall, winter, and spring months. Anglers fishing warmwater outlets should find the seam where the cold and warm water meet. Many times smallmouth will hold on the warm side of the seam.

BIRDS

In addition to finding fish by looking for structure, you can also borrow a page from a saltwater fly fisher's playbook and look for birds. Birds play an important role in the food chain, and they can serve as a visual aid to locating feeding fish.

Birds of interest to smallmouth anglers include various species of herons, egrets, terns, and gulls. Where baitfish are abundant and school together, smallmouth will attack these schools and push them to the surface. The commotion on the surface from the feeding bass and escaping baitfish attracts the birds, which capture and eat the baitfish. On many large smallmouth rivers, gulls concentrate over busting fish and noisily dip and dive while feeding on the baitfish pushed to the surface. A concentration of birds such as a gathering of herons and egrets can also be a sign that baitfish are abundant, and where there are lots of baitfish, there's a food supply for hungry smallmouth. I have seen groups of almost two dozen herons perched in trees along a certain stretch of shoreline or gathered around grass beds and islands. Observe the birds and watch where they go to feed.

MUD STREAKS

During hot summer days, looking for bass feeding behind bottom feeders that stir up mud, such as carp, catfish, or suckers, could be the best—and perhaps the only—way to consistently catch big smallmouth. Lefty Kreh and his son Larry targeted big smallmouth on mud streaks one hot August day and caught and released five smallmouth from two and a half to over four pounds.

Big smallmouth bass follow bottom-feeding fish as they scour the bottom for food, leaving streaks of muddy water trailing downstream. Smallmouth move in and out of the streaks to feed on crayfish, hellgrammites, and small baitfish stirred up in the process. While they feed, they change colors, as do many predator fish species. Big smallmouth often become jet black while feeding in a mud streak and are easy for trained eyes to spot. One day in early July, as I poled a client toward a mud streak created by a feeding carp, the black silhouette of a four-pound smallmouth appeared from the streak and took position above the carp's back. Without hesitation, my client cast the fly about two feet in front of the carp. The fly landed on target, and the smallmouth darted forward and inhaled it.

Anglers who spot a mud streak should locate the fish making it and observe its movement before approaching. All bottom-feeding fish, whether suckers, catfish, or carp, become very wary in clear, shallow water and are easily spooked by sounds or movement. Waves, ripples, or even a pressure change from an approaching boat can spook them. At times, it's best to leave the boat and approach the mud streaks by careful wading. Noise or an abrupt change in the surrounding environment spooks not only the bottom-feeding fish, but the big smallmouth as well. Good presentations and long, fifty- to eighty-foot casts are critical in these situations.

SIGHT FISHING

Sometimes the easiest and most productive way to find fish is to spot them in the water. In smallmouth fisheries with clear water, sight-fishing provides the ultimate challenge—and reward—of bass fishing. The fish can see you

Bass follow carp around, looking for an easy meal that the carp root out of the stream bottom. MIKE O'BRIEN

In rivers with clear water, sight-fishing for bass offers the ultimate challenge— and reward.
ROSS PURNELL

High sun, clear water, and no wind combine for perfect sight-fishing conditions. JAY NICHOLS

easily, but you can see them as well. Besides the reward of having a fish come to your fly, you also are able to watch one of nature's predators track your fly pattern and inhale it, which is exhilarating.

Sight-casting to a big smallmouth is thrilling, but the conditions must be right. The water needs to be clear and calm, and the levels should be low. You must have high sun, as occurs between 10:00 A.M. and 4 P.M. Wind can disturb the surface of the water, making it hard to see the fish. Favorable conditions most often occur in July through October.

The time of day, position of the sun, and location you intend to fish are critical. Try to keep the sun above and behind you to help you spot fish more effectively, but beware of casting shadows over your intended target. A river that twists and turns through a valley has many curves and bends with opportunities for optimal lighting.

Bright, sunlit days can be productive, but only if you use the sun's rays to your advantage. Always try to be in a position where the smallmouth will not have to look directly into the sun to spot your fly. The sun should illuminate the fly but not shine into the fish's eyes. One positive scenario would be to have the sun overhead and shining slightly upriver. This will both help you spot the bass and help the bass see the fly without looking into the sun.

CHAPTER 4

What They Eat

A pack of hungry smallmouth herds baitfish in the shallows.

JAY NICHOLS

Smallmouth will eat just about anything that moves, and that's one of the reasons they are a sought-after gamefish. On any given stream, besides the regular foods that make up the bulk of the bass's diet—baitfish, crayfish, and aquatic insects—there are also occasional food items such as ants, grasshoppers, ladybugs, frogs, snakes, leeches, small mammals, and birds. Bass also take advantage of infrequent events such as periodic cicada emergences that bring hundreds of big-bodied bugs to the water's surface. In short, bass are not fussy eaters, and if it looks like food, they'll give it a try.

While matching the hatch is fun, it is rarely necessary. Often when there is abundant food available, such as during a hatch of whiteflies, larger bass focus more on the smaller fish partaking of the feast than on the insects. It also sometimes helps to show the bass something different from whatever the abundant food is. If it gives you satisfaction to fish a size 16 White Wulff when smallmouth are feasting on whiteflies, do it, but with smallmouth, you can also use a Clouser Minnow or a popper if you feel like it.

BAITFISH

Baitfish are any fish eaten by other fish. Smallmouth bass feed on everything from the eggs, sac fry, and young of their own species to twelve-inch or larger fallfish and

Smallmouth bass take a wide range of flies, and that's what makes them a sought-after gamefish. Flies that match baitfish (above) consistently catch my biggest bass. JACK HANRAHAN

suckers. Because most smallmouth streams have an array of minnows, dace, darters, sculpins, and other forage fish, including young trout, bass, and sunfish, baitfish are the most important food items for smallmouth bass. By the time a smallmouth bass is about three inches or so, it becomes primarily piscivorous, feeding mostly on fish smaller than itself, and supplements its diet with crayfish and aquatic insects. For me, baitfish are interesting natural foods to imitate because of their wide range of colors and behaviors. They are also the most rewarding—year after year, my largest fish are caught on baitfish imitations.

Just as trout anglers match mayflies with suggestive fly patterns, a match-the-hatch approach to baitfish imitations is an exciting and successful way to fish. Baitfish range widely in size, shape, color, and general habits, and understanding these characteristics well enough to tie and fish baitfish patterns effectively is a challenging part of fly fishing. Most of the time it's not necessary to match any particular baitfish to catch bass, but being able to match the important characteristics such as shape, size, color, and behavior of the prevalent bait will probably increase your success.

Choosing and fishing baitfish imitations is similar to matching and fishing insect hatches. Although you can tie on a suggestive pattern and catch fish, you need to understand what foods are on the table if you want a shot at smarter and larger fish. Various kinds of baitfish frequent different parts of a stream. Minnows swim throughout the stream and often feed on the surface; others, like darters, swim in short, erratic movements on the stream bottom. Understanding the general differences and habits of these fish will help you tie and fish imitations more effectively.

In many river systems, baitfish may have seasonal or localized importance for smallmouth bass. Because no two rivers are alike, the key is to observe your surroundings and try to figure out what the bass are eating and pattern the behavior of both the bait and the bass. One stretch of river I fish has a warmwater outlet from a nearby power plant. Gizzard shad are abundant there because of the warmer water. On other rivers, alewives are important. On many Great Lakes streams, bass gorge on emerald shiners and gobies, an introduced species that is rapidly becoming the major food base for smallmouth here.

How Bass Feed on Baitfish

Unlike fish with teeth, such as barracuda or brown trout, bass do not try to cripple their prey before eating it. Instead, they use a burst of speed to help them overcome their prey, and then inhale baitfish with powerful suction created by the rush of water through their gills when they open their mouths. They approach their prey from behind, and then quickly dart to the side or meet them head-on, opening their mouths quickly to create suction.

Depending on the habits and availability of prey, bass either roam a river chasing the bait or lie in ambush along shorelines, rocks, deadfalls, and other structure. Smallmouth following schools of baitfish usually try to trap them by corralling them in the shallows or using structure to limit their escape routes.

Just because you find schools of baitfish doesn't necessarily mean bass will be feeding on them. Water temperature plays an important role in how long and how many times a day smallmouth need to feed. At water temperatures below 70 degrees, large smallmouth do not have to feed as often as when the water temperatures go above 80 degrees. There is an old saying: "The hotter the water, the better the smallmouth fishing." This is so because the hotter the water, the higher the bass's metabolism, causing them to search for food.

Some large bass wait for smaller ones to bust up a school of bait, and then cruise in to consume stunned or crippled prey. I've watched this happen frequently when bass are blitzing schools of gizzard shad. To catch fish in these situations, cast and let your fly flutter toward the bottom with only an occasional twitch.

One day I spotted fish feeding along a shallow shoreline laced with protruding ledge rock. I headed the boat to that location, and as my clients and I approached, we watched three small bass, around twelve inches long, attacking a school of gizzard shad. I prepared one client's tippet with a 6-inch-long fly while we waited and watched the area carefully. Just as the commotion started to ease, a large smallmouth appeared. Slowly, with displayed authority, it swam toward the hubbub. Two injured shad lay quivering on the river bottom. As the large smallmouth slowly swam toward them, I instructed my client to cast the fly between the bass and the injured shad and let it sink. As the fly slowly descended, the big smallmouth inhaled it.

Although we could have caught the smaller bass by casting flies to them when they were feeding, we chose not to. Hooking the smaller bass would have ruined our chances at the larger fish. It may sound obvious, but patiently watching something from beginning to end provides more knowledge than just observing the beginning.

In this section, I discuss the most important baitfish that I've had experience with; there are so many kinds that it would be hard to include them all. I have designed specific imitations for the following baitfish: shiners, dace, and minnows; darters; immature gamefish; fallfish; gizzard shad; and sculpins. I provide more detailed descriptions of those for which I have created patterns, because most of them belong to important groups of baitfish that occur in smallmouth habitat throughout the United States. There's a lot to say about each type, but I'll focus on those things most important to anglers and fly tiers: range; physical characteristics, such as size, shape, and color; major defining features; habitat preference for feeding and spawning; and swimming behavior.

Most smallmouth anglers have experience fishing for trout and a rudimentary understanding of aquatic insects, the backbone of trout fly fishing. Most trout anglers do not seem to know as much about baitfish as they do about mayflies and caddisflies, however, so I will spend more time in this chapter discussing baitfish than bugs.

The following are only short descriptions, but armed with information such as this for your local baitfish will make you a better angler. It's important to study the baitfish in your own home streams. Check your local fishing-regulations handbook and state fish commission website or publications. For the information below, I am indebted to the Pennsylvania Fish and Boat Commission's publication on the state's baitfish.

Flies tied with dumbbell eyes are very effective because they help sink the fly to the fish's level and also cause it to dip and dart like the naturals. More often than not, action and presentation are more important than color. JAY NICHOLS

Darters come in a wide range of colors. They have broad heads tapering to thin tails and swim along the stream bottom. I designed the Purple Darter to imitate these overlooked baitfish. ROB CRISWELL

CLOUSER PURPLE DARTER

JAY NICHOLS

Hook:	Size 4 Mustad S71S SS
Thread:	6/0 olive Uni-Thread
Eyes:	⅟₃₀-ounce metallic dumbbell eyes
Belly:	Olive calf-tail fibers
Middle (tail):	Purple calf-tail fibers
Back:	Olive calf-tail fibers
Flash:	Purple Flashabou and red Krystal Flash

Darters

Freshwater darters are often overlooked and under-imitated. As a group, they are the most colorful freshwater baitfish species, and the males in their brilliant spawning colors rival any colorful and exotic aquarium fish.

Darters are members of the perch family, and there are more than 140 species in North America. They live everywhere but the extreme northeastern United States, eastern Canada, and the waters west of the Continental Divide (except where they have been introduced). Most darters range from one to two inches long, though two species reach at least six and a half inches.

These fish forage for food on the stream bottom, and as their name implies, they dart along the bottom of the stream in erratic bursts. Many do not have swim bladders, the buoyant sacs in many fish that aid in flotation. Their lack of buoyancy helps darters stay near the bottom of the stream, as does the water rushing over their flattened, downward-sloping heads.

Darters spawn over several months in the spring and summer. During this period, they are brilliantly colored. Darters have two dominant dorsal fins and wide pectoral fins. These traits create a broad and wide silhouette, unlike the slim profile of minnows.

Sculpins are also bottom fish that are at home in trout and smallmouth streams across the country. Zoo Cougars, Muddler Minnows, and sculpin-colored Clouser Minnows imitate these baits. ROB CRISWELL

Sculpins

Sculpins live in smallmouth waters across the country but are most often found in habitats with cool, fast-flowing water. They reach four or five inches in length. Sculpins have broad heads tapering to relatively thin tails and prominent fanlike pectoral fins. They do not have scales. Like darters, sculpins do not have swim bladders and swim tight to the bottom of the stream with short, erratic darts. They prefer the faster-moving sections of a stream, such as the heads of pools, and they spawn in the riffles in the spring.

All sculpins are mottled in brown, olive, or black tones that closely match the overall color of their habitat, with lighter bellies ranging from white to tan to yellow. Like many creatures in nature, they are camouflaged, taking on the appearance of the stream bottom for protection. The most common species in the waters I fish is the mottled sculpin, a light to dark brown fish with darker mottling on its back and sides and a pale brown or whitish belly.

CLOUSER DEEP MINNOW
(Orange and Brown Sculpin)

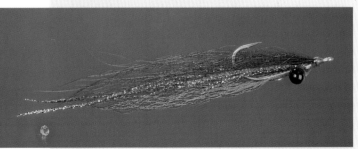

JAY NICHOLS

Hook:	Size 2 Mustad 71S SS
Thread:	6/0 light cahill Uni-Thread
Eyes:	$\frac{1}{30}$-ounce metallic dumbbell eyes
Belly:	Orange deer-tail fibers
Middle:	Gold Krystal Flash
Back:	Brown deer-tail fibers

CLOUSER DEEP MINNOW
(Olive and Tan Sculpin)

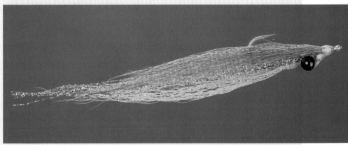

JAY NICHOLS

Hook:	Size 2 Mustad 71S SS
Thread:	6/0 light cahill Uni-Thread
Eyes:	$\frac{1}{30}$-ounce metallic dumbbell eyes
Belly:	Tan deer-tail fibers
Middle:	Gold Krystal Flash
Back:	Olive deer-tail fibers

Madtoms, also called stonecats, look like baby catfish. Retrieve Clouser Madtoms or marabou or rabbit-strip Muddler Minnows along the bottom to catch fish feeding on madtoms. ROB CRISWELL

CLOUSER MADTOM

JAY NICHOLS

Hook:	Size 4 Mustad S71 SS
Thread:	6/0 rust brown Uni-Thread
Body:	Rusty brown wide-cut rabbit strip
Belly:	Dark brown calf-tail fibers
Head:	Rusty brown rabbit-fur fibers
Head covering:	Small clump of dark brown calf-tail fibers
Eyes:	1/30-ounce metallic dumbbell

Catfish

Many anglers call most small catfish madtoms or stone-cats, but technically, these are different species in the same family. For fishing purposes however, all of the small catfish behave similarly.

The common name stonecats reflects their preferred habitat beneath flat rocks in riffles and runs. They live in a range of water types throughout the United States and Canada, from warmwater creeks to large rivers.

The origin of the name madtom is unknown. Some say it's because of this baitfish's erratic motions; others say it has something to do with their ability to sting. One thing is for sure: Wherever they are found, big bass eat them. More big smallmouth are caught on these small fish than with any other bait—at least, where I fish. They are relatively unknown to fly anglers, however, because they are not often seen in streams during the day. Like most catfish, madtoms feed at night and eat aquatic insects as well as crayfish and other small invertebrates. Madtoms have poison glands at the base of their pectoral fins, and if you handle them improperly, you can be stung.

All of the small catfish swim along and close to the bottom. They have flat, broad heads similar to sculpins; dark backs ranging from brown or black to olive or gray; and lighter bellies from white to tan to yellow. The most common size range that bass feed on is from two to six inches.

Emerald shiners are slim baits common in the Great Lakes and their tributaries. The Clouser Silver Shiner; blue over white or olive over white synthetic-hair Clouser Deep Minnows; or epoxy flies like Bob Popovics's Surf Candy imitate these baits. ROB CRISWELL

Minnows

Many people refer to any small baitfish as a minnow, but minnows are a large, diverse family of fish that encompasses small fish like the native black-nosed dace to common carp that can weigh thirty pounds.

The members of the minnow family that are most important to my fishing—and those for which I have designed flies—are the shiners, fallfish and chubs, and black-nose dace.

Shiners. Shiners are a large group of baitfish ranging from small, slim fish such as the emerald shiner, which is an important species in the Great Lakes smallmouth fisheries both for lake and tributary bass, to large, robust fish such as the common and golden shiners, which live in bass waters across the country. Common shiners can grow to ten inches long, golden shiners twelve inches.

On my home river, I imitate the common shiner, which we call the Susquehanna or river shiner, and golden shiner. I also have an imitation I call the Silver

Common shiners are widespread baitfish. The Clouser River Shiner is my imitation for this bait. ROB CRISWELL

Some mistake golden shiners for goldfish. When they are young, slim baitfish patterns work well as imitations, but as they get older, they take on a more robust shape better imitated by Half and Halfs or Lefty's Deceivers. ROB CRISWELL

CLOUSER DEEP MINNOW
(Susquehanna Shiner)

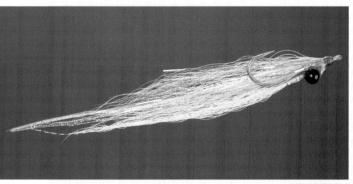

JAY NICHOLS

Hook:	Size 2 Mustad 71S SS
Thread:	6/0 gray Uni-Thread
Eyes:	⅟₃₀-ounce metallic dumbbell eyes
Belly:	White deer-tail fibers
Middle:	Silver Krystal Flash and pearlescent Flashabou
Back:	Gray over blue deer-tail fibers

Shiner, which is not a precise imitation for the species of that name, but a generic pattern that imitates the overall coloration and profile of many young shiner species. Though some species such as the common and golden shiners grow robust and large, and the golden shiner takes on a distinctive yellowish gold cast as an adult, shiners are silvery in color when they are young, and my generic imitation with its darkish gray back and white belly with flash imitates most juvenile or small adult shiners.

Common shiners are found as far west as the Rockies, as far north as southern Canada, and as far south as Virginia. They average three to four inches long but can grow as big as six to ten inches. The common shiner has an olive green back, white belly, and a prominent purple or bluish gray stripe along each side. The heads of males swell, turn pink, and are covered with bumps (like those of the chubs) when they are spawning. Common shiners prefer streams with cool, clear water. They spawn over gravel beds when water temperatures reach 60 to 65 degrees.

Right: Chubs (creek chub shown here) and fallfish belong to a group of minnows called stonerollers, because they build nests by moving small rocks in the stream. ROB CRISWELL

Golden shiners are widely distributed, from the Canadian maritime provinces, throughout the eastern and central United States, to South America, as well as in many parts of the western United States. Adults can reach seven to twelve inches and may live as long as eight years. The golden shiner has a deep body with gold-colored sides and an olive-brown back. The sides sometimes reflect a silver color. The fins are yellow or light olive in adults and silvery in the young. The young smaller than about four inches appear silvery all over, as do other shiners. Golden shiners prefer quieter portions of rivers and streams with clear water, a bottom of sand or organic debris, and much aquatic vegetation, where they feed on zooplankton, midge pupae, algae, and aquatic insects. They spawn in late spring through about midsummer in water temperatures of 68 to 80 degrees near submerged vegetation.

A shiner's scales reflect brilliant silver or brassy gold tints, giving the fish a shining appearance. Shiners feed, travel, and spawn in groups.

Chubs and Fallfish. Chubs and fallfish are part of a group of eastern minnows once called *Awadosi,* or stone carriers, by the Indians of the Hudson Bay region. These fish, known as chubs and fallfish today, are unique among North American minnows in that they build spawning nests from gravel and small pebbles in the streams by picking up stones with their mouths and placing them in piles. The piles can vary in size, some large.

Chubs are stout-looking, cylindrical minnows, with large, reflective scales and moderately large mouths. Dur-

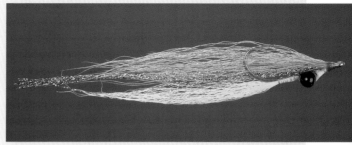

CLOUSER DEEP MINNOW
(Silver Shiner)

JAY NICHOLS

Hook:	Size 2 Mustad 71S SS
Thread:	6/0 gray Uni-Thread
Eyes:	$\frac{1}{30}$-ounce metallic dumbbell eyes
Belly:	White deer-tail fibers
Middle:	Rainbow Krystal Flash
Back:	Gray deer-tail fibers

ing breeding time, in the spring when water temperatures reach 55 degrees, the heads of male chub swell and develop bumps on top. Some species, such as creek and river chubs, develop rose-colored bands along their sides when they spawn.

Creek chubs are common in central and eastern United States smallmouth water. They can be as long as ten inches but average around four inches. They have light olive backs and silvery white bellies with shades of purple and blue. Creek chubs prefer the deeper pools

When chubs spawn, they develop hornlike bumps on their heads and take on a distinct pink coloration (breeding male river chub shown here). *My Spring Chub Deep Minnow imitates this prominent feature.* ROB CRISWELL

CLOUSER DEEP MINNOW
(Spring Chub)

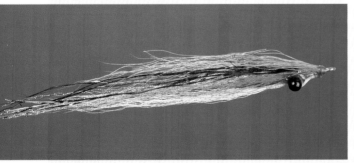

JAY NICHOLS

Hook:	Size 2 Mustad 71S SS
Thread:	6/0 light cahill Uni-Thread
Eyes:	¹⁄₃₀-ounce metallic dumbbell eyes
Belly:	White deer-tail fibers
Middle:	Red Flashabou and pearlescent Krystal Flash
Back:	Gray over pink deer-tail fibers

of small and medium-size streams. Young creek chubs are more silvery than adults and feed on aquatic invertebrates. Adult creek chubs eat small fish, larger invertebrates, and immature crayfish.

Fallfish are the largest native minnows in the northeastern United States, growing as long as eighteen inches but averaging six to eight inches. It is for these enormous baitfish that I designed my Half and Half (see recipe on page 88). They have olive-brown to black backs, silvery sides, and white bellies. Fallfish less than four inches are almost completely silver, with a prominent wide, dark band extending along the middle of each side. They prefer clear, clean, gravelly pools and slower-flow areas of large streams. Fallfish spawn when water temperatures reach about 58 degrees. Their nests can be as large as six feet across and two feet high.

Right: Black-nose dace live in a wide range of water types, from small streams to large rivers, but they thrive in clear, cool water, one of the reasons they are also an important food for trout.
ROB CRISWELL

Fallfish are the largest native minnow in the Northeast. They can grow as long as eighteen inches but are more commonly between eight and twelve inches. I designed my Half and Half pattern to imitate the fallfish that the big bass feed on. When fishing in shallow water, a Deceiver provides the same profile but doesn't sink as fast. ROB CRISWELL

I have often caught surface-feeding chubs and fall-fish on flies, both surface and subsurface.

Black-Nose Dace. Black-nose dace are common small minnows distributed throughout the Mississippi and Great Lakes watersheds and along the Atlantic coast to North Carolina. They live in a wide range of water types, from small streams to large rivers, but thrive in clear, cool water, which is one reason the black-nose dace is also an important food for trout. These slender minnows grow to about three inches long and have brown backs, black side stripes, and white bellies. When spawning in the spring, May to June in Pennsylvania, males have rusty orange or red stripes immediately below the black side stripes, and their pectoral and pelvic fins become yellow-white or orange. They spawn in shallow sandy or gravelly riffles. Black-nose dace feed on the tiny invertebrate animal life they find on the stream bottom, including blackfly and midge larvae.

CLOUSER DEEP MINNOW
(Black-Nose Dace)

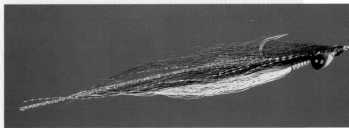

JAY NICHOLS

Hook:	Size 2 Mustad 71S SS
Thread:	6/0 brown Uni-Thread
Eyes:	1/30-ounce metallic dumbbell eyes
Belly:	White deer-tail fibers
Middle:	Silver Krystal Flash
Back:	Brown over black deer-tail fibers

Juvenile smallmouth bass are a prime target for any bass larger than they are. My Baby Smallmouth Bass Deep Minnow is one of my favorite flies to use all season long. ROB CRISWELL

Juvenile Gamefish

A bass will eat any fish it can get into its mouth, which includes juveniles of other common gamefish that share stream space with smallmouth bass, such as baby walleye, pike, and trout. Bass hunt for these small fish around cover such as large rocks or rock rubble, underwater grass, sunken logs, tree branches, and other debris. Many walleye, pike, and trout can be found along the shorelines of main rivers and their islands. Bass also may eat smaller fish of their own species. I have seen large adult smallmouth capture and eat six- to nine-inch-long smallmouth.

Gizzard Shad

Gizzard shad are schooling fish common in stillwaters and the deep, slow pools of river and streams. They live in the brackish water of tidal zones and estuaries as well. Gizzard shad have also been introduced into many freshwater impoundments and rivers across the United States, either by accident or on purpose as a forage fish.

Gizzard shad look like other members of the herring family but have short, soft-rayed dorsal fins on the center of the back. The rear ray is a long, trailing filament, longer than any of the other rays. The gizzard shad's back is bluish green to gray. It has silvery sides that

CLOUSER DEEP MINNOW
(Baby Smallmouth Bass)

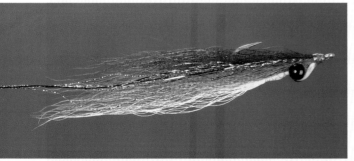

JAY NICHOLS

Hook:	Size 2 Mustad 71S SS
Thread:	6/0 light cahill Uni-Thread
Eyes:	1/30-ounce metallic dumbbell eyes
Belly:	White deer-tail fibers
Middle:	Root beer Flashabou and gold Krystal Flash
Back:	Brown over green deer-tail fibers

CLOUSER DEEP MINNOW
(Baby Pike)

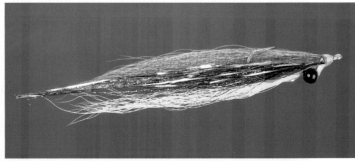

JAY NICHOLS

Hook:	Size 2 Mustad 71S SS
Thread:	6/0 light cahill Uni-Thread
Eyes:	1/30-ounce metallic dumbbell eyes
Belly:	Yellow deer-tail fibers
Middle:	Gold Krystal Flash and gold Flashabou
Back:	Olive over black deer-tail fibers

can reflect blue, green, brassy, or reddish tints, depending on light and water conditions. These fish grow rapidly, as much as seven inches in the first year, and can reach twenty inches. Adult gizzard shad are broad from top to bottom but narrow from side to side. Young shad are long and slender. Gizzard shad have large eyes, which may be an important trigger for bass. A size of one to two inches long in early summer and four to six inches by late summer is a good rule to follow when imitating young shad. Anglers should be aware of the remaining adult shad in the area, of which many can be longer (up to sixteen inches) than what is reasonably imitated by a fly. Match the size of shad you see in the river at the time up to that size.

These fish are filter feeders, straining small animal organisms and plants from bottom mud and organic deposits. Gizzard shad have an unusual digestive process, with a gizzardlike stomach that grinds the vegetable material they eat. Shad are often found over a mucky bottom, which they filter when feeding. Schooling shad stir up silt from the bottom as they feed or move across these muddy areas. The mud and silt they stir up is similar to the mud streak carp leave behind them, but a school of shad leaves a much wider trail that can attract many bass.

Gizzard shad spawn when water temperatures reach the mid-sixties to mid-seventies. Spawning fish gather in large schools to broadcast their eggs in water several feet deep, near the shore. Shad die-offs can occur after they

CLOUSER DEEP MINNOW
(Baby Walleye)

JAY NICHOLS

Hook:	Size 2 Mustad 71S SS
Thread:	6/0 brown Uni-Thread
Eyes:	1/30-ounce metallic dumbbell eyes
Belly:	Tan deer-tail fibers
Middle:	Gold Krystal Flash
Back:	Brown deer-tail fibers

CLOUSER DEEP MINNOW
(Gizzard Shad)

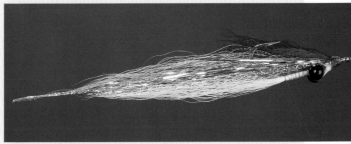

JAY NICHOLS

Hook:	Size 2 Mustad 71S SS
Thread:	6/0 gray Uni-Thread
Eyes:	1/30-ounce metallic dumbbell eyes
Belly:	White deer-tail fibers
Middle:	Silver Krystal Flash and silver Flashabou
Back:	Gray deer-tail fibers
Throat:	Red deer-tail fibers

spawn or as a result of cold water conditions in late fall and winter.

As water temperatures drop toward the sixties in the fall, gizzard shad migrate downriver until they find suitable water temperatures. Many of them stay in and around the warmwater outlets of power plants. These areas usually provide good fishing in the fall, winter, and early spring, while the rest of the river is shut down by cold water temperatures.

Birds follow schools of gizzard shad just like they do saltwater baitfish. One of my strategies on the Susquehanna in late August is to look for birds feeding on a school of gizzard shad. You can see these birds hovering and diving from a long distance, especially if you are actively searching for them.

Schools of gizzard shad also give away their presence in other ways. In clear water, you can see silver reflections from their sides as they move from one area to another. As a school, they rotate in the water like a spinning top when they swim. This movement is a trait of survival. All of the shad want to be in the center of the school for security from predators, and those on the outside of the school move toward the center, pushing fish that were in the center to the margins. Gizzard shad are continuously on the move. As a shad school moves close to the surface, it creates "nervous water." The surface above the school displays a wavy, ripple-type motion different from the surrounding area. This nervous water is sometimes very subtle, so it takes some practice to recognize it.

Schools of small shad—and other schooling minnows, for that matter—moving just under the surface create a shadow that anglers call dark water. At first it may just look like a patch of dark river bottom, but if you watch closely, you will see movement along the fringes, and at times the whole shadow may move.

Traveling gizzard shad choose routes of less resistance. When the school is on the move, it tends to travel alongside obstacles instead of going over them. Anglers that locate these crossings—around grass beds, logs, rocks, or shallow gravel bars—increase their chances for smallmouth action. Smallmouth bass are familiar with this behavior and often attack the shad at these ambush points. One of their favorite spots is alongside a ledge where the river becomes shallow. Shad following the ledge become trapped between the ledge and the shallow water, and the bass feast on them. I have cast flies to smallmouth chasing shad in water so shallow the bass's backs were out of the water. Gizzard shad, where they live with smallmouth bass, provide exciting fishing.

CRAYFISH

On some rivers where crayfish are abundant, I've looked down a bass's mouth as I was removing a hook, to see pincers protruding from the fish's throat. Crayfish are crustaceans that thrive in rivers with semisoft bottoms strewn with rocks, rubble, sunken wood, grass, and other types of structure. They are mainly nocturnal feeders but won't pass up an easy meal during the day.

Water temperatures, length of days, and sunlight determine activity periods. During the winter, crayfish hibernate by burying themselves in mud or under layers of decaying leaves. In the spring, as water temperatures rise, crayfish prepare to spawn. Female crayfish carry an orange egg mass under the abdomen near the tail.

Crayfish colors vary when they spawn, with their habitat, and after they molt. Crayfish living around grass are greenish olive, and I've seen them in many other colors, including variations of blues, grays, dark browns,

Along with baitfish, crayfish are another smallmouth mainstay. Crayfish colors can vary with their habitat and the time of year.
BOB CLOUSER

My favorite crayfish colors are olive, tan, and brown. I fish these in various sizes. JAY NICHOLS

rust, greens, and splotched orange. Like all crustaceans, crayfish must periodically molt their exoskeletons as they grow. Immediately after they molt, crayfish are at their most vulnerable stage. These softshell crayfish are ghostly pale, and light tan or pale olive imitations work well at this time.

Crayfish are most available to bass and other fish species from late spring through fall. Even though they are available in great numbers, there are certain times of the season where size is important. In early spring, I use the largest patterns, in size 2, to imitate adult crayfish coming out of hibernation, or the very smallest, in size 12 or 14, to imitate the young of the year. As the summer progresses, the average size of the crayfish increases. Ninety-nine percent of the fish I catch with a Clouser Crayfish (see recipe on page 93) are on size 4 through 8 hooks.

Many crayfish die during and after spawning. At times, smallmouth feast on them when they are in the final struggles of life on stream bottoms and along shorelines. I have seen bass tight to the banks with their backs out of the water eating dying crayfish.

AQUATIC INSECTS

Although large bass prefer meals of minnows or crayfish, aquatic insects, by virtue of their sheer numbers, make up a significant part of a smallmouth's diet. When insects are available in great quantities, even the large bass feed on the relatively tiny bugs.

But many of the aquatic insects bass feed on are not tiny at all. Numerous rivers and lakes across the country have populations of damselflies, dragonflies, mayflies, and stoneflies. The nymphal forms of many of these aquatic insects are large, such as yellow, green, and brown drakes; big *Isonychia;* and *Hexagenia limbata,* or Hex.

Mayfly nymphs, emergers, and adults make up an important part of a smallmouth's menu, and when they are emerging in the spring, summer, and fall, they can provide excellent opportunities for surface fishing with either imitations of the aquatic insects or other surface flies such as Floating Minnows and poppers. I rarely encounter situations where a generic surface fly won't work on a bass rising to mayfly adults, though many anglers carry specific imitations with them. One benefit of fishing smaller mayfly imitations is the ease with which you can cast the flies. It's much easier to cast a size 10 White Wulff than a size 4 bass popper, and when bass are feeding on surface insects, it's an excellent time to use light tackle such as 3- to 5-weight rods. A twelve- to fourteen-inch smallmouth puts up a great fight on a 4-weight.

Stoneflies are abundant in many rivers with fast-flowing water that is of good quality, and bass feed on them. Small Woolly Buggers in all black or brown and yellow or specific stonefly imitations can be fished dead drift or twitched through the shallows. STEVE MAY

When smallmouth are feeding on hatching insects, you do not normally need an exact imitation or size. I use a few general, multipurpose dry flies that are durable and float high. Most of the flies that work for trout work equally well for smallmouth.

The whitefly hatch on many eastern rivers can be an exhilarating experience. At first the river is quiet, but then mayflies begin to emerge—first one here, another one there, then a few more, until they blanket the water. After a few minutes, as the hatch progresses, the air is filled with insects, at times twelve feet thick stretching from shoreline to shoreline. When the mating ritual begins, the entire surface of the water is covered by the dying insects and turns grayish white with their carcasses. Whiteflies get into your open tackle pack, down your shirt, and in your eyes, and the dying insects can be four inches deep on the floor of the boat. The bass—and many other fish species—are in a feeding frenzy.

In the early 1900s, this insect emergence was so thick it would drive anglers off rivers and stop locomotives on railroad bridges over the Potomac and Susquehanna. Lefty Kreh recalls fishing these hatches on the Potomac River in 1949 and says that the hatches were two to three times heavier than today. Nevertheless, it is still the greatest hatch of the season for smallmouth bass anglers.

The whitefly *(Ephoron leukon)* is also called the white miller. The whitefly hatches on many eastern rivers and

This nice bass fell for a dead drifted large Clouser Drake, before the whitefly hatch even came off. In the summer, bass are conditioned to feeding on the surface and are always looking up for a meal. JAY NICHOLS

streams from July through August. The emergence begins in the lower reaches of a river or stream and travels upstream as water temperatures increase. This is the only mayfly I know of with a five-minute life span. In this short time, it emerges, mates, and dies. Unlike some other mayflies that go to the trees, rocks, or shorelines to transform from dun to spinner, the whitefly completes its life cycle in the air within minutes of hatching.

During the hatch, other species besides smallmouth feed on whiteflies, and each makes distinct riseforms. Sunfish usually dimple the surface, and rock bass make a sucking or snapping-type sound while feeding on the surface. Carp make a small, nearly perfect circle with every little rise. Fallfish and chubs stay close to the surface

when feeding, and this causes the riseform ring to be elliptical or erratic. Catfish appear on the surface after dark and skim the surface with their upper jaws exposed. When you first see this feeding form, it can fool you into thinking something is swimming across the surface, such as a muskrat or snake. Catfish prefer to feed in slower currents. Look for them tight against banks where spent whiteflies are concentrated or at "chum seams," places where a concentration of flies passes along rocks or at the seam of water at the rear of a grass bed. Another hot spot is often at the downstream side of a break in a rock ledge that funnels and concentrates the fallen spinners.

Other large mayflies, such as yellow, brown, and green drakes, can provide excellent surface dry-fly fishing for smallmouth bass. These flies hatch in the late spring and summer on many smallmouth rivers. Another important summer hatch on streams across the country are the cream- or yellow-colored mayflies ranging from size 12 to 18. On the Susquehanna River, there are many species of yellowish flies commonly called light cahills and sulphurs. In my experience, it's not critical to match the exact size or color, but sometimes—especially in slow pools where bass often sip these insects—it doesn't hurt to come close.

Where there are big hatches of mayflies, especially large ones like Hexagenia limbata, *bass of all sizes feed on the surface.* KEN COLLINS

Hellgrammites

Hellgrammites are the larval stage of dobsonflies, large, winged insects that emerge around dusk through the summer on many streams across the United States. They are an important year-round food source for trout, bass, and other fish, especially in the spring and early summer. Some fish feed on the winged adults, but they gorge on the nymphal form. The larva has a robust, yellowish to brown, segmented body; large, pinching mandibles; six legs on the thorax; four claws at the rear of the abdomen; and eight feathery appendages on the abdomen.

Hellgrammites are usually on the move from late May until mid-July. On Pennsylvania's Susquehanna River in the Harrisburg area, hellgrammite patterns work all summer, but the first three weeks in June are best. The ugly hellgrammite is most active at this time of year, as it crawls from its nymphal habitat in fast-moving riffle water to the streambank, where it eventually matures into the equally homely dobsonfly. During this precarious trip, many hellgrammites are swept off the river bottom and drift helplessly in the water's currents. At this time, fish key on these insects.

Hellgrammites live in a wide variety of habitats, from small streams to stillwaters, but they generally prefer cool rivers and streams with good water quality and highly oxygenated water. They spend their nymphal stage living under rocks and prey on a wide range of other aquatic insects, such as mayfly, caddis, and stonefly nymphs. Hellgrammites can grow up to five inches long, though they average two to three inches. In rivers where hellgrammites live, bass and trout show a strong preference for the one-quarter- to three-inch-long brown and black nymphs.

After mating, female dobsonflies lay their eggs on a dry surface near water, usually on an exposed rock, bridge abutment, or overhanging vegetation. The white, circular, nickel-size egg masses usually consist of a large number of eggs that take from a few days to a few weeks to hatch. When they hatch, the larvae drop into the water, where they spend an average of one to three years under rocks and logs. The nymphs crawl onto land near the water and burrow two to four inches into wet soil, moss, decaying vegetation, or beneath logs, where they pupate for about two weeks. They emerge as adult dobsonflies and live only about two weeks before they mate, lay eggs, and die.

You can scout rivers for these large insects by wading and tipping over flat stones in freestone streams. The nymphal hellgrammites cling to the bottoms of stones. Beware of the pincers at the head, mandibles that help them catch and eat aquatic insects and can also nip your fingers if you pick them up carelessly. The best place to

Some anglers swear that if given a choice between a crayfish and a hellgrammite, the bass takes the hellgrammite every time. Either way, a black Woolly Bugger or a Clouser Hellgrammite fished dead drift or swung through the shallows catches bass. BOB CLOUSER

Close-up of hellgrammite cocoon. BOB CLOUSER

grab them is behind the back of the head, the way you'd grab a snake.

Adult dobsonflies can be five inches long, with a wing span of four to five inches. Males have long pincers that they use to grasp the females during mating. Adults look for cover in the trees near water and hide there during the day. They are weak fliers.

Good flies for the larval forms include Woolly Buggers and Clouser Hellgrammites (see recipe on page 95) in size 4 through 8. Smallmouth will eat adult dobsonflies if they fall on the water's surface at night and helplessly flutter their wings. A popping bug steadily worked across and down currents imitates this action.

Damselflies and Dragonflies

Both the larval and adult stages of dragonflies and damselflies are important foods for bass. Damselfly larvae have slender, cylindrical bodies ending in three leaflike gills; dragonfly larvae are robust and bullet-shaped or sometimes flat, depending on their habitat. They can be in the larval stage from three months to four years or more. They feed on fish eggs, tadpoles, and the larvae of smaller insects.

When the larvae finish developing, they migrate from the water to land. Most species use a vertical surface such as a reed in the water to climb up and molt. Once attached to the stalk, the adults emerge and fly off to nearby fields, where they can spend from a few days to three weeks maturing. When they are ready to mate,

Smallmouth feed on damselflies (shown here) and dragonflies both above and below the surface. RALPH CUTTER

they return to water, where anglers often see them flying about in tandem during mating and egg laying.

Adult dragonflies typically are strong fliers and have eyes that touch on top of the head. Their fore- and hindwings differ in shape, and when at rest, the wings are held away from the body at approximately a 180-degree angle. Adult damselflies are weaker fliers and have separated eyes. Their fore- and hindwings are similar in shape, and the wings are held close to the body when at rest.

Damselfly and dragonfly larvae live in a wide variety of environments, but they are most common in stillwaters, shallow areas of streams, and slower stretches of rivers. Generic thin nymph patterns tied on long-shank hooks in olive and brown do a good job of imitating damselfly nymphs, and more robust patterns in olive and brown imitate dragonfly larvae. The Clouser Swimming Nymph tied to imitate local insects is a good choice. For most smallmouth bass fishing, Woolly Buggers in a range of sizes imitate dragonfly larvae, and thin-profile Woolly Buggers that lack the palmered hackle and have marabou tails imitate the damsels. Fish these imitations near grasses where the naturals are migrating, and use an active retrieve with long strips punctuated by short ones.

When adult damsels and dragons are mating over the water, they trigger aggressive surface-feeding activity. Imitative damsel patterns like Whitlock's Damsel and John Betts's Foam Dragon Fly are good choices, as are simple poppers such as the EZ Popper. The Henshall Bug, named after Dr. James Henshall, whose *Book of the Black Bass* was published in 1881, is one of the oldest bass-fly patterns preserved in print and possibly was tied to imitate an adult damselfly.

OTHER CRITTERS

Smallmouth will take advantage of any opportunity for a meal. They eat frogs, salamanders, snakes, leeches, baby birds, cicadas, and just about anything else that winds up in the water and makes a commotion.

Poppers fished early in the morning or at night may imitate the floundering of small frogs or other small animals, such as mice, that happen to fall into the water or attempt to swim across the river. The thrashing of these small food items creates sound and disturbances that attract predators like smallmouth bass.

When I was a youngster, my dad collected live mice and used rubber bands to attach them to hooks. He'd set a mouse on a piece of tree bark, strip line off the reel, and let the bark with the mouse on it drift downstream toward a good holding spot such as a brush pile. When the bark and the mouse got close to the brush pile, he'd pull the mouse off the bark. The mouse would try to swim to the brush pile, and as my dad kept the line tight,

Deer hair has long been a favorite material to imitate frogs. Though these flies are beautiful, I have found that a foam popper can be just as effective. JAY NICHOLS

I remember seeing my dad catch big bass with live mice. Flies that float and create a disturbance on the surface of the water at night catch big fish. JAY NICHOLS

Left: Poppers fished early in the morning or at night may imitate the floundering of small frogs or other small animals, such as mice that happen to fall into the water or attempt to swim across the river. STEVE MAY

This nice bass took a large, black rabbit-strip fly fished deep on a sinking-tip line. It may have struck the fly thinking it was a leech, a snake, or simply something that looked like food. JACK HANRAHAN

MOST COMMON BAITFISH AND CLOUSER FLIES

Darters and Perch — Clouser Darter

Catfish (Stonecats, Madtom, Immature Catfish) — Clouser Madtom

Sculpins — Clouser Sculpin Deep Minnow, Darter, or Madtom

Gizzard Shad — Half and Half, Clouser Gizzard Shad Deep Minnow

Minnows

Black-Nose Dace — Clouser Black-Nose Dace

Common Shiner (aka River Shiner, Susquehanna Shiner) — Clouser River Shiner

Silver Shiner — Clouser Silver Shiner

Sucker — Clouser Silver Shiner/Half and Half (gray and white)

Fallfish — Half and Half (olive and white, gray and white)

Baby Carp, Rock Bass, Carp Minnow, Golden Shiner — Clouser Golden Shiner

Horned Chub — Clouser Spring Chub

Juvenile Gamefish

Walleye — Clouser Baby Walleye

Pike — Clouser Baby Pike

Bass — Clouser Baby Smallmouth

a big bass would come from under the pile of brush and inhale the mouse. I saw my dad catch smallmouth of twenty inches or more using this technique.

Rabbit-strip flies in various colors and lengths stripped slowly under the surface can do a good job of imitating salamanders and leeches. A hopper, cricket, or cicada can provide a nice meal, but bass also feed on smaller terrestrials such as ants and inchworms. During flying-ant migrations in the fall, I do well fishing a small popper. No, it doesn't match the ants, but the bass are looking up in anticipation of the flying ants, and they won't often refuse an easy meal. Remember, one of the nice things about fly-fishing for smallmouth bass is that you can keep your fly selection simple and still catch a lot of fish.

One of the nice things about fly-fishing for smallmouth bass is that you can keep your fly selection simple. A chartreuse and white Deep Minnow catches most bass most of the time. JAY NICHOLS

CHAPTER 5

My Fly Box

JACK HANRAHAN

Some of the most common questions I get from anglers, both new and experienced, are what flies I carry with me and what colors and sizes I use. First off, let me state that this chapter is my attempt to answer that question as accurately as I can by sharing the patterns I carry and use for bass. This is not a comprehensive list of all the effective patterns that catch smallmouth bass. Many fly designers, such as Dave Whitlock, John Barr, Larry Dahlberg, Al Troth, Lefty Kreh, Russ Blessing, and Don Gapen, have patterns that are proven

fish catchers and are covered in many books and magazine articles. I would like to share with you the system that I have developed over the years, and I hope this will inspire you to develop a system of your own. Maybe you will even create your own series of flies to match the baits in your area.

Because bass eat a wide range of foods, it would be impractical to carry specific imitations of every type and size of baitfish and impossible to carry flies for all the different types of food bass eat. My solution is to carry

Though I carry and fish flies that imitate a wide range of food that smallmouth eat, Clouser Deep Minnows in various colors with different size lead eyes are the backbone of my fly box.

BASIC TIPS FOR BUILDING A STREAMER BOX

More important than copying all of the flies that I use, my best advice is to emulate my decision-making process when choosing flies for my boxes. This governs my philosophy for everything from minnows to crayfish imitations.

• Carry a few basic imitations that cover the general shapes of the different baits in your area. I use Deep Minnows for slim to medium-size baitfish, Half and Halfs for large or robust baitfish, and Clouser Darters or Madtoms for bottom-dwelling baitfish. In a pinch, Deep Minnows work almost as well as Darters or Madtoms. Other anglers use different basic fly designs and modify the colors.

• Carry several sizes of each imitation.
• Carry a few basic color combinations. There is no need to go overboard. An all-white, a chartreuse over white or chartreuse and yellow, and a brown or tan fly will cover most every situation. As you learn more about your stream and the food there, you may derive satisfaction by creating more exacting imitations, as I have.

• Study the bait in your area, and fish your fly like a nervous or wounded natural—in the habitat the bait prefers, but always swimming away from the bass. If the baitfish swims on the bottom, make sure your fly has enough weight to get it to the bottom.

---

a range of patterns in a variety of sizes, profiles, and actions throughout the water column. I make sure I have heavily weighted flies for fishing the bottom, unweighted flies for fishing just under or on the surface, and several floating flies, some that make a lot of noise and some that are more subtle when I retrieve them in the water. Armed with all these choices, I'm certain one of these flies will catch a bass. Over time, I think it's important to develop a stable of flies that you feel confident about. You catch more fish when you have confidence in your flies.

I will list recipes only for those flies that I carry with me and use religiously or those that are a little different from the common Zonkers and Woolly Buggers. The fact that I don't have to include recipes for flies such as Muddlers, Zonkers, and Woolly Buggers testifies to their universality. They are common because they work extremely well. A pattern like the Red and White Hackle is known to relatively few anglers, but I hope that including it in this book will inspire others to use it. I am also providing a little background about how I came to create the patterns I designed. For complete tying steps, see *Clouser's Flies* (Stackpole Books, 2006).

Left: At times, bass demand a baitfish pattern that closely matches the naturals they are feeding on, but often it's more important to stick with one pattern and match the movement of the baitfish. This fish fell for a chartreuse and white Clouser Minnow. JACK HANRAHAN

IMITATING BAITFISH

Whether you are trying to design effective flies at your vise or shopping for the right patterns to match local bait, the shape and profile of the baitfish are important considerations. In his classic *Guide to Aquatic Trout Foods,* Dave Whitlock breaks down forage fish into four major classifications: wide-bodied, thin-backed, schooling, silvery fish; oval-bodied, free-swimming fish that are solitary or swim in small groups; wide-bellied fish with large heads tapering to relatively thin tails that live along the stream bottom; and eggs and newly hatched egg-sac and swim-up fry of trout and suckers. The silvery schooling fish include shad, smelt, herring, alewives, and shiners. The free-swimming fish include chub, dace, whitefish, sticklebacks, carp, and trout. Most of these fish take on colors of their habitat. The fish found on the bottom of the stream usually have broad heads tapering to thin tails, and include sculpins, catfish, and darters. These fish also take on the colors of the habitat in which they are found and are most often shades of browns and olives.

When choosing flies to match these basic profiles, I like to keep it simple. I use Clouser Deep Minnows to imitate slim to medium-bodied fish, Half and Halfs or Lefty's Deceivers for broad fish, and Clouser Darter or Madtom imitations to match the bottom-dwelling species with fat heads and thin tails. I don't need to imitate the eggs or newly hatched fry. Most of the large fish that I try to target would prefer a larger meal if given a choice.

Matching the predominant size of the baitfish that bass are feeding on can be important. For each color combination, I carry three sizes of each fly pattern. BOB CLOUSER

Behavior

Many baitfish swim and move in different ways. Whether moving around to feed or escaping a charging predator, each baitfish species moves in a distinct way. Free-swimming minnows move in short, darting spurts or long, fast dashes. Bottom-dwelling baitfish dart erratically while seeking out places to hide. Both types, when escaping from predators, head for cover on the bottom or elsewhere. These same baitfish, when injured, move in a completely different manner. At certain times, some baitfish, such as gizzard shad killed by cold water temperatures, float downstream motionless.

Even if you knew the exact baitfish motion that triggers the bass to strike, you probably would not be able to perfectly imitate the subtleties of its movement with a fly. Since we can only suggest life with our patterns, and we rarely know what bass are thinking, the best strategy for imparting motion to your baitfish imitations is to vary the retrieve. If long, slow strips aren't working, try long, fast strips or short, erratic ones, until you find an effective combination. When your retrieves no longer catch fish, start the process all over again.

Often it's not the movement of the bait that attracts the predatory bass, but rather the stops and pauses in between that may signal hesitation, weakness, or change of direction. Smallmouth attack their prey when they think it is most vulnerable. Though a sculpin darts from rock to rock, eventually it has to stop. If the bait stops within eyesight of the predator, it's a goner. On the Susquehanna River, shiners hang in schools, and when something comes after them, they dart toward safety. When they have to stop to change direction to go under the rocks, that's the key for bass to attack.

Size

Selecting the right fly size is often important. Matching the average size of the predominant bait makes sense, but at times, fish prefer baits smaller or larger than the naturals, and I like to carry three sizes of any given pattern when I go fishing—one small, one average, and one large. In a pinch, I've often had to trim long, heavily dressed patterns to get a smaller, thinner fly profile.

Though there are no hard-and-fast rules, I generally fish small flies, two to three inches long, in the spring to match the young-of-the-year baitfish, and I fish increasingly larger patterns through the season. By the time fall rolls around, I fish baitfish imitations almost half a foot long to imitate the average size of the bait that has matured since spring.

Where it is legal, some anglers fish two different size streamers at once to try to figure out what size the bass prefer. They simply attach another twelve to sixteen inches of tippet to the bend of the hook of the first streamer, and then tie on another streamer of a different size, color, or both. Though this rig can sometimes be awkward to cast, especially with two heavily weighted flies, it is an effective method for figuring out a fish's preference. It makes the most sense to use two flies with different sizes, profiles, or color.

When I encounter fish that refuse a fly but still roll on it, jump over it, or just nip it, I often increase or decrease the size of the pattern to get a strike. In clear water where you can spot the fish's reaction to your fly, you have a real advantage. If the fish doesn't commit to the fly or shies away from it at the last minute, you can learn from these clues and modify your tactics and fly choice. I have seen smallmouth roll over a large popper on the surface and inhale a size 6 on the next presentation. In addition to the size of the fly, hook size is also important. If you are fishing for small-stream bass, which tend to be small, though there are exceptions, a fly or hook too large for the fish to get into its mouth deters strikes and hinders hookups.

Weight

Though size and profile of the fly are critical, a baitfish pattern's weight can often determine its success. Adjusting the amount of weight in a fly allows you to fish the

Often, adjusting the amount of weight you use will help you catch larger fish. Here, Bob Clouser Jr. had to switch to a smaller Baby Pike Clouser Deep Minnow with a larger dumbbell eye, so that it would sink to the right depth where this bass was feeding. BOB CLOUSER

It's rewarding to match your local baitfish, but for many anglers, chartreuse is the best color. Here the author holds a nice bass that took a chartreuse and white Clouser Minnow. As Lefty Kreh says, "If it ain't chartreuse, it ain't no use." JACK HANRAHAN

fly at various depths, and the positioning and form of the weight influence the movement of the fly. Most of my subsurface flies have weight, whether in the form of lead wraps around the shank or a bead, such as with the Clouser Swimming Nymph, or dumbbell eyes, critical components in my Clouser Deep Minnow and other minnow imitations. On a Clouser Minnow, the metallic eyes positioned on the forward half of the fly help imitate the fleeing movements of a panic-stricken baitfish.

The amount of weight I use in each fly depends on the type of baitfish I want to imitate. If I want to match bottom-dwelling baitfish, such as sculpins, darters, stonecats, baby catfish, or suckers, I add a lot of weight to the fly so that it swims on the bottom. If I want to match baitfish that swim throughout the water column, such as shiners, dace, chubs, or shad, I add less weight so that I can retrieve the fly at various depths, depending on where I am catching the most fish. A moderately weighted fly will swim near the surface if I use a quick retrieve, but I can still get it deep if I allow it time to sink before beginning a slower retrieve. Because bass feed on many types of baitfish in any given river, I carry flies in a range of weights so that I can fish at various levels and imitate the behavior of different baitfish.

Color

In the water, baitfish reflect hundreds, if not thousands, of hues depending on light conditions, water clarity, and other factors, such as the color of the stream bottom. Bright, silvery baitfish such as the appropriately named shiner at times look iridescent blue or purple, and the bright reflections from the fish's body as it turns make it easy to see why adding different colored flashes to flies is sometimes effective. Some baitfish, such as the brilliantly colored darters, look like aquarium fish. Many baitfish also change colors when they spawn, adding to the complexity of your fly-tying palette.

Color, though not as crucial as size, profile, and weight, can be important at times. Baitfish colors vary as a result of habitat, light reflections, and water depth and clarity. Most colors appear dark below relatively shallow depths and as clarity diminishes. I don't have any answers as to why at some times certain colors work better than others. I just know that they do, so I always carry several colors of each fly.

Many baitfish species manifest basic reflective colors, which usually appear as various pearlescent shades, gold, silver, and even chartreuse. Not only do the basic colors change, but their hues also vary and include numerous shades of black, gray, brown, olive, white, green, purple, and blue. Colors and reflections also change with light refraction and at various water depths.

Adding some flash or using synthetic materials that reflect light are less-than-perfect attempts at truly capturing the wide range of colors in any baitfish. But we do our best, or we do just well enough, by matching the predominant colors. Most of my Clouser Minnows consist of two or three colors of bucktail and flash to imitate the overall color of the natural. When I look at a small shiner, for instance, I see, more or less, a grayish back, a flash of silver down the side, and a whitish belly. Though a sculpin may be ten shades of brown and yellow with mottling, a basic brown fly shaped and fished like a sculpin is good enough to make the bass bite. If the pattern doesn't do a good job of looking like something to eat, the fish will tell you!

Part of the beauty of fly tying is that you can take it as far as you want to go. Some tiers attempt to match every mark, fin, and other feature of the bait they are trying to imitate. Whether you like to tie superimitative flies or simple representations, it's important that you look at the fly when it's wet. The colors and shape of the fly are different when it's dry and in the vise or the fly-shop bins than when it's in the water. Bucktail and dubbing darken when wet, and the materials often compress. The best tests of an effective fly are how it looks in the water, how it casts and fishes, and how well it catches fish. Everything else is just window dressing.

Imitating the exact color of the natural is not always the most effective strategy. Many times it pays to change the color of the fly, depending on light conditions, water clarity, and the reaction of the fish. As a general rule, in low, clear water, sparse, light-colored flies with just a few strands of flash seem to work the best. At this time, I often fish Clouser Deep Minnows tied with synthetic fibers. In high or dirty water, or when fishing at night, dark flies with more flash work best. Over the years, I've found that chartreuse is a good all-around choice, because it's easy to see in a wide range of water clarity.

CLOUSER DEEP MINNOW

Clouser Minnows in hook sizes 2 through 6, from 1¾ to 4½ inches long, are my go-to patterns for imitating baitfish. At times, large smallmouth prefer bigger patterns tied on size 1/0 and 1 hooks. The imitative Clouser Minnows that I tie appear in the preceding chapter, where I also include recipes. Though I carry a wide assortment of color combinations, the most important colors for me are all white, chartreuse and white, chartreuse and yellow, brown over tan (Baby Walleye), olive over tan (Baby Sculpin), brown over green over white (Baby Smallmouth), and red and white. The Baby Smallmouth has caught the most smallmouth for me and draws strikes through the season in all types of clear-water conditions.

Some of these color combinations, such as the Baby Smallmouth, Baby Walleye, and Olive Sculpin, are imitative; others, like chartreuse and yellow and chartreuse and white, have proven themselves as great color combinations that consistently catch fish. At first you may not think anything in nature looks chartreuse, but many insects have shades of chartreuse in them, and a lot of baitfish show hints of chartreuse in their sides in certain lighting. Chartreuse is also an easy color for fish to see under various water conditions.

CLOUSER DEEP MINNOW
(Chartreuse and Yellow)

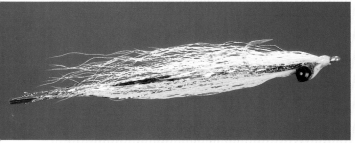

JAY NICHOLS

Hook:	Size 2 Mustad 71S SS
Thread:	6/0 light cahill Uni-Thread
Eyes:	1/30-ounce metallic dumbbell eyes
Belly:	Yellow deer-tail fibers
Middle:	Gold Krystal Flash and gold Flashabou
Back:	Chartreuse deer-tail fibers

I tie my Clouser Minnows sparse to allow more light to penetrate through the fibers, which adds sparkle and suggests life. Sparsely tied flies also sink faster than heavily dressed ones and have more action in the water. Action and sink rate are also changed by the size of the dumbbell eyes. For bass, I use eyes that weigh from 1/80 through 1/24 ounce, depending on how deep I want the fly to swim. There are no set rules for eye size. Tie some patterns with heavy eyes and some with lighter eyes for different water conditions.

In low and clear water, when brighter colors stop working, I use a more subdued pattern, such as my Baby Smallmouth, which has a white belly, green middle, brown back, and subdued flashes (see page 66 for recipe). That fly has saved the day during late September and October when the water is low and clear. Also at this time, brown and tan, olive and yellow, and brown and tan mixed together are good combinations. Super Hair Deep Minnows (facing page) also work well.

Because the Clouser Deep Minnow represents a style of tying, the best presentation is one that closely copies the movements of the food you want to imitate. It helps to understand the bait you are trying to imitate and, if using a strip retrieve, to experiment with it to find out what works best. You can also fish the fly dead drift with intermittent strips in flowing waters of rivers or saltwater currents. The weighted fly noses to the bottom, and as it comes down through the currents and bounces along the bottom, it looks like an injured minnow trying to hide.

CLOUSER DEEP MINNOW
(Chartreuse and White)

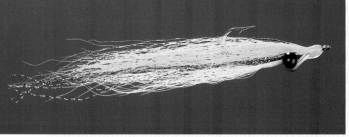

JAY NICHOLS

Hook:	Size 2 Mustad 71S SS
Thread:	6/0 light cahill Uni-Thread
Eyes:	1/30-ounce metallic dumbbell eyes
Belly:	White deer-tail fibers
Middle:	Rainbow Krystal Flash
Back:	Chartreuse deer-tail fibers

CLOUSER DEEP MINNOW
(White)

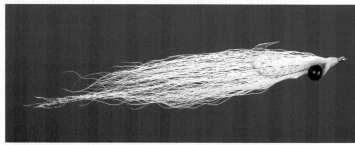

JAY NICHOLS

Hook:	Size 2 Mustad 71S SS
Thread:	6/0 yellow Uni-Thread
Eyes:	1/30-ounce metallic dumbbell eyes
Belly:	White deer-tail fibers
Middle:	Pearlescent Krystal Flash
Back:	White deer-tail fibers

CLOUSER DEEP MINNOW
(Red and White)

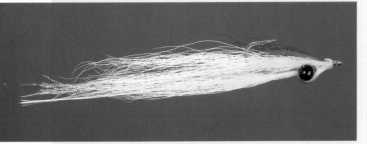

JAY NICHOLS

Hook:	Size 2 Mustad 71S SS
Thread:	6/0 light cahill Uni-Thread
Eyes:	1/30-ounce metallic dumbbell eyes
Belly:	White deer-tail fibers
Middle:	Pearlescent Krystal Flash and pearlescent Flashabou
Back:	White deer-tail fibers
Throat:	Red deer-tail fibers

CLOUSER SUPER HAIR
MINNOW (River Shiner)

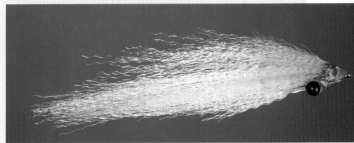

JAY NICHOLS

Hook:	Size 2 Mustad S71 SS
Thread:	6/0 gray Uni-Thread
Eyes:	1/30-ounce metallic dumbbell or hourglass eyes
Belly:	White Unique or Super Hair
Middle:	Pearl Flashabou and silver Krystal Flash
Back:	Smoky Gray Unique or Super Hair over blue Super Hair

SUPER HAIR DEEP MINNOW
(RIVER SHINER)

The Super Hair Deep Minnow is nothing more than a Clouser Deep Minnow tied with synthetic hair, such as Super Hair or Unique Hair. I use these flies in late fall or anytime there is low, clear water. Cold water temperatures affect fish's vision differently than warm temperatures. In clear, cold water, a fish's eyes are sharp enough to distinguish a lot more things than they can in warm water. Based on my experience on the river, translucent flies tied with synthetics seem to catch more fish in clear water. Perhaps this is because the way they reflect light looks more realistic to fish. I think this is also why we have to use lighter, 4- to 6-pound-test tippets on the river in the clear water of the fall, but we can use 8- to 12-pound-test tippets in the spring and summer.

Like regular Clouser Deep Minnows, I carry these flies in sizes 2 through 6 and use eyes that weigh from 1/80 through 1/30 ounce, depending on how deep I want to fish the fly. I fish the following combinations most frequently: tan over white with gold flash (Golden Shiner), gray over white with silver flash (Silver Shiner), and gray back over light blue middle and a white belly with pearl flash, which looks like the river shiner, one of the predominant minnows in the Susquehanna River.

Right: Here are some popular color combinations for Clouser Deep Minnows tied from synthetic fibers such as Super Hair.

JAY NICHOLS

CLOUSER DARTER (PURPLE DARTER)

Darters have two dominant dorsal fins and wide pectoral fins. These features create a broader and wider silhouette, unlike the slim profile of other minnows represented by the Clouser Deep Minnow. I tie this pattern with calf tail, and it has an extra section of hair on it, which helps it maintain its robust form underwater. I let the flash materials extend out of and beyond the calf-tail fibers by one inch, often longer, and they enhance the darting motion of the fly when it is retrieved. This flash accents the color of the fly and also helps imitate the darter's vibrant colors, which are located midway on the body, starting behind the gills and extending into the tail.

Though I have about thirty variations of this fly pattern, I fish the purple most frequently. I carry this fly in sizes 2 through 6, but I most often fish size 4. I use eyes that range from 1/50 through 1/30 ounce. See the preceding chapter for a photo of the fly and the recipe. In off-color water, I fish a black and purple darter. I fish darter imitations with short strips along the stream bottom using floating, intermediate, or density-compensated full-sinking fly lines. Though a floating line and 9-foot leader will work, I like to fish darters on full-sinking fly lines. In high water, I use a medium- to fast-sinking density-compensated full-sinking line to get the fly down. With all sinking lines, I attach the fly to a 4-foot piece of 8- to 12-pound-test monofilament leader.

FOXEE REDD MINNOW

The Foxee Redd Minnow is a version of the Clouser Deep Minnow that has become a staple for many species of fish. I do not leave home without this one, and I carry it in a variety of sizes. It has become my favorite fly for trout and carp.

Darters come in a wide range of colors and I tie flies to imitate most of them. However, my two essential colors are all purple and black and purple. JAY NICHOLS

Fish darters along the bottom with either a floating line and long leader or a sinking line (full-sinking or sinking-tip) and short leader. JAY NICHOLS

I was looking for some type of material to make a shorter Clouser that would give me the same type of action in the water as deer-tail fibers. If you try to shorten deer tail and tie it onto the hook shank, it is stiff and has no action in the water. Because I always liked the colors of the different guard hairs on red fox tail, I decided to give them a try.

My first attempt was a disaster. I cut a clump of the hair from the tail and tied it onto the hook shank without first removing all of the soft underfur. Fox tail has a lot of underfur, which makes good dubbing for nymphs and dry flies, but it caused the fly to have a bulky head, look horrible, and matt when wet. One day it dawned on me to remove the underfur and just use the long guard hairs, which have black tips, reddish centers, and creamy brown bases. With all the underfur removed, the guard hairs of red fox tail make a small, neat-looking Clouser Minnow, don't tangle or mat, and have the right consistency for the size so that they look just like deer tail going through the water.

The Foxee Redd Minnow is a good imitation of sculpins and crayfish. Lefty thinks it looks like a baby carp or rock bass. I love to fish this pattern for trout in sizes 2 through 8 in coldwater rivers and carp in sizes 2 through 6 on the Susquehanna from late July to September.

CLOUSER FOXEE REDD MINNOW

JAY NICHOLS

Hook:	Mustad R74 4XL for sizes 8 and 10; sizes 4 and 6 can be tied on Mustad 3366
Thread:	6/0 light cahill Uni-Thread
Eyes:	Wapsi Presentation eyes, 1/32- and 5/32-diameter for sizes 8 and 10; 6/32-diameter for sizes 4 and 6
Belly:	Cream-colored guard-hair fibers from a red fox tail
Flash:	Gold Krystal Flash and bronze Flashabou
Back:	Black-tipped red fox guard-hair fibers that have a reddish brown area below the black tips

CLOUSER HALF AND HALF

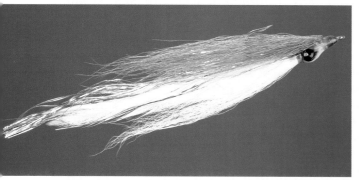

JAY NICHOLS

Hook:	Size 1/0 Mustad S71 SS
Thread:	6/0 white Uni-Thread
Tail:	Long white saddle hackles
Collar:	White deer-tail fibers
Belly:	White deer-tail fibers
Middle:	Pearl Flashabou
Back:	Gray deer-tail fibers
Eyes:	1/30-ounce metallic eyes

HALF AND HALF

Whereas the Clouser Deep Minnow is the ideal imitation for slim-bodied baitfish, the Half and Half provides the other part of the equation. It has the flash and silhouette of many large-bodied baitfish, such as gizzard shad, as well as the many broad forms of panfish and other robust species, such as fallfish, chubs, suckers, and adult shiners.

I first designed this fly to imitate the large fallfish, up to 8 inches long, on the Susquehanna River, which the 3-pound and larger smallmouth eat. Lefty Kreh once said to me that if you want those big bass to eat a fly, you'd better give them the groceries. The Clouser Minnow didn't have the bulk or the flashy sides that I felt were necessary for a good imitation, so I combined the rear saddle hackles and collar of Lefty's Deceiver for length and bulk, added a lot of flash to the fly, and put the Deep Minnow's eyes and deer tail in the front of the fly.

I tie the Half and Half on a variety of hook sizes, from 2/0 to 4, using 2/0 and 1/0 for really big smallmouth. The eyes range from 1/30 through 1/24 ounce,

The Half and Half was a combination of my Clouser Deep Minnow and my friend Lefty Kreh's (right) famous Deceiver.

BOB CLOUSER

depending on how deep I want to swim the fly and how fast I want it to sink.

I carry two color combinations of the Half and Half, chartreuse and white and red and white. Though these colors aren't exactly imitative, I think that with this fly, the motion and profile are more important than the color. The fly is large enough to trigger the striking instinct of a large bass.

The Half and Half is also the fly I use when I'd rather catch a few large fish throughout the day than a bunch of them under sixteen inches. I generally leave this up to my clients: Sometimes people just feel like catching lots of fish, and a standard Clouser Deep Minnow hooks great numbers, but a large Half and Half helps keep the smaller fish off your hook and often attracts bigger ones. I'd tie longer Clouser Minnows, but I'm limited by the length of the bucktail, and you'd have to have a lot of long deer-tail fibers to replicate the broad profile of some of the larger baits in the river. Adding broad saddle hackles to the deer tail, along with ample amounts of flash, makes for a chunky fly that sinks well and is easy to cast.

DECEIVER

Like the Clouser Minnow, Lefty's Deceiver is a style of tying a baitfish imitation, and it has probably accounted for more fish species caught around the world than any other fly. I tie and fish Deceivers to imitate just about every size range of baitfish, from 3 to 8 inches long. I use this fly most often when fish prefer a shallow-running or very slow-sinking baitfish imitation. When they want something a little deeper, I'll fish this fly on a sinking line or use a Half and Half, for which Lefty and his Deceiver was an inspiration.

BENDBACK

Lefty Kreh introduced the Bendback to me. This fly, by virtue of its design, is almost weedless and very useful when smallmouth are holding over grass or around sunken logs and other woody debris. You can cast this fly into the limbs of a tree that has fallen and sunk into the water and by using a slow retrieve, you can pull the fly through the limbs without it snagging. If a weedguard is added to this design, Lefty claims it would make the "ultimate weedless fly."

When retrieving the Bendback through and over sunken debris, you only need to strip the fly slowly without jerks so that the fly slides over the debris and drops. Expect strikes to come when the fly is dropping. The Bendback is a necessity for fishing around woody cover.

LEFTY'S DECEIVER

JAY NICHOLS

Hook:	Size 1/0 Mustad S71S SS
Thread:	Red
Tail:	White saddle hackles
Collar:	Red and white deer tail
Eyes:	Painted

BENDBACK

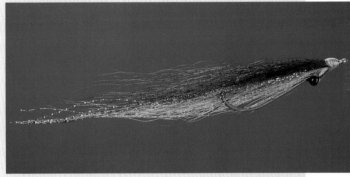

JAY NICHOLS

Hook:	Size 1 Mustad S74S SS
Thread:	6/0 light cahill Uni-Thread
Eyes:	7/64-inch diameter, black
Belly:	Tan deer-tail fibers
Middle:	Gold Krystal Flash
Back:	Brown deer-tail fibers

Bendbacks, Red and White Hackle flies, and Lefty's Bugs. These flies have stood the test of time and have influenced my fly designs.
JACK HANRAHAN

Group shot of madtoms. JAY NICHOLS

MADTOM

When I was creating the Madtom, I needed a fly that would sink quickly and bounce along the bottom with the hook point up to help prevent snags. I was also looking for a catfishlike shape, bulk, and silhouette without having to use a lot of different kinds of materials. Rusty brown, dark brown, black, and dark olive are my most effective colors, although sometimes white, yellow, and chartreuse work well. I fish them most frequently on size 4 hooks, but I tie them in sizes ranging from 2 through 6 with ⅟30- and ⅟50-ounce eyes. This fly works for me throughout the season. For the recipe, see the preceding chapter, page 60.

Madtom imitations must be bounced or stripped slowly along the bottom. Impart action to this fly by dropping the rod tip to about six inches from the water and making short, quick one- to two-foot-long strips with short pauses in between. For this method to be effective, make sure the fly is on or close to the bottom before you retrieve it.

FUR STRIP CLOUSER

The Fur Strip Deep Minnow, or simply Fur Strip Clouser, is an easy adaptation of the deer-hair pattern that takes advantage of the proven fish-catching properties of rabbit strips. Rabbit strips move enticingly in the water, and the individual fibers breathe in the current, making them excellent for patterns in fresh or salt water.

The Fur Strip Clouser is longer and chunkier than the deer-hair minnow and is a good choice to imitate everything from eels to large baitfish. Anglers across the country report that this is a good muskie and pike fly.

In clear water, I fish a Fur Strip Clouser with light eyes such as ⁴⁄32- or ⁵⁄32-ounce metallic eyes on hook sizes 2 through 1/0. Bass take the fly when it is dropping. To spruce up your fly, you can purchase barred rabbit strips or use a black or brown permanent marker to add bars to the rabbit strip.

Wide fur strips work best on large Clouser Minnows. These are often sold as Magnum strips. For smaller

FUR STRIP CLOUSER

Hook:	Size 2/0 to 8 Mustad S71S SS or a Tiemco equivalent
Thread:	6/0 gray Uni-Thread or color to match fly
Eyes:	⁶⁄₃₂-inch Wapsi hourglass eyes; change size depending on fly size
Belly:	White deer-tail fibers
Flash:	Pearl Flashabou
Back:	Gray deer-tail fibers
Tail:	Grizzly-colored rabbit-fur strip, ¼ inch wide

Below: Zonkers, Woolly Buggers, and Muddler Minnows (and all their variations) are extremely popular trout patterns that also match a wide range of bass foods. JAY NICHOLS

flies, you can use regular Zonker strips made from rabbit, mink, or pine squirrel.

ZONKERS

Flies tied with rabbit strips seem to work like magic for bass, and I used rabbit-strip patterns such as Zonkers for many years. Rabbit strips pulse in the current when stripped through the water, and when they are at rest on the bottom, the individual hairs wave in the water. My rabbit-strip Clouser and other rabbit patterns came about because of my positive experience with Zonkers.

You can tie Zonkers in a wide variety of colors ranging from white to black and with many kinds of furs, not just rabbit. Pine squirrel and mink strips also make nice flies.

MUDDLERS

I have had great success during my years of smallmouth bass fly fishing using Muddler Minnows in various colors and sizes. The Muddler Minnow was designed by angler Don Gapen for use on his home smallmouth rivers. I fish them on a 4-foot leader on a type 3 sinking line, working it deep around rocks and other debris or just dead drifted along the bottom. I also dress this fly with dry-fly floatant and fish it on the surface to imitate

a large fly or grasshopper. I think it also looks like a surface-feeding minnow.

I also liked the design of Al Troth's series of bullhead patterns; in fact, they influenced the design of the Crippled Minnow. Al's bullhead patterns were some of the first effective sculpin imitations that I used to catch smallmouth. I found that during a hatch of insects, many small varieties of fish would feed on them, and an imitation of Al's bullhead pattern would work wonders on smallmouth that were feeding not on the insects, but on the smaller fish that were eating the insects.

WOOLLY BUGGERS

The Woolly Bugger is a Pennsylvania pattern designed by Russ Blessing that catches fish just about everywhere. It was designed as a trout fly but has also proved itself on steelhead and salmon, as well as all kinds of warmwater fish, such as carp, pike, panfish, and bass.

Smaller dark brown, olive, and black Woolly Buggers imitate leeches, larger mayfly nymphs, stonefly nymphs, hellgrammites, dragonflies, and other aquatic insects. A size 6 or 8 olive Woolly Bugger is a deadly damselfly imitation on stillwaters and slow-moving bass and trout streams across the country.

The slim profile of a Woolly Bugger also represents the streamlined shape of most minnows and many larger baitfish, and in low-light conditions or if the fly is strongly silhouetted against a light background (the sky), it doesn't matter if the fly color exactly matches a specific prey. The important part of this fly is that predators find its movement in the water irresistible. With the addition of beadheads, coneheads, dumbbell eyes, flash, or rubber legs, you can jazz this fly up to fish at any depth, dead drifted or actively retrieved, and in dirty or clear water.

Black is the most popular Woolly Bugger color because of its strong contrast against most backgrounds. A black Woolly Bugger is easy for fish to find and see, especially in dirty, turbulent water. For smallmouth bass in clear water, I prefer more drab olive, brown, and tan Woolly Buggers for exactly the opposite reason. Most prey species match the color of the river substrate. Even most leeches are not jet black, like a black chenille Woolly Bugger; they are dark mottled hues of reddish brown, olive, and dark gray. Although I prefer Clouser Crayfish and my specific darter imitations, small tan Woolly Buggers with contrasting hackle colors are good imitations of fleeing immature crayfish, and olive and mottled brown Woolly Buggers are regularly eaten by smallmouth feeding on sculpins, darters, and other bottom fish.

CLOUSER CRAYFISH

I designed the Clouser Crayfish to be fished dead drift along the bottom. The placement of the lead wire on each side of the hook shank helps this fly bounce, rock, roll, and tumble along the bottom, portraying a crayfish in trouble. It looks like easy prey to a bass.

I prefer to use a crayfish imitation when the water temperatures rise above the mid-fifties. This usually occurs in late spring. Water temperatures in July through September are usually stable, and this is my favorite time for nymph-fishing this fly. Smallmouth seem to take the imitation regardless of water color. You do not have to be put off by discolored water conditions as long as the fly is on the bottom and drifting slowly along it.

I carry the crayfish in three colors—drab olive, olive, and tan—in sizes 4 through 8 and lightly weighted. A crayfish out in the open is vulnerable, and smallmouth take advantage of any opportunity to grab a crayfish imitation bouncing along the bottom of the stream. I tumble the Clouser Crayfish along the bottom through pools and along seams of eddies formed by rocks, ledges, and other structure blocking or deflecting the downstream flow of water.

CLOUSER CRAYFISH

JAY NICHOLS

Hook:	Size 4 Mustad R74
Thread:	6/0 light tan Uni-Thread
Weight:	.025- or .030-inch lead wire
Claws:	Hen mallard flank feather
Antennae:	Pheasant-tail fibers
Carapace cover:	Tip from hen mallard flank feather
Back:	Olive-drab Furry Foam
UnderBody:	Pale green dubbing
Legs:	Bleached grizzly saddle hackles, honey dun, or ginger

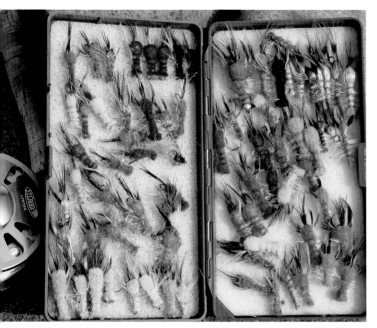

Different colors and sizes of crayfish patterns. BOB CLOUSER

The Clouser Crayfish is my favorite pattern when I am wade-fishing. It's extremely effective, and it's a lot easier to fish crayfish dead drift when wading than it is to fish streamers with an active retrieve. I most often fish this pattern by casting upstream or upstream and across, allowing it to sink to the bottom and drift downstream with the current. This is particularly effective if you allow the fly to drift over the drop-off below a gravel bar or anywhere else bass lie in wait to ambush their prey.

Many anglers add a strike indicator to the leader to help detect strikes or suspend the crayfish at a specific depth just above the bottom of the stream. Sometimes adding a twitch or a short strip and pause to the crayfish imitation will increase its success. In slower water where bass are cruising in search of food, you may have to try a more active retrieve. Short-stripping and pausing a crayfish imitation across a shallow-water gravel bar brings aggressive strikes from smallmouth. This is also an effective carp pattern.

HELLGRAMMITE (BLACK)

On the Susquehanna River, hellgrammites are most active from June through August. I fish this fly dead drift in riffled waters. Though I tie this pattern with olive Furry Foam and grizzly hackle, I have several color variations of this fly. I most often fish the all-black version in sizes 4 and 6.

Hellgrammites are adept at clinging to rocks, but they sometimes get swept away in fast water or turbulent riffles. In these areas, use a dead drift presentation, with or without a strike indicator. Cast quartering upstream, and let the water funnel your fly to the waiting bass. Hellgrammites migrate toward the shoreline in late spring and early summer, and during these time periods, it's effective to fish the edges and margins of a river with a side-swimming technique. Use a lightly weighted pattern, and cast the nymph quartering across and upstream. Lift the rod tip while stripping line to swim the fly toward shore in these slower waters.

For a photo of the natural and the eggs, which are good indicators of prime habitat, see the preceding chapter, page 71.

CLOUSER SWIMMING NYMPH

I use the robust Swimming Nymph in sizes 6 and 8 to imitate large mayfly and dragonfly nymphs that swim through the water, moving along the bottom during their journey toward emergence on the banks or grass beds.

This fly is heavily weighted so that it swims near the bottom. With the heaviest portion of the weight tied in at the front of the fly, you can make the fly undulate by using a short, jerky speed-up-and-stop stripping retrieve. With soft tail material such as marabou and rabbit fur, even when dead drifting the fly, a slight shake of the rod tip adds motion to the rear portion of the drifting fly. I have a beadhead version that works well, but my favorite color combination has a fire orange head. For some reason, that seems to catch more fish than any other color combination.

Generally, colors should closely match the natural you are imitating. Insects tend to adopt the coloration of the habitat in which they live, and large swimming nymphs burrow into mud-silted bottoms. During emergence, and as the silt washes from their bodies, their true colors are revealed.

The most effective colors for the Clouser Swimming Nymph are rusty brown, dirty yellow, and gray. I

Left: Don't try to imitate the large natural crayfish with your fly patterns. Fish most often feed on the smaller, more vulnerable crayfish that are molting, though there are exceptions. BOB CLOUSER

CLOUSER HELLGRAMMITE
(Black)

JAY NICHOLS

Hook:	Size 4 Mustad S71S SS
Thread:	6/0 black Uni-Thread
Weight:	.020- or .025-inch lead or lead-alternative wire
Tail:	Black marabou or rabbit-fur strip
Body:	Black rabbit fur in dubbing loop
Legs:	Grizzly hackle
OverBody:	Black Furry Foam

CLOUSER SWIMMING NYMPH

JAY NICHOLS

Hook:	Size 8 Mustad R74
Weight:	.020-inch round lead or nonlead wire
Thread:	6/0 fire orange Uni-Thread
Tail:	Dark brown marabou or rabbit fur and bronze Flashabou
Body:	Dark rusty dubbing
Wing case:	Peacock herl from eye
Legs:	Speckled brown hen-back feather

Bob Clouser Jr. lifts a nice carp. Swimming Nymphs and Foxee Redd Minnows are great carp patterns. BOB CLOUSER

use dirty yellow to match many of the damselfly nymphs found in the area where I fish. Use dark grays or dark olives if dragonfly nymphs are prevalent.

Although this pattern is effective throughout the water column, I catch most of my fish near the bottom. I like to fish the Swimming Nymph across and down-stream, with a slow strip or crawl across the bottom. When wade-fishing, I search for pools with slow-moving water and cast the Swimming Nymph slightly up and across stream, let it sink to the bottom, and retrieve it with short, slow strips. When fishing from a drifting boat, cast toward the shoreline and drop your rod tip to about six inches from the surface. Allow the fly to sink to the bottom, and retrieve it in short, slow strips. These strips breathe life into the marabou or rabbit-fur tail. Strikes from bass or trout are easy to detect when using this type of retrieve.

The Swimming Nymph is also effective when fish are rising to emerging insects. Cast the fly just above the ring of the riseform, and retrieve it before it has a chance to sink. Be alert and ready to strike, because often a bass takes the fly as soon as it hits the water. Along with the Foxee Redd Minnow and Clouser Crayfish, the Swim-ming Nymph is one of my best carp flies.

SUSPENDER

The Suspender is a relatively new invention of mine. I have no idea what the fly represents, and it's the only pattern I've developed that doesn't imitate something I've observed in nature. It has caught many species of fish, including snook, redfish, smallmouth, largemouth, trout, albacore, striper, pike, and a Susquehanna River muskie. I now carry a few Suspenders on all my fishing trips.

I usually retrieve it using two different techniques. One is to cast it out onto the surface, give it a short twelve-inch strip, stop, and let it sink slowly. The Sus-pender flutters as it sinks and can also be twitched dur-ing the slow sinking process. The other method is to make one to three long strips, one to three feet in length, then stop the fly and let it sink slowly. Most takes come during the slow descent.

I like fishing this fly because in the clear water con-ditions in which it is most effective, I can see the fish attack the fly. I can watch smallmouth rise from the bot-tom and inhale the Suspender as it hangs almost motion-less under the surface film. This is the only fly that I designed solely for the manner in which I fish it rather than for its imitative qualities, though in my experience,

CLOUSER SUSPENDER

JAY NICHOLS

Hook: Size 4 to 1/0 Mustad Signature S71S SS
Thread: 6/0 white Uni-Thread
Flash: Mixed pearl and silver Flashabou, 15 to 20 strands of each color
Tail: Yellow and white or chartreuse and white marabou
Body: Silver Metallic Estaz (extrawide)
Head and collar: White sheep fleece or lamb's wool

RED AND WHITE HACKLE

JAY NICHOLS

Hook: Size 1/0 to 4 Mustad S71S SS
Thread: 6/0 white Uni-Thread
Tail: 6 to 8 white saddle hackles
Flash: Gold or pearl Flashabou
Body: One red, one white, and one red palmered saddle hackle

white and yellow have always been good colors. A lot of anglers have asked me what it represents, and I tell them I have no idea. I don't ask those kinds of questions when the bass start eating it.

You can vary your retrieve when fishing this fly, depending on the fish, but always be ready for the take when you stop pulling and the head of the fly starts to bob upward and the entire fly turns.

The head on this fly is not very durable, but if you coat it for extra durability, you sacrifice some of the buoyant qualities of the fly. For me, one fly is worth four or five good fish, and then I tie on a new one, because when this fly is working well, sometimes nothing else works.

RED AND WHITE HACKLE

Lefty Kreh introduced this fly to me in the early 1980s. I understand that the Red and White Hackle was used by anglers as far back as the late 1880s, and its originator is unknown. It has since been renamed the Seaducer.

I was convinced to add this pattern to my fly box when I watched Lefty catch large smallmouth with it on a consistent basis, and it has proven itself again and again. The Red and White Hackle filled the gap between deep-running and surface offerings. The fly can be easily

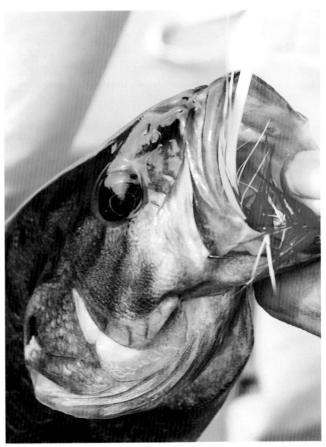

The Red and White Hackle fools a lot of bass. Though I'm not exactly sure why, the fact that this fly isn't as popular as it used to be might have something to do with its effectiveness.

BOB CLOUSER

fished and is most effective in the surface film or two to four inches below when used on a floating fly line. The fly attracts smallmouth that are busting baitfish or sipping mayflies from the surface. Lefty and I have tried many other color combinations, but we've found the red and white combination to be the most effective.

CRIPPLED MINNOW

I designed the Crippled Minnow based on the effectiveness of Larry Dahlberg's Diver patterns. The red and white color combination is a proven one, and it is not a coincidence that it has the same overall coloration of the deadly Red and White Hackle Fly.

Along with the Clouser Crayfish, the Crippled Minnow was one of my first bass fly patterns back in the early 1980s. When I designed this fly, I was inspired by Al Troth's bullhead patterns. Many know Troth as the inventor of one of the most popular dry flies ever, the Elk Hair Caddis, but the streamers he designed for Montana trout were well ahead of his time and inspired many, including me, to learn how to work with deer hair. I copied the head style of some of his deer-hair baitfish patterns. I just trimmed the head differently with a rounded bottom, like a canoe, so it sits in the film.

CLOUSER CRIPPLED MINNOW

JAY NICHOLS

Hook:	Mustad R74 or Tiemco equivalent
Thread:	6/0 white Uni-Thread for the body; white Danville Flymaster Plus for spinning the deer-hair head
Body:	Peacock herl and white Antron or Sparkle Yarn
Throat:	Red wool or yarn
Tail:	Red and white marabou blood feathers
Flash:	Pearl Flashabou
Head:	Red and white deer-body hair

I designed this fly to dive under the surface when retrieved and rest on the surface with only a portion of the head above water. The most effective spinning and casting surface lures were always the ones that hung in the surface film with only the head exposed. I wanted this trait in a surface fly. The rear portion of the fly is tied with materials that soak up water, and the front of the fly is deer-body hair, which floats. With this combination, the fly hangs in the surface film like a feeding or injured baitfish.

If you trim the bottom of the head flat, the fly doesn't hang in the film, but floats high on the surface. For the fly to sit properly, trim the bottom close to the bottom of the hook shank, with the top edges of the round bottom above the hook shank. The top portion of the head could be trimmed in a semioval half the distance of the head's length. The remaining deer-hair fibers on top of the rear portion of the head are trimmed to form a collar similar to that of the Dahlberg Diver. The collar allows the fly to dive and also creates a surface disturbance.

My favorite color combination is red and white, although Crippled Minnows can be tied in many colors. Sizes 4 and 6 get the most attention from Susquehanna River smallmouth.

The Crippled Minnow fishes better after it becomes waterlogged, and even better still once it has caught a few fish and the fish slime pulls the fly down so that it hangs low or even slightly under the surface film. I dress the head on the trimmed portion if I want to fish it high, but it generally sinks only four to six inches undressed.

An effective technique is to fish this fly on intermediate or sinking lines like a Muddler Minnow. When fishing this fly underwater, the quicker you use the Susquehanna Strip on this fly, the more erratically it swims. Sometimes that motion is just what is needed to get the fish to hit the fly.

GARTSIDE'S GURGLER

Jack Gartside's Gurgler is a special fly worth mentioning, not only because it's deadly for many fish species, but also because it's incredibly easy to tie. Like my Floating Minnow, the Gurgler is a low-riding fly that disturbs the water just enough to get the bass's attention, but not enough to scare it. Effective colors are white, yellow, and black, though you are limited only by your imagination. You can tie this fly with clear packing foam or 2-millimeter craft foam that is sold in a fly shop or craft store. The tail can be synthetic hair or deer tail, but it's important to add a little cement to the base of the fibers where the tail extends from the hook bend to prevent it from fouling around the hook bend.

Gartside's Gurgler (top right) belongs to a group of what I call low-floating surface flies. These flies create less disturbance on the water than a full-fledged popper, but they still create an enticing wake that attracts bass. JAY NICHOLS

FLOATING MINNOW

Fallfish, chubs, and young bass are a few of the baitfish that feed on aquatic insects when they are emerging. When this happens, large smallmouth eat the fish feeding on insects. Instead of matching mayflies, anglers targeting large bass should imitate the smaller fish feeding on the insects.

One of my favorite tactics during an insect hatch is to fish a Clouser Floating Minnow or an EZ Popper blind or through the ring of the rise. If there are any large bass in the area, they will often take the large surface fly, perhaps because it represents one of the many small baitfish coming to the surface to take advantage of the hatching insects. Large bass do feed on insects during a heavy hatch, but they rarely refuse a minnow imitation or a popper.

The Floating Minnow's slender design causes only a slight disturbance on the surface during a retrieve. It imitates the movement of many types of baitfish either feeding on the surface or struggling from injury. When it is at rest, the foam head keeps the fly afloat in a semi-vertical position. The rear portion of the fly remains submerged during slow, tantalizing twitches of the fly. A

CLOUSER FLOATING MINNOW

JAY NICHOLS

Hook:	Size 1 Mustad S71S SS
Thread:	6/0 white or light cahill Uni-Thread
Head:	Two white sponge spider bodies (Size 10)
Eyes:	Stick-on prismatic eyes
Body:	White and chartreuse deer-tail fibers; Super Hair or Unique Hair can be used instead
Throat:	Red Krystal Flash
Flash:	Pearl Flashabou
Adhesive:	Zap-A-Gap CA+

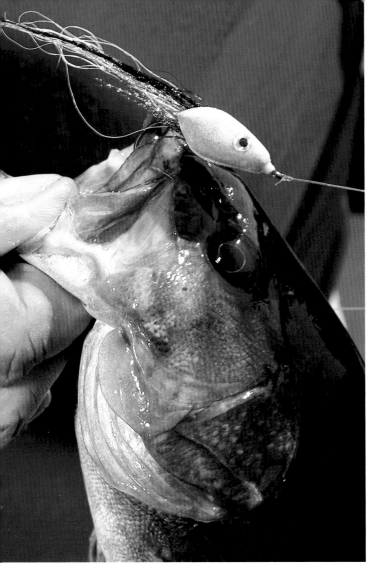

Floating Minnows are my favorite pattern for surface smallmouth. BOB CLOUSER

I carry an assortment of light and dark Floating Minnows in different sizes. JAY NICHOLS

well-tied fly should hang at a 45-degree angle or near-vertical position in the surface film, with the forward portion of the head tilted upward. This is a trait in all of the most productive surface lures used by successful conventional tackle bass fishers. The Floating Minnow suspends nearly vertical in the surface film and triggers strikes from wary smallmouth bass.

Sometimes surface patterns that cause commotion on the surface, like the EZ Popper or flat-faced hair bugs, can spook wary bass, especially in low, clear water. In these conditions, I use the Floating Minnow, a more suggestive pattern that provides a silhouette of a surface-feeding baitfish. This fly moves through water with little surface disturbance, but you can twitch it if necessary, depending on the fish's mood.

You can fish the Floating Minnow in several ways. If you are using a floating line and a 9- to 12-foot leader, try stripping it across the surface with occasional pauses or letting it drift with the current. My favorite presentation is to give the fly a fast strip, stop, and let it dead

drift, then make a few fast, erratic strips and let it dead drift again. This imitates the erratic motion of an injured or struggling baitfish. As with many other patterns, smallmouth often strike during the pause, rather than during the retrieve. A balanced Floating Minnow dives just under the surface when you strip it and floats back up into the surface film during the pause. It has the opposite action of a Clouser Deep Minnow, which sinks during the pauses and rises toward you when you strip it. You can use this action to your advantage with a full-sinking line and a short, 4-foot leader. During the pause, the fly rises, imitating an injured baitfish struggling to reach the safety of the bottom. Smallmouth most often hit when the fly starts rising.

One bright, sunny afternoon, while fishing in five feet of clear water, I watched a client make a sixty-foot cast with a sinking line and Floating Minnow toward a submerged ledge rock. We could clearly see the floating fly as it was pulled down by the sinking fly line. The angler started to strip the fly back, and the fly would rise toward the surface during the pauses of the strip. This rising action of the fly brought on strikes from large, wary smallmouth that otherwise ignored a standard presentation.

Some of my favorite color combinations are chartreuse and white, tan and white, gray and white, blue and white, all black, and black over white. You can mix and match to your needs. You can easily color the white foam heads with marking pens if you want them in various colors. I fish this fly in sizes that range from 1/0 to 4, but size 1 is my favorite all-around size and the one that I fish the most.

BRIGHT SIDES MINNOW (SILVER)

The Bright Sides Minnow sits somewhere between the Floating Minnow and the EZ Popper. It is quieter on the surface of the water than the EZ Popper but provides a stronger body profile than the Floating Minnow. I designed this fly first for salt water but now use it frequently on the Susquehanna River.

The long foam body looks like a baitfish from below. I think this shape plus the bright flash along the sides give the illusion of a struggling, injured baitfish. The full length of the body lies half submerged in the surface film, which I believe is an important trait to imitate, as some injured baitfish struggle while lying in this position.

The Bright Sides Minnow can be fished using the same techniques as the Floating Minnow. I fish this fly in sizes ranging from 1/0 to 2.

CLOUSER EZ POPPER

I have found no other pattern that is as simple to tie and as effective as the foam EZ Popper. The flat face along with the proper placement of the hook allow the popper to generate disturbance on the water's surface when retrieved in short strips. On the Susquehanna River, my favorite times are when low, clear water conditions are combined with water temperatures 50 degrees and above. These conditions usually occur in June through mid-November.

The EZ Popper can be retrieved in several ways that will entice a smallmouth into hitting it. You can rip it across the surface, creating a massive commotion, or you can tease it so that it makes only a subtle ripple. Experiment with retrieves.

If you reverse the head and use it for a diver, you can replicate a crippled minnow. Minnows struggling or feeding at the surface are usually quiet and don't create much disturbance. Because the diver fishes quietly, it often catches fish in low, clear water. Often a smallmouth will softly sip in the fly when the diver lies motionless on the surface. Many times I have seen large smallmouth come

BRIGHT SIDES MINNOW

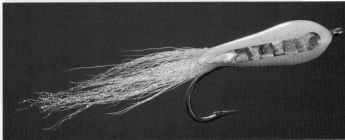

JAY NICHOLS

Hook:	Size 1 Mustad S74S SS
Thread:	6/0 Uni-Thread, any color
Adhesive:	Zap-A-Gap CA+
Body:	White closed-cell foam perfect ant bodies in sizes 175 or 150
Side Flash:	⅛-inch-wide strip of adhesive-back Witchcraft Lure Tape, metallic fish scale design
Eyes:	³⁄₁₆-inch metallic Witchcraft adhesive-back stick-on eyes, color to match the flash on the sides
Tail:	Blue over white calf tail
Flash:	Pearlescent Krystal Flash

EZ POPPER

JAY NICHOLS

Hook:	Size 1 Mustad S71 SS
Thread:	White Danville Flymaster Plus and 6/0 red Uni-Thread
Head:	½-inch-diameter white foam cylinder
Legs:	Yellow rubber
Eyes:	Adhesive-back prismatic eyes
Glue:	Zap-A-Gap CA+ or Fishin' Glue
Tail:	Yellow hen hackles

Light-colored poppers are easy to see in low light—when poppers are often most effective. STEVE MAY

to investigate and sip in the fly only after all ripples from the fly landing on the surface have dissipated.

I generally carry white, yellow, and black to experiment with both fish preferences and my ability to see the fly under changing light conditions. In low light, light-colored poppers are easier to see; in glare, black poppers are easiest to see.

Carry several different sizes of poppers. For bass, I use sizes 8 through 1/0 on wide-gap hooks. At times, large smallmouth will take a size 8 or 10 popper while ignoring larger sizes, and when they do, they simply suck it in like an insect. I like to use the smaller sizes for bluegills and add rubber legs to the bodies. One of my favorite bluegill EZ Poppers is yellow with bright yellow rubber legs and small yellow hackle tips for the tail.

Over the years, fly tiers have built poppers from a wide variety of materials, ranging from balsa wood to cork to deer hair spun on a hook and trimmed to shape. Though painted cork poppers are meticulously clipped, deer-hair flies are part of the colorful history of small-mouth bass flies, and many anglers still use them with great results, I prefer flies tied from foam for my popper fishing. Widely available in many different shapes, sizes, and colors, closed-cell foam is easy to work with and durable.

Though deer-hair flies (right) work well, they are much more time-consuming to tie than my simple EZ Popper (left).
JAY NICHOLS

Poppers are tied from all sorts of materials and come in countless variations. I won't go into those variations here, because I don't think they make much of a difference to bass. But a few design points are worth mentioning. People frequently ask me about the difference between a popper with a flat face and one with a cupped-out face, and which works better. Though poppers with cupped-out faces push water differently than ones with flat faces, I don't think a flat-faced popper moves any less water. I prefer flat-faced poppers because they are easier to tie and, when designed properly, are easier to pick up on the backcast than a popper with a cupped-out face.

With any popper, good design is important for it to perform as it should. The most critical step in designing a popper is placing the body in the correct position on the hook. A properly finished popper should rest on the water's surface with the forward portion slightly elevated so that the fly has the right action and is easy to pick up on the backcast. Poppers with straight heads do not fish well, and because many commercially tied flies are made this way, it pays learning the few easy techniques required to tie an EZ Popper.

Poppers tied with 3XL hooks usually will hook more fish, depending on the design of the popper body. Some poppers have longer bodies than others or have rear portions the same diameter as the front. These require longer-shank hooks, making hooking up easier. A short popper body with a slanted rear section does not need a longer-shank hook in order to do its job. In general, I've found that a popper that has a downward slant to its rear portion aids in hooking ability. The blunt or large-diameter front portion of the popper forces the mouth of the fish to open during the strike, and the downward slant of the back portion allows the mouth to close down on the hook shank. Most hooks that are glued into a popper need at least one-half to three-quarters of an inch of bare hook and shank protruding from the rear of the body. This allows for easy hooking and room for application of materials.

Poppers can be squat or long and thin, and though I don't fish them much, Pencil Poppers deserve mention because many anglers use them to imitate feeding or scurrying schools of baitfish. This fly was original tied out of balsa, but now you can buy tapered foam for these patterns.

Sometimes bass prefer patterns with rubber leg material either in the tail or on the sides of the fly. Rubber legs on a fly usually aid in its movement and also add bulk to the pattern. I often carry a few patterns with rubber legs, especially for panfish.

CLOUSER GREEN DRAKE DUN

JAY NICHOLS

Hook: Size 10 Mustad R72
Thread: 6/0 light cahill Uni-Thread
Wing: Dark natural brown deer-body hair from the back of the deer
Tail: Dark, brownish black moose body hair fibers
Body: Pale yellow rabbit dubbing
Hackle: Dry-fly-quality saddle hackles. Rear hackle: light ginger. Front hackles: one grizzly and one ginger for the green drake dun; one ginger, one grizzly, and one brown for the female green drake spinner

CLOUSER DRAKE

The Clouser Drake is my generic pattern for all large mayflies; I just change the size and color to imitate the mayfly in question. It gives the proper silhouette for most mayflies and rides high on the water. The heavy hackle from one end to the other was inspired by the effectiveness of one of my favorite trout flies, the Bivisible. The high wing makes the fly easy to see and helps balance it when it lands. I also use long, dark, blackish brown moose body-hair fibers for the tail to balance the fly, and I cut a V-shape out of the bottom of the hackle fibers so the fly will land upright. Trimming the bottom of the hackle helps the fly sit on the surface like the natural on most every cast.

Properly dressed with a dry-fly floatant, these large imitations sit high on the surface. Conventional trout patterns that imitate a lot of insects do not float very well. The film in many warmwater rivers like the Susquehanna contains a lot of dirt. A traditionally dressed dry fly has a life span of a couple casts in this type of water, even when treated with a floatant. A treated heavily hackled fly with a large deer-hair wing floats like a cork.

Larger flies are more buoyant than small flies. I tried fishing size 16 dry flies to rising bass sipping little sulphurs, but if I could get a three-foot float out of those small flies, I was lucky. Even when the small mayflies are hatching, the bass take the larger flies, so why bother with the small stuff? The big, meaty form and wing silhouette draw bass and trout to this fly. Another advantage of these large drake imitations is that they are easily seen in the fading light at dusk.

These big flies catch bass regardless of what is hatching, because all summer long the fish are used to seeing brown, yellow, and green drakes and *Isonychia*. This is also true for large flies on trout streams such as Penns Creek or the upper Delaware. Once the big flies start hatching, it can be a good idea to fish a large dry fly, because the fish seem to remember the large insects.

One of my favorite surface flies for smallmouth is the Brown Drake. I designed this pattern so that it floats high off the water and has a pronounced silhouette. The single high deer body-hair wing adds to the large fly's form, and the split tails ensure that the fly lands on the water's surface upright.

On my home river, brown drakes appear during the whitefly hatch of late July and early August. I also carry these patterns for the smaller bass waters I fish, even if they don't have brown drake hatches. These flies are effective in sizes 8 through 12. I like size 10 for all-around use, either as a searching pattern or for fishing the hatch.

WHITE WULFF

The White Wulff is the other imitation I use for whiteflies. Dry flies in the Wulff series are durable and great for bass. They float higher and longer than any other patterns tied with natural materials. I have caught more than twenty smallmouth on one Wulff before it was destroyed. These flies have a strong silhouette and are easily seen at twilight, when the fishing is often the best. I carry them in sizes 8 through 12. When the smallmouth start to feed heavily on the spinners, I trim the hackles on the bottom and top and spread out the fly's calf-tail wings so they are touching the water.

WEEDLESS FLIES

I also carry a few weedless Clouser Deep Minnows, EZ Poppers, and Floating Minnows in my fly box. I prefer simple weedguards made of a single strand of 15- or 20-pound-test Mason hard nylon monofilament. I crush the tip of a short, 3-inch piece of mono with the jaws of needlenose pliers to create a textured surface that won't slip out from under my tying thread. Holding the tip of the monofilament in the jaws of the pliers, I use my thumb to bend the mono to a 45-degree angle, and then tie in the "foot" of the weedguard under the hook shank just behind the hook eye with my tying thread. The monofilament guard should be about half a hook-shank length long and extend below the hook point. There should be a gap between the guard and the point of the hook equal to the gape of the hook. This will ensure that the weedguard does not also become a bite guard.

Sometimes a weedless fly is critical, such as when fishing on bottoms with rock rubble or woody debris or over submerged grassbeds, or when casting against tree-lined banks—often where bass live. Weed guards not only prevent hanging up, but also allow you to fish your fly through grassy areas and over sunken limbs without interruption. A fly without a guard fished under these same circumstances would not be as effective. In fact, any debris hung up on the hook or fouling the fly's actions could render it useless.

CHAPTER 6

Casting Tips

JACK HANRAHAN

At times, smallmouth bass fishing can be very for-giving. When the bass are hungry and on the grab, they sometimes throw caution to the wind and chase every fly you put in front of them, regardless of how poor your casting may be. As long as you get the fly out there, they hit it. At other times, such as when the water is low and clear and bass are spooky in the bright sun, you must have excellent casting skills with both accuracy and good presentation of the fly to catch larger bass.

In many situations, you do not need to cast far to catch smallmouth; however, when you are fishing to large fish or in low, clear water, forty-foot casts are usu-

ally not long enough. In fact, it's a general rule of thumb that if you can see the bottom at forty feet, the bass are at forty-one feet. In other words, if you can see a small-mouth and it can see you, it generally moves to a spot where you are not visible. Big smallmouth are intimately aware of their surroundings and can become defensive at the slightest change to their living quarters. Many large bass will slowly move away from an intruder when they sense that something is different in their territory.

Under these difficult conditions, you can catch more large smallmouth by making long casts. Anglers able to cast sixty or more feet are most successful. Lefty Kreh has demonstrated to me time and again how necessary

Good casting skills are essential to consistently catch big bass. Here, Bob Clouser casts to bass while master caster Lefty Kreh poles the boat.

Lefty Kreh's basic principles of casting will help you with the large flies and heavier rods necessary for serious bass fishing.
BOB CLOUSER

long casts are to fool clear-water smallmouth. One particular instance that proved this point occurred when I was fishing with Lefty one hot August afternoon. A large smallmouth was holding in rock-strewn shallows along a shady shoreline, and we could not get closer than ninety feet without spooking the bass. Lefty looked over the distance carefully and picked a spot of sunlit water just above the shade-covered area where the smallmouth was holding. He made the long cast and, as the fly was travel-

ing toward the target, immediately dropped the rod tip to inches above the water. This ensured that the fly line would lie straight on the water without any slack between the rod tip and the fly. As the fly entered the shady area, he twitched it once, and then hooked the five-pound smallmouth. I will never forget Lefty's words: "Presentation starts with the cast and not after the fly is in the water."

Weighted flies catch more smallmouth. The oval cast will help you cast these heavy patterns effectively. JACK HANRAHAN

Entire books have been written on casting, and I recommend reading them. In this chapter, I cannot cover all the details required to make a good cast, but I suggest that you read Lefty Kreh's books on the subject. In my opinion and that of many others, Lefty is one of the best casters in the world. He is also the most diverse angler I know, having experience with multiple species and a master at fishing casts. By fishing casts, I mean that it's not good enough to be able to make perfect casts out in the yard with a piece of yarn on your tippet, though that's a start. Fishing casts require reading the water and the currents and knowing how to manipulate your line while casting to get the most effective presentation to the fish. Learning these types of skills requires dedication and lots of practice on the water.

Though I won't cover the basics of casting, I think a good place to start this chapter is by summarizing Lefty Kreh's basic principles of fly casting. He'll tell you that these are not his principles, but basics of physics; yet he was the first to start using them in his teaching methods. These principles are as relevant to bass fishing in a big river as they are to trout fishing on a spring creek. When casting short distances with a light rod, many anglers can get by with a simple karate-chop cast, but many times fishing for bass requires heavy flies, relatively heavy rods and lines, and long casts. Adhering to these basic principles is critical for efficient casting:

• You cannot make any cast until you get the end of the line moving on either your backcast or forward cast.

• Once the line end is moving, the only way to load the road is to move your casting hand at an ever-increasing speed and then bring it to a sudden stop.

• The line goes in the direction in which the rod tip speeds up and stops.

• The longer the distance the rod travels on the back and forward casting strokes, the less effort is required for the cast.

CASTING WEIGHTED FLIES

In a normal cast with a dry fly for trout, you can use short, quick strokes. Many anglers advocate casting as tight a loop as possible and false-casting several times, presumably to help *dry* the dry fly. People are often taught to pick up line for the backcast and stop the rod tip abruptly as the line unrolls behind them. Just as the candy cane or J shape unfurls, you are instructed to begin your forward cast in the same plane as the backcast, stopping your rod tip high. This basic ten o'clock to two o'clock casting approach works okay for beginners fishing dry flies. But with weighted flies, you have to do things much differently, and those who have a hard time breaking these dry-fly habits can have trouble fishing weighted flies and heavier rods.

Many of the flies I use for smallmouth bass are either heavy or wind-resistant. When casting these flies, I most often use a special cast designed for weighted flies. This cast is also useful for sinking-tip lines and shooting tapers. Often called the Belgium, oval, or elliptical cast, the basic idea behind it is to smoothly pull the fly line, leader, and weighted fly around in an oval with a low but upward-moving backcast and a higher forward cast. Unlike dry-fly casting, you want to keep your loops relatively wide—though not so wide that the cast is inefficient—and minimize false casting.

HOW TO CAST WEIGHTED FLIES

Begin with a wide, stable stance, in which your left foot is forward if you are a right-handed caster. Your rod tip should be low to the water. This allows you to begin your backcast with the greatest efficiency, because as soon as you start moving the rod tip, you begin to move the line.

As you bring the rod tip back slowly in an upward sidearm position, focus on the end of your line to see when the fly is about to leave the surface of the water.

Keep bringing the rod back until the fly is just about ready to leave the water.

At this point, the rod should be loaded and ready to begin your backcast.

JAY NICHOLS

Begin the cast and come back smoothly in a sidearm position, with only a slight upward angle. Cast only hard enough to get the line moving in the air on the backcast. This is a slow cast, and you don't want to create a lot of line speed on the backcast. Do not stop your rod hand as you would with a dry-fly cast.

JAY NICHOLS

Through this casting motion, you should be able to feel the rod pulling the weighted fly around in an oval. Lift the rod tip by tilting the rod hand from its 45-degree position to about 90 degrees, bringing it around in an oval. One way of thinking of this cast is picturing a weighted ball at the end of a rope. To throw the ball in the direction you want it to go, you have to swing it around with the rope while maintaining tension on the line. It's difficult to make something with so much weight change directions quickly, so to effectively cast weighted lines and flies, you need to pull the fly and line around in an oval.

JAY NICHOLS

Speeding up the acceleration as you move the rod hand forward, smoothly accelerate to a stop on the forward cast. You can haul on the forward cast for distance.

JAY NICHOLS

With this cast, it is preferable not to cast too tight of a loop. After the stop, follow through and drop your rod tip, opening the loop.

Follow the line and fly down toward the water.

Dropping your rod like this helps you stay in contact with the fly line and keeps your line straight on the water. Your stripping hand should be close to the line, ready to strip or set the hook if a bass strikes immediately.

Lefty Kreh uses a roll cast to pick up his fly and prepare for a cast. BOB CLOUSER

THE LIFT-OFF

For efficient casting with all flies, it's important to lift the fly off the water before starting the full force of the backcast. This is especially important when fishing poppers. Too many anglers begin the backcast while all their line and the heavy fly are still on the water. Not only does friction of the line on the water rob the cast of energy, but the popper also digs into the water, making it extremely difficult to get a good backcast. The key is to first retrieve all the slack line on the water, and then start the pickup with your rod tip low to the water. Accelerate slowly as you lift the rod tip, and do not begin the actual backcast until you see the fly lift off the water. Having a long stroke on your backcast helps get the fly moving and also helps load the rod for a good backcast.

To efficiently lift line off the water, make sure that all the slack is out of your fly line and it is straight in front of you on the water. If your line is in curls on the water, roll-cast your line out ahead of you. It's critical for a good cast that the line is straight in front of you before making the cast, because you want to be able to start moving the fly as soon as you begin lifting the rod. With a floating line, you can use a roll cast to straighten the line on the surface of the water. When fishing a sinking line, this roll cast is necessary to bring the weighted line to the surface of the water; it's a lot easier to pick up the line if it's on top of the water than if it's a few feet under the surface.

LINE CONTROL

Controlling the fly line while casting and presenting your fly can help you catch more fish. Let's assume that you need to make a fifty-foot cast to a two-foot-square area behind a protruding rock where you have seen a big bass. The best way to make an accurate cast is to pull off more line from the reel than you need. Cast beyond the target, and drop the fly directly above the target by stopping the line. As the line and fly reach the target, you only have to pinch the fly line between your thumb and forefinger. The pinch stops the fly line, causing the fly to drop on or near the target. To master this technique, you should form a circle with the thumb and forefinger of your hauling hand to control the line while it shoots. Too many anglers develop the bad habit of letting go of the line when they shoot it. Not only does this create a lot of line slap and extra friction as the line is pulling through the guides on the cast, but it also causes you to lose track of the line. If you let go of the line while casting, you will have to exert greater effort over the course of the day, will have more tangles, and won't be as able to stop the fly accurately when it reaches the target. But if you proficiently control the line during the shooting phase of the cast by running it through your looped fingers, you will avoid these problems and won't have to fumble for your line before beginning your retrieve. The fly stops, hits the target, and you immediately begin stripping the fly because the line is already in your hand.

If you have contact with the line as soon as the fly hits the water, you are also able to set the hook on any fish that might happen to hit your fly immediately. Sometimes bass can strike a fly so quickly it seems as if they hit it in the air on the way down. You need to be ready for these fast strikes.

Contrary to the belief of many anglers, you can set the hook on a fish at long distances as long as you have complete control of the cast and presentation, as well as proper rod position. I've watched Lefty hook and land many four-pound and larger smallmouth with casts of seventy to a hundred feet in my twenty years of fishing with him. To hook fish at these distances, you must be prepared for the strike as soon as the fly hits the water. This means that when the fly hits the water, your stripping hand should be in control of the line and raised near your rod hand and ready to strike. The line should be straight on the water with no excess slack. Too much slack will prevent you from setting the hook on a fish. If your cast does not lie out straight, remove the excess slack quickly with one or two long strips on the line. It's also important to keep your rod tip low to the water and pointed at the fly. When the fish strikes, make a long haul with your stripping hand and quickly lift the rod at the same time. Using this combination, you can set a hook on a bass at distances over sixty feet without a struggle.

Another problem I see after a day of casting is that the running line—the thinner part of the line behind

Forming a loop with your fingers when you shoot line helps you maintain control of the fly line. JAY NICHOLS

If you let go of the fly line when you shoot line, you won't be able to cast as far and your line may tangle. LEFTY KREH

the head—twists. Many casters pull the thirty-five feet or more of the fly-line head off the reel and another forty feet of the running line with it. The trouble begins when the caster doesn't use all the fly line during the cast. Some types of flies twist the leader, which twists the fly line. These twists in the leader and line move back along the line toward the reel and into the thin running line that is off the reel lying in coils but not being used. These line twists accumulate and soon tangle the running line, which eventually gets caught in the line. To prevent this, you should have only the line you are using in your stripping basket or on the boat deck. If you are

fishing a shoreline sixty feet away, then you should have only sixty feet of line out of the rod tip. The twists cannot twist the line on the reel, and if you cast the whole line and strip the fly line back to you, it forces the twists out of the line. I know this works because I've watched many anglers use both methods, and those who cast the amount of line they have out of the rod have fewer tangles. By the way, stretching a tangled line will just cause more problems. Stretching a twisted fly line will permanently set the twists in the line. It is okay to stretch a new fly line or remove coils set by the reel, but first make sure the line is not twisted.

TIPS FOR DISTANCE CASTING

• Keep your lines clean. Fly lines today are slicker and resist dirt better than they used to, but they still need to be cleaned frequently with a washcloth and mild soapy water and then rinsed completely. Dirt and grime can rob distance from your casts and make you work harder than necessary. Cracks and abrasions in your fly line can also interfere with your casting and fishing. Inspect your lines regularly, and replace them when needed.

• Use a stripping basket or Line Tamer when fishing from a boat to help manage and control the shooting part of line so it doesn't tangle when you are making long casts or blow off the boat deck into the water. Wading anglers should also consider a stripping basket to make fly line handling easier. The stripping basket prevents the fly line from being washed away by the current's flow as you retrieve it during stripping.

• Eliminate obstructions on and in the boat that can catch your line. I often take my shoes off when I'm casting because the line snags on the laces. Keep as clean a boat as possible, and cover any obstructions such as cleats and the transom.

• Reduce false casting. Though it may seem counterintuitive, generally speaking, the more you wave the line around, the worse your cast is going to be. When casting weighted flies or sinking lines, you must minimize false casting. The more you false-cast, the greater chance you have of introducing slack into your line or making an error. This is especially true in windy conditions. Excessive false casting also can spook fish and wastes your energy and fishing time. All the time you spend waving the line around in the air is time your fly isn't being retrieved in front of fish.

• Shoot line on the backcast to help reduce false casting.

• Use the shortest leader the fish will allow, and one that is designed for the size of fly being cast.

• Make sure the shooting or running line has no coils or twists in it.

• Take the muscle out of your stroke, and practice good timing and smooth casting. To help with your timing, look at your backcast.

If your backcast is poor, your forward cast suffers. Looking at your backcast helps you not only improve your timing, but also determine whether you are forming tight loops. BOB CLOUSER

Aim your forward casts at eye level or above for the best presentations. When you are casting long distances, you need to have a low backcast and a high forward cast. JAY NICHOLS

STEALTH PRESENTATIONS

If you cast aiming down at the water, the fly and line crash to the water near your target. By aiming at eye level or slightly upward, the fly line and fly fall to the water's surface with less force and don't splash as much. When I finish my forward cast, I point the rod down the line and then lean forward or push the rod tip toward the cast. This frees the rod of the line and prevents backlash vibrations in the rod and thereby avoids sending shock waves traveling down the fly line. If you continue to lower the rod tip with the falling fly line, the fly line lies straight on the water without slack.

Of course, making a silent cast is hard to do with a fly that has dumbbell lead eyes. Because of the inevitable noise your fly makes when it hits the water, there are times when it is best to lead the fish by anticipating the direction in which it is moving and making your cast well ahead of the fish, so that it can find the fly. With a stationary fly in moving water, leading the fish means aiming your cast upstream of the bass so that the combination of your retrieve and the current will bring the fly to the bass. Bass will spook if you crash the fly down right on top of them. In shallow water, it's best to use flies with lightweight dumbbell eyes or plastic or metal bead-chain eyes to reduce the chances of hanging up on the bottom before you reach the fish or spooking it. These types of eyes are usually associated with fishing for

bonefish in shallow water, but I often use bead chain for bass or carp in low, clear water conditions.

In addition to good casting skills, a long leader definitely helps your presentation, because it distances the fly from the line.

SAFETY

The benefits of a low backcast, having the rod positioned at a 45-degree angle away from you, and a high in-plane forward cast are many. This method of casting reduces the chances of hitting yourself in the head with a heavily weighted Clouser Minnow. It also helps prevent your rod from becoming "Clousered," a term that is now universally used for hitting your rod with a dumbbell-eyed fly, thereby damaging and weakening it. This is such a common occurrence that some rod manufacturers specifically mention in their care instructions to not hit your rod with weighted flies. With high line speeds and heavy flies, one good whack with a Clouser Minnow can weaken the rod enough that it might break when you are fighting a fish or even on the next cast.

It makes sense to wear a hat, not only to help you see better by shielding your eyes from the sun's glare, but also to protect your head. To reduce the chances of a serious injury, debarb all your hooks and wear sunglasses at all times. When fishing with a partner or guide in the same boat, think carefully about your casting. If you are

The large, weighted eyes on many of my fly patterns require careful casting so you don't hit yourself or your rod with the heavy fly.
JAY NICHOLS

in the stern of the boat, for example, keep a careful eye on what the angler in the bow is doing. Don't cast your line over the middle of the boat on either the forward cast or backcast—your fishing partner is standing in that direction. When the wind is blowing toward your casting arm, turn around and present the fly on your backcast or fish the other side of the boat. Learning to make long casts using the backhand method also adds to your catch rate. I watched Bob Popovics and his buddy Lance Erwin make seventy- to ninety-foot backcasts from my

boat on a windy day that would have stumped many fly casters. They caught as many nice smallmouth as would have been caught on a day without wind. It pays to learn how to make long, accurate casts in all conditions.

Learning how to cast with both hands allows you to cast with greater degree of safety and catch more bass. If you can cast with either hand, you can always keep the wind blowing the fly away from your body as you cast, and at times you can make presentations to areas that would not be options otherwise.

CHAPTER 7

Presentations

Even if you can cast a mile with a fly rod, under most circumstances you are better off getting as close to your target as the fish allow. Just because you can cast eighty feet does not mean that you should. You will probably catch more fish by being quiet, planning your approach, using good line-control techniques, and getting within forty feet of the fish. Being able to cast far and having good presentation skills gives you the advantage either way.

GETTING INTO POSITION

Whenever you fish for bass, you should get as close to the fish as conditions permit before casting. When fish-ing faster pocket water, riffle sections, or other broken water, you can usually get close to the bass—often within thirty feet. However, when fishing in low, clear water, bass are wary, and in slow, low, clear water, they most likely can see you if you can see them.

To avoid being seen by fish while wading, approach them from behind. This decreases the chances of the fish seeing you, and the downstream flow of the water pushes your wakes and the sound of your approach away from them. Think of it as talking into the wind. Your voice can carry a long distance if there's a slight breeze behind it, but if you're talking into the wind, you have to yell to be heard.

Try to get as close to the fish as you can before making your cast. Sometimes in low water, a long cast is necessary even with a stealthy approach.

Because fish under most circumstances face upstream, it's wise to approach a good fishing spot from downstream. JAY NICHOLS

When approaching a fish or a likely area where a fish might hold, keep a low profile. STEVE MAY

When you must approach a fish from the front, such as when drifting down toward it in a boat, stay as low as possible and minimize your casting movements. It's better to cast short and not be seen than to make an Olympian cast that rocks the boat and scares away the bass. Whether you're in a boat or wading, wearing flashy items or bright clothes can send wary smallmouth scurrying for cover.

Keep a low profile. Anglers floating downriver when the water is clear and low are usually more successful fishing from a sitting position. Standing up on the casting platform of a boat, high above the water, and waving a 9-foot fly rod back and forth can spook fish. On the other hand, I have watched wading anglers standing chest-deep in clear water hooking fish only four feet away from their feet while nymphing.

Though it may seem obvious at first, one of the most important things to remember when getting into position is not to walk through water you intend to fish. Similarly, when floating, do not motor upstream through the water you plan to fish on the way back down, and if at all possible, plan your route down the river to prevent floating over fish.

You have to worry about the fish seeing not only you, but also your shadow. When you approach fish, be aware of where your shadow is, and never do so with the sun shining at your back. Also be aware of the shadows your fly line makes when you are false-casting. Think of this from the perspective of a fish that has been hunted by overhead and flying predators such as herons, mergansers, and osprey all its life. When a predator passes over the fish, or at least between the fish and the sun, the shadow acts as a warning signal. Large fish have learned to respond to these types of danger signals, and when your fly line casts flickering shadows over a smallmouth bass, though the fish may not be intelligent enough to realize there is an angler nearby attempting to catch him, he will receive the danger signal loud and clear and spook to safer quarters.

The best anglers I know false-cast to the side of the fish, working out enough line until they have the proper distance measured, and then fire the final cast so that

Even when fishing from a boat, you need to think about stealth and presentation. Poling a boat into position is often the best way to get close to feeding fish. BOB CLOUSER

In slow-moving water, it's easy to send waves ahead of you that will alert fish to your presence. JAY NICHOLS

they don't spook the fish with shadows or sprays of water from the fly line. Position yourself so as not to cast shadows over the area you intend to fish.

Whether wading or in a boat, try not to make unnecessary wakes on the water. When wading in slow water, walk slowly so that your waves dissipate between steps. Make sure that each foot is firmly planted before taking the next step. Any missteps or slips can mean disaster. Anglers casting from the bow of a boat need to be careful not to rock the front of the boat back and forth. Smallmouth feel these vibrations with their lateral lines and can spook. I have seen fifty surface-feeding smallmouth disappear because of wave action rolling over their feeding area. Moving gear around or walking in a boat sends shock waves through the water. Sometimes these disturbances do not affect the smaller fish but will warn the larger ones.

Besides being careful not to make waves, it is also critical that you be quiet. Whether you are in a boat or wading, sounds you make travel through water more efficiently than through the air. When wading, be as quiet as possible. Boots will make noise as they crunch

the gravel on the bottom. Felt-soled wading shoes are quiet and also allow for easier movement over river bottoms.

All sorts of things can spook fish if you are in a boat. If you're fishing from an aluminum johnboat, be careful not to drop anything on the hard surface of the boat. Hitting a rock can damage your boat and also ruin the fishing in the area. Motors and anchors splashing into the water can also put down feeding smallmouth. Drifting anglers might consider soft-soled footwear or something that won't slip or cause unnecessary noise when they move about the boat.

When approaching a fishing spot in a boat, common sense will tell you how close you can get. In a fast riffle or when fishing a funnel between two rock ledges, you may be able to run the boat close to where you plan to anchor. In a quiet back bay or calm side channel, I often cut my motor fifty yards or more from where I plan to fish, glide for a distance, and then pole quietly to my destination. A poorly timed scraping of a pole or a screeching ungreased oarlock can send big smallmouth scurrying for cover.

When I pole into a productive fishing area, I like to pause and let all telltale signs of my entry subside before beginning to fish. One year my son Bob Jr. was guiding Bob Popovics. He knew where there was a trophy smallmouth, but in low water, a quiet approach was almost impossible. He carefully pushed the boat over a shallow gravel bar and used a large grass bed to block the noise and waves. He settled the boat against the grass and instructed Bob Popovics to wait until things settled down. After five minutes, Bob Jr. said, "See the top of that large rock under the water about sixty feet out to the right? Put the fly on the water just a couple feet above the head of the rock." The fly landed at the right spot, and the large form of a five-and-a-half-pound smallmouth rose undisturbed and inhaled the lure.

You must also be careful not to disturb the water when casting or picking up your fly. Try not to cast directly to the fish or cast a line over them. Sometimes the noise of the lure hitting the water spooks fish. If this happens, keep the lure motionless for a while before moving it. A poorly cast fly and line crashing down onto the water's surface will make smallmouth bolt toward shelter. Along these same lines, a poorly lifted fly leaves a lot of disturbance on the water and can spook fish. Use a roll-cast pickup, or if you use a regular pickup, make sure the fly is moving and almost leaving the water before you begin the fast part of your backcast. If you begin the power part of your backcast while some of your line and all of your leader are still on the water, the popper will dig into the water before it lifts off, robbing your cast of power and creating an alarming disturbance that scares fish.

Good trout anglers have mastered the technique of laying down a dry fly over a rising trout as quietly as possible. Even though bass anglers use larger flies, it's still important to aim for a spot above your target so the line straightens in the air and then falls to the water with as little disturbance as possible. Avoid carelessly slapping the line and fly down on the water. Large, wary smallmouth will flee from this—or develop a bad case of lockjaw— just as surely as a trout will.

When fish are spooky, do not use noisy topwater flies such as poppers. Instead, fish a Floating Minnow or slider with little or no retrieve. Your choice depends a

When fishing from a boat, drive to within a reasonable distance of where you want to fish and then cut the motor. JAY NICHOLS

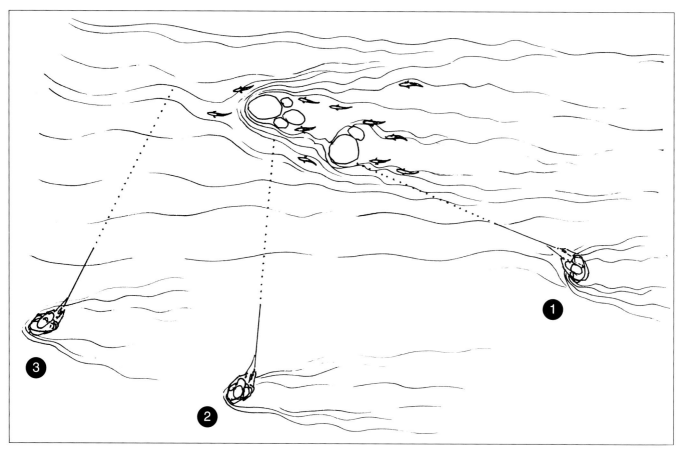

Before you get into position, plan your approach to minimize the number of different currents your leader and fly line go over. For instance, it is much easier to get downstream of an eddy and fish straight upstream (1) or upstream and across (2) than it is to try to get a dead drift by casting across stream and placing your line and leader in three or more currents. On the other hand, when fishing streamers, it's often easier to swing the fly downstream (3) or cast across stream (2) than it is to fish upstream (1). To get a good drift you often have to move—either closer to your target or in a position where there are fewer different currents to complicate your drift.

great deal on the conditions and the attitude of the fish. If a breeze is blowing and the fish are only moderately spooky, a Floating Minnow with an active retrieve may be a good choice. In flat, calm conditions, when the water is low and clear, you may have to fish a slider with the faintest wiggle or no retrieve at all. Often a silent dead drift or subtle retrieve has brought smallmouth to the surface in five to ten feet of water. In many other instances, smallmouth take the fly only if it is lying perfectly still on the surface. I have seen smallmouth rise to the surface and drift along with a dead-drifting Floating Minnow, inhaling it only after it drifted ten feet. Those same smallmouth completely ignored a stripped fly.

One other important aspect of getting into position is planning your approach to fishing any given area to reduce the amount of drag on your fly by minimizing the number of different currents your leader and fly line go over. For instance, it's much easier to get downstream of an eddy and fish straight upstream or upstream and across than it is to try to get a dead drift by casting across

stream and placing your line and leader in three or more currents. Of course, you can combat drag by using a lot of special casts and mends designed to get better drifts, but then your line isn't in a straight line to the fish and makes hooking fish a challenge.

LINE CONTROL
Controlling your fly line effectively is a skill that all good anglers master. Learning a few tips and following a few rules will make this easy for you most of the time, but other times, such as during a high wind, you can only do your best. What does controlling your fly line mean? It includes controlling how you handle your line while you walk upstream or wait on the bow of a boat for the perfect cast; control over your line with your line hand while you are casting; how well you take up the slack line while you're fishing so you can fish your fly effectively and set the hook; and how you manipulate the line on the water to beat drag. Let's take a look at some important elements of line control, starting first with

how you strip in line and handle that line before you make another cast, followed by line control while casting, and then while fishing the fly.

After you cast and begin stripping in line with a streamer retrieve, or gathering in slack as you keep a tight line when following a nymph back while employing the high-stick technique, you need to do something with the line that you take in. Many saltwater wading anglers use stripping baskets, and that's also a good idea for bass fishers if you are making a lot of long casts, especially with sinking lines. Having a stripping basket or something else in which to strip your line on a boat also makes a lot of sense. Fly lines always seem to find something to tangle around on a boat deck—especially when you are making the cast to the fish of a lifetime.

On a boat, be aware of how you handle the slack line as you retrieve it. You should drop the line in loose coils on the stripping platform of the boat, with each coil lying on top of the previous one. Do not kick the line pile or move it around with your feet. This may damage the line, and your chance of a tangle when you are shooting line greatly increases if coils from the top of the pile end up underneath coils from the bottom of the pile.

When you are wading in stillwater, the same principles apply. In moving water, line management is easier—the current drags your line downstream below you in one large loop that rarely tangles unless debris in the water, such as drifting weeds, catches on it. However, this loop of line is difficult if not impossible to shoot off the water, especially if the swirling currents below you drag it under the water. In this case, you have to bring this slack line upstream into castable coils or make excessive false casts to get the line in the air. A stripping basket eliminates both of these problems.

The next important thing for line control is to learn how to cast weighted flies properly. I covered this in more detail in chapter 6, but the most important thing in your cast that sets you up to begin stripping the fly immediately is to make sure your line straightens out at the end of the cast. This is necessary only when you are fishing flies with an active retrieve, such as a Clouser Minnow or Half and Half. If you are dead drifting a crayfish imitation, nymph, or dry fly, it is often best to purposely introduce slack into the line during the cast to get a good drift.

Another tip is to follow through on your forward cast, following the fly's descent to the water's surface with your rod tip. When you do this, your rod tip is low to the water as soon as the fly hits the surface, and you are ready to begin your retrieve, make a mend, or set the hook if the fish immediately grabs the fly. Take another

A stripping basket helps keep your line under control when you retrieve the fly and allows you to shoot more line on the cast. When not in use, you can put it behind you. JOHN RANDOLPH

look at the last few steps in the casting sequence on page 112. The one major exception to this is when you are high-stick nymphing. After you cast, you most often stop your rod tip high and pull out the slack through a combination of stripping line with your line hand and raising the rod.

Drag

Floating lines and sinking-tip lines with floating running lines are the most popular for freshwater fishing. In moving water where its speed changes throughout the water column—generally fast on the surface, slow on the bottom—the floating line and leader move faster than the weighted fly, so it's necessary to control the drift of the fly by manipulating the line at the surface. Because the surface currents move faster than those at the bottom of the stream, it's important to be able to control your fly line and leader to help minimize drag, which is a general term for any unnatural movement in your fly.

A dry-fly fisher's worst enemy is drag. When drag takes over, it pulls your fly, and you lose control of it. When a floating fly drags, it's easy to see the fly pulling across the surface unnaturally. Drag also happens underwater, though it's more difficult to detect, but it's equally

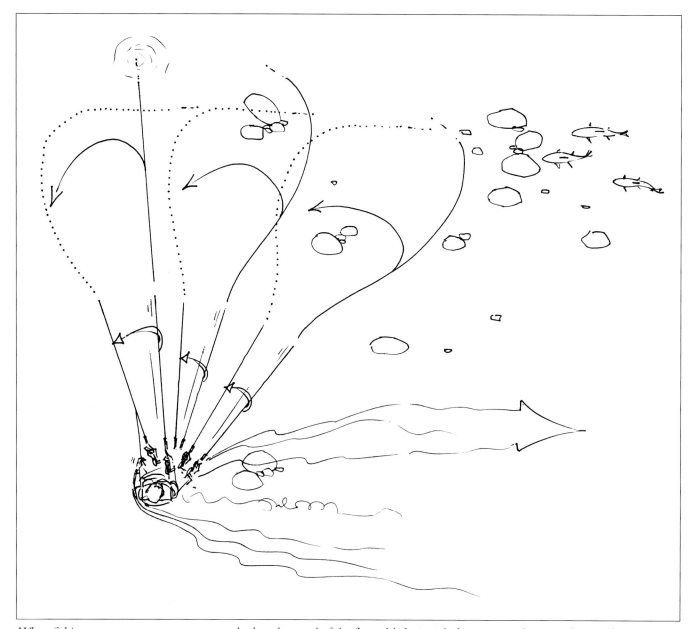

When fishing across currents, upstream mends slow the speed of the fly and help it sink deeper. I use these mends most frequently when fishing Clouser Deep Minnows. Mends minimize the drag the current has on the fly, and repeated mending through the swing helps swim the fly effectively through a larger area.

important to counteract because most underwater foods move in a way that you can't copy with drag on the line. With drag, the fly swings and pulls and moves unnaturally through the water.

Drag is caused by water pressure pushing on the fly line, allowing the line to move downstream faster than the fly. This happens because the rod, line, and fly are moving downstream at different speeds. To help counteract drag, cast only as far as you need to. Most anglers cast from very far away, and all that line on the water can wreak havoc with a good drift and make it hard to set the

hook when the fish takes your fly. Also attempt to set up your presentation so that you can avoid casting over water with widely varying current speeds. Try moving to a different location for a better presentation. For instance, if you are standing in midstream, facing across stream at a slow pocket of water behind a boulder, your best approach would probably be to get directly or almost directly below the boulder and cast straight upstream. If you don't, you will have to cast over faster-moving water. The faster water will start pulling on your line as soon as it hits, dragging your fly too.

Mends come in handy anytime you want to control the speed of the fly underwater, and on the surface as well. Generally, upstream mends slow the fly; downstream mends speed it up. Most of the time, you'll want to make upstream mends, but in some instances with slow water, you may want to use downstream mends to keep your fly swimming in a natural-looking manner.

To make an upstream mend, simply lift the belly of the fly line off the water and place it upstream. You use more of a lifting motion to place the line upstream or flip it with your rod tip. If you cast a fly straight upstream from you, throwing lots of slack into the line will help it sink unhindered by the tug of the fly line. When you make an upstream mend, try not to disturb or interrupt the drift of the fly. Many times you will have to make as many as three or five mends just to control one drift over a three-foot span of bottom.

The photo sequence illustrates a basic across-stream cast with an upstream mend. After you cast across stream, lift line from the water and place it upstream of the fly. This allows the fly to sink. As the floating line travels downstream, it will catch up with the fly and eventually be downstream of it, pulling on it, speeding it up, and causing drag. To counteract this, throw upstream mends in your line as the fly drifts downstream, and do not allow the floating portion of the line to get below the point where the leader enters the water.

I mend streamers differently than I do dry flies. With a streamer, I tend to pull all the slack from the line when I mend the line upstream. Though this moves the fly a bit, I'm careful to not pull so hard that I move it away from the area that I want to fish. By having a straight line, I can strip more effectively and set the hook easier. You can use mends to achieve a dead drift or in combination with a stripping technique such as the Susquehanna Strip.

With a dry fly, it's often better to shake slack into your line with your rod tip before throwing the upstream mend, so that you are mending only the line in front of you and not affecting the drift of the fly. Even if you don't shake slack into the line, you can focus on flipping just the line in front of you upstream so that you don't move the dry fly. Of course, few hungry bass mind a surface fly that skitters a little bit.

BASIC UPSTREAM MEND

JAY NICHOLS

Cast across stream toward your target.

Lift your rod tip and the line off the water. The more you lift your rod tip, the more line you will mend.

Flip the line upstream with your rod tip. The more line you want to mend upstream, the more you have to lift the line deeper into the butt section of the rod. For small mends, you can usually just use the rod tip.

Stop the rod tip as the loop forms. Instead of flipping or casting the line upstream, as shown in this sequence, you can also just lift and place the line upstream, but this method moves the fly less.

The upstream mend is formed on the water. The current will have to remove this upstream bow of slack line before it can begin to drag the fly. The rod tip is high, but you want to start lowering it to begin your retrieve.

The rod tip is low to the water, and the angler is ready to start stripping. This single mend helps sink the fly. You can strip a few times and then repeat this process in faster water.

Retrieving the Fly

Anglers with complete control of a fly line at all times usually have more hookups. A tight line is required to both effectively impart action to a fly and set the hook. If there is a lot of slack in the line, the fly won't move when you strip the line or it won't move the way you want it to. If the line is slack, you may not feel a strike, or if you see the fish strike, you won't be able to set the hook. When you have a tight line, you will feel more strikes and hook more fish. Sometimes fish even hook themselves! If you have no slack and a low rod-tip position when retrieving a fly, the smallmouth can pull against a solid connection during the strike, thus enabling easy hook penetration. Anglers using a dead drift nymphing method should also experience increased hookups after learning proper rod and hand positioning and how to control slack. Hook setting increases dramatically as well when you lower the rod tip and manipulate a popper with the line hand instead of using the rod tip.

You can set the hook in two major ways; both involve taking all the slack out of the fly line. The method favored by saltwater anglers, and one useful for bass fishing, is the strip strike. In this method, you keep your rod tip pointed at the fly and fish and make a long strip with your line hand to set the hook. This works well if you have no slack in your line, because it allows you to tighten on the fish but doesn't pull the fly completely away from the bass if it happens to miss on the first strike. This gives the bass another chance to strike.

The other method is setting your hook by lifting the rod tip. This is the method used by most trout anglers, because it is effective at removing a lot of slack very quickly. The downside is that because the rod tip bends, you cannot exert maximum pressure on the hook point. You also often will pull the fly away from the bass when you use this type of strike.

SUBSURFACE PRESENTATIONS

Bass readily come to the surface to take a fly—one reason they are considered such great gamefish—but they, like most every other fish species, eat most of their food underwater. This food can range from mayfly nymphs to baitfish to crayfish, and you must learn to imitate the behavior of each to be successful.

When fishing subsurface flies, it's important to match the mood of the bass, which is determined by a number of factors, including water temperature. Because bass are cold-blooded, their body temperature and metabolism are regulated by water temperature. When the water temperature increases, their metabolism speeds up, requiring the fish to eat more. Conversely, in cold water, their metabolism slows down, and the fish become lethargic. Because of this, water temperature is often a good gauge to determine the aggressiveness with which smallmouth feed. The lower the temperature, the shorter the distance the fish moves to catch its food, and the less likely it is to chase fast-moving prey. In cold water, you need to drift a nymph or streamer slowly over the bottom to the fish, but in warm water, you can aggressively strip a fly and the fish may follow from six feet to eat it.

Smallmouth come to the surface to feed in low current speeds and in clear water. Many times, the energy required to come up through the water column—through turbulent and fast currents—would be more than the food would provide, so most large bass feed subsurface.

Another important thing to consider when fishing subsurface flies is that water moves at different speeds throughout the water column. Whereas currents are relatively simple to spot on the surface, subsurface turbulence causes your fly and leader to move in ways that you need to be aware of to be a consistently successful angler. In some areas, usually where water flows over structure, turbulence causes water to move in all sorts of directions. At times, although surface currents may be moving downstream, the currents underwater are moving upstream. These current changes can wreck a good presentation of any fly by creating drag and lots of slack in the line, preventing a natural appearance and causing poor contact with the fly.

A lot of different streamer and nymphing presentations that people have developed for trout, salmon, and saltwater fish work for bass. Like most anglers, I use combinations of different techniques depending on the

Lefty Kreh strip strikes a bass by lifting on the rod and simultaneously stripping in line with his left hand. JACK HANRAHAN

circumstances. For bass, it's important to experiment with presentations and retrieves to determine what works best. But for simplicity's sake, the main subsurface presentations that I use are strips with baitfish and a dead drift with crayfish and mayfly and hellgrammite nymphs. Sometimes I pulse or swim nymphs at the end of a dead drift. This not only extends the amount of time I can fish my flies before picking them up and casting again, but also gives the flies a tantalizing motion that may sometimes look like an escaping item of food. Adjusting to different water depths and conditions is a bit of a challenge, and two important things to know about how to sink your flies and get a good drift are weight and understanding how drag affects the drift of your fly and how you can mend your line to counteract that effect.

Bottom-Bouncing Techniques

Bottom bouncing is a presentation in which your fly drifts unimpeded by drag along the bottom of the stream, occasionally hitting bottom. This presentation is most effective for fish that are lethargic because of cold water temperatures or those feeding on prey at or near the bottom of the stream, such as crayfish or hellgrammites. If you are not hitting bottom and occasionally snagging your fly, you are not fishing deep enough. When fished effectively, the fly tumbles into pockets of slack currents where fish hold, waiting to pick off food that washes

toward them. Bottom bouncing is also a deadly technique for Woolly Buggers, Clouser Swimming Nymphs, and aquatic nymphs such as mayfly and stonefly. An overlooked but effective technique is to bottom-bounce a Clouser Minnow with short hops and twitches. Simply add enough split shot to the leader about eighteen inches above the fly to counteract the buoyancy of the fly and sink it to the bottom, and the fly will ride just about a foot off the stream bottom.

When bottom-bouncing a fly, it sometimes helps to use an indicator placed above the fly about one and a half times the depth of the water. As the fly bounces along the bottom, watch the indicator for any slight hesitations or movements that might show that a fish has taken your fly. Indicators are also helpful when you want to fish a fly at a specific depth, such as when bass are holding in a deep hole. Suspend your fly by adjusting an indicator large enough to float your fly and the weight at the depth you need.

Besides using lead wraps on the hook shank or adding beads made of different materials, such as brass or tungsten, I often adjust the fly's sink rate and depth it will reach by adding or taking away B or BB split shot. Good nymph fishers change weight more frequently than flies. If the fly sweeps downstream as fast as the speed of the surface currents, then you need more weight to get it down into the slower current that flows along the bottom. If I am not getting to the bottom or achieving a slow downstream bottom bounce with my fly, I add more split shot to the leader about one foot above the fly. When I add shot to sink the fly, I space them along the tippet at intervals of eight to twelve inches. When I fish a shallower or slower-moving area, I take the shot off. Matching the weight to the current speed and water depth is a never-ending affair. In some rivers, you'll have to change the amount of weight you use only two or three feet from your previous position. In addition to split shot, I sometimes use various lengths of flat metallic strips twisted around the leader.

But adding enough weight to sink your fly like an anchor is only part of the equation. Though I fish a lot of weighted flies, I don't think you should go overboard. You'd be surprised how well you can sink a fly with just a little strategically placed weight and good mending techniques. The weight you add to a fly and the manner in which you add it affect how the fly swims in the water. If it is heavily weighted, it will drift naturally only in strong, fast currents. The same fly would become lodged

on the bottom in slower-moving currents, so you should use less weight when fishing in slow or medium currents.

When fishing these flies, it's important to make a cast that leaves enough slack in the line that your fly has time to sink before tension on the line starts to pull it downstream. If the line is pulling on your fly, it can drag your fly from the bottom regardless of how much weight you have. Some anglers make a tuck cast to improve their dead drift along the bottom. By making a low backcast and coming forward with an upward trajectory, you stop the rod tip hard on an upward angle. The forward momentum of the weighted fly causes it to stop quickly and tuck under the line. This technique throws a lot of slack line ahead of where the weighted fly sinks in the water, allowing it time to sink.

I seldom make a tuck cast, but I do make another slack-line cast that achieves similar results. Starting with a low backcast, I come forward with an upward trajectory and stop the forward cast abruptly, shocking the fly and causing it to bounce back a few feet. This creates slack in the line and gives the fly time to sink.

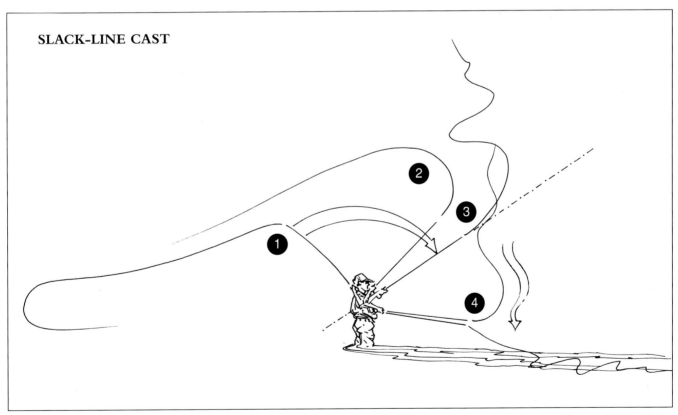

SLACK-LINE CAST

When fishing crayfish or hellgrammite imitations upstream, it's important to make a cast that leaves enough slack in the line so that the flies have time to sink before tension on the line starts to pull the flies downstream. Begin the slack line cast the same way as the oval cast (1) but stop the forward cast with a stronger upward trajectory (2) and more abruptly, shocking the fly and causing it to bounce back a few feet. This creates slack in the line and gives the fly time to sink. After stopping abruptly, follow through by dropping the rod tip (3 and 4).

This photo shows the high-stick, dead drift technique when casting to a target upstream and slightly across from you. JAY NICHOLS

Dead Drift Wading Presentations

When I am wade-fishing, I prefer to use dead drift bottom-bouncing techniques rather than fish streamers. Wading lets me get into the best position with the best angle of approach. I have two main casting positions for bottom-bouncing a fly: casting upstream, either straight or at a 45-degree angle, and stripping in line as the fly drifts back to me, or casting across stream and high-sticking as the fly drifts back toward me.

For a basic dead drift presentation when you are below the target, cast your fly upstream, drop your rod tip, and strip in line so that it doesn't have a lot of slack and you can feel the fly tick on the bottom. Pull in only as much slack as is required to stay in contact with the fly, and allow it to drift naturally. I like to cast far upstream with this technique so that I get a long drift and show the fly to as many fish as possible. With a long dead drift, it's possible to use less weight, because your flies have more time to sink to the bottom.

To fish a target across stream from you, cast your fly slightly upstream of the target, throw an upstream mend to let your fly sink, and follow it through the drift with your rod tip, throwing upstream mends in your line as you feel necessary so the fly stays on the bottom. If I am fishing a nice run or pocket upstream and to the side of me, I'll use a high-stick nymphing technique. In high-stick nymphing, you hold the rod tip and your arm high to keep the line off the water, preventing it from being pulled by the water's currents, as you follow the fly through the drift. This technique works best with short casts and heavier weight on the leader because of the short drift.

After the fly enters the water and settles to the bottom, you should point the tip of the rod at the area where the fly line enters the water. It is not necessary to lower the rod tip as you would when stripping back the fly. Now follow the drift of the fly line with the rod tip, never allowing the line to drift past the tip. If a bow of line does begin to form downstream of the rod tip, mend upstream a little, and again follow the drift of the line with the tip.

I fish the first half or two-thirds of the drift on the bottom, and then let the fly swing up in the current at the end of the drift with a technique called the Leisenring Lift, named after Pennsylvanian James Leisenring. To do the Leisenring Lift, fish the first part of your drift high-sticking, and drop your rod as the line moves downstream. Let the current swing your fly up through the water column at the end of the drift, and as the fly is lifted up by the currents, slowly pulse your rod tip so the

This photo shows an angler high-sticking a run along a downed tree directly across from him. JAY NICHOLS

fly undulates on its upward path. This technique brings the fly to the surface like a nymph rising into the surface film. It is an especially good technique when fishing the Clouser Swimming Nymph.

Dead Drift Boat Presentations

Another effective method to catch bass is allowing the imitation to freely drift along the bottom while fishing from a drifting boat. From either end of the boat, cast ahead of you at approximately a 45-degree angle, and take up most of the slack in the line so that you can feel the fly tick along the bottom. Because the boat is moving faster than your fly along the bottom, you may have to make some upstream mends to continue the drift, and eventually the boat will catch up to and pass the fly. When this happens, pick up and cast again. Using this technique, you can get incredibly long drag-free drifts. Generally, the farther downstream you cast, the longer drifts you can get.

This nice bass took a hellgrammite imitation fished dead drift from a drifting boat. Because the boat can move at the same speed or slower than the current, you can easily get your fly drifting naturally on the bottom. KEN COLLINS

STREAMER FISHING

When you are fishing a streamer, keep in mind how bass feed on baitfish. They like to intercept the fly as it drops during the pause of the strip. A bass doesn't chase down a fish and hit it running like a lion chases a gazelle. Fish without teeth—like bass—wait to take the bait when it's at a disadvantage. Detecting a strike like this can be challenging at first. Sometimes it's just a slight tug on the line as the bass inhales or sucks in water trying to consume the bait. Sometimes it will swallow the fly during the pause and give a more definite pull as it turns with the bait.

Bass ambush baitfish, so good places to fish streamers are in front of and behind large rocks, against banks, through deep cuts, at the heads of pools, and in front of and behind ledges. When you are setting up the cast for your streamer, keep in mind what Lefty Kreh once said: "I have never seen a fleeing baitfish stop, face the predator, and ask to be eaten." Make your fly appear as though it is trying to get away from an attacker. Move it *away* from a fish or fishy-looking lie. Do not cast the fly past the fish and then swim it toward the bass, as this is perceived as a threat. It goes without saying that you don't want to hit the fish on top of its head with a dumbbell-eyed streamer.

It's important to follow the drift of the fly with your rod tip. After you cast across stream or slightly up and across stream, you can either mend your line or not, but as your fly drifts downstream, don't leave your rod pointing where you just cast; let it follow the drift of the fly. This helps you stay in better contact with the fly and

will let you strike and hook the fish more effectively. The longer the fly is swimming broadside to the bass, the better your chances of getting a strike. Sometimes this requires lots of mends—either upstream or down—to swim the fly across the currents.

Susquehanna Strip

The Susquehanna Strip is named after a stripping technique I developed on the Susquehanna River after being unsatisfied with the standard streamer retrieves. This technique accelerates and pauses the fly during the retrieve so that it darts like a fleeing baitfish. I often get more strikes when retrieving the fly with this technique than with a steady stripping retrieve. The fly darts during the strip and dips during the pause, portraying the behavior of an escaping baitfish. Lefty Kreh once told me, "Bob, the reason your fly is so deadly is that it never stops moving, and neither does a baitfish that is trying to escape a predator."

To be able to do this technique for a long period of time, I think it's important to move your stripping hand in line with your rod hand. This prevents the line from chafing your right forefinger, which you use to control the line. If you hold the rod on your right side and strip line from your left, the line can burn your forefinger from the friction.

After you strip once, pause before stripping again, and be ready to set the hook. Smallmouth will follow the fleeing streamer and inhale it the instant it pauses and starts to fall slowly toward the bottom.

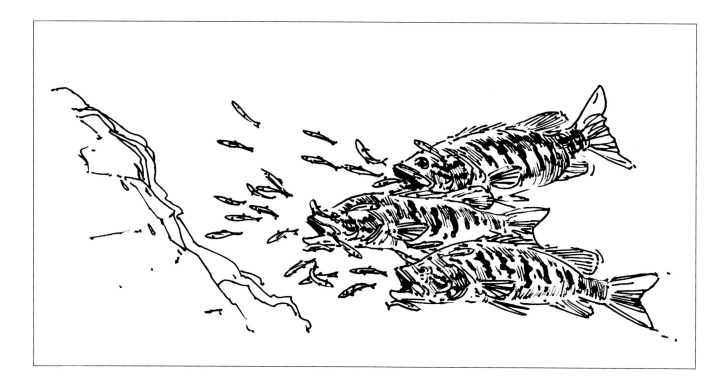

After you cast and your fly hits the water, drop your rod tip to within six inches of the water so that it is pointing straight at the fly. Trap the line under the pointer finger of your rod hand. With your rod hand on the same side of the body as your stripping hand, reach up with your line hand and grab the line just behind where you have it trapped with your rod hand. JAY NICHOLS

Begin a strip by dropping your line hand down to your thigh. Movement should accelerate smoothly.
JAY NICHOLS

Once your line hand reaches your leg, increase the speed of the strip until your line hand is extended behind you. I also abruptly push my thumb back to further accelerate the fly. The bass usually strike just as the fly stops and starts to drop because of the weighted eyes. The fast dart forward frees the fly from the tension of the line and leader. JAY NICHOLS

When fishing streamers, it's important to keep as straight a line as possible between your rod tip and the fly and also to keep your rod tip low. JAY NICHOLS

Slow-Drop Technique

A technique that is the opposite of the Susquehanna Strip, what I call the slow drop, can also be an effective way to fish streamers. You simply cast your fly and let it sink slowly in the water without moving it. Anglers who use this tactic should carry an assortment of various weighted flies. This slow-drop tactic is favored by smallmouth guide Mike O'Brien when fishing underwater minnow imitations to large smallmouth in clear water.

I'll never forget watching an angler cast to a smallmouth holding in a deep depression behind a rock. He was stripping the fly back to him after it entered the water, but even after several casts and retrieves, the bass still ignored his fly. The angler made another cast, and the fly fell to the water about two feet in front of the smallmouth. The smallmouth inhaled the fly as it sank, and as we watched in amazement, the fish spit it out. This happened quickly well before the angler had time to strip the fly. That instance taught us a new tactic that has produced many a large smallmouth when other methods failed. Since then, I found that bright-colored flies that sank slowly could easily be seen as they sank toward the bottom. Another advantage of these flies when using the free-falling tactic is that their visibility aids in striking the smallmouth. You might not always see the small-mouth take the fly, but the fly disappears as it is sucked into the mouth of the bass. It pays to strike instantly when the fly disappears quickly.

Flies that are weighted lightly sink much more slowly toward the bottom. An example of this would be a Clouser Minnow dressed with extra small or mini eyes instead of a larger size.

Streamer Presentations while Wading

Though fishing streamers while wading is a lot more work than fishing streamers from a boat drifting at the same speed as the current, it does have benefits. First of all, you don't need a boat to do it. Second, and most important, you can work a particularly productive spot from many different angles to get the fish to take, whereas in a drifting boat, you usually have only a few shots at a particular spot or fish before you drift on to other water.

The most basic streamer retrieve is to cast across and slightly downstream, and then strip the fly back to you as it swings downstream. From this position, you can make farther casts to cover more water or take a few steps downstream. This is a good technique for searching lots of slow to moderately moving water.

If you cast across a current and do not mend, the fly swings around at a relatively steady speed, because the line and leader are always under tension. A better technique in my opinion is to mend your line upstream after you cast and in between your strips. Though it takes a lot of work, this technique makes your fly look like a baitfish swimming across current, darting, twisting, and acting hurt, and it swims the fly broadside to the fish for the longest period of time. The upstream mend relieves the fly from the unnatural pull of the line and leader by the downstream current. With the fly free from the leader, it bounces and jigs in the current.

You can also fish a streamer straight upstream or down. I'll often approach a large eddy or pool, cast straight upstream, and strip the fly back down. I like to get thirty or forty feet below the target, cast, drop the rod tip, and strip the fly as fast as the current is moving. But that's hard work. You can also get upstream of the bass and feed your fly down to it, teasing the lure with short strips or subtle pulses with your rod tip.

Curve casts are fun to make and provide another tool that allows you greater flexibility in many fishing situations. For instance, if I am opposite a bank where I think bass are holding, I can make a left or right curve cast so the fly lands along the bank, and then swim the fly either up or downstream along the bank for a short distance. Similarly, if I want to cast a fly around an obstruction such as a rock, I can do that with a curve cast. The benefit of this is that you can swim your streamers in front of or behind rocks while you use the obstruction to prevent the fish from seeing you. This cast is worth practicing.

When streamer fishing, I like to spend as much time fishing the most productive water. That means not fishing out the entire drift if I know that the bass are hiding behind the rocks. If I don't get another hit after a few strips and mends in the prime water, I pick up the line and cast it back into what I think is the sweet spot or the fish's lie. I situate myself about ten feet below the lie and cast upstream, which gives me the chance to work that area productively, rather than standing straight across from it.

Streamer Presentations while Boating

Streamer fishing from a boat is simple and highly effective. Because you are drifting at the same rate as the current, you can easily get a good retrieve without much mending. I tell my clients to cast in a straight line to the shoreline or a little downstream of them for the best retrieves with a subsurface fly.

When you anchor and cast across current, you need to mend your line as you would wading.

Bombing the banks from a drifting boat is an exciting and productive way to fish streamers. BOB CLOUSER

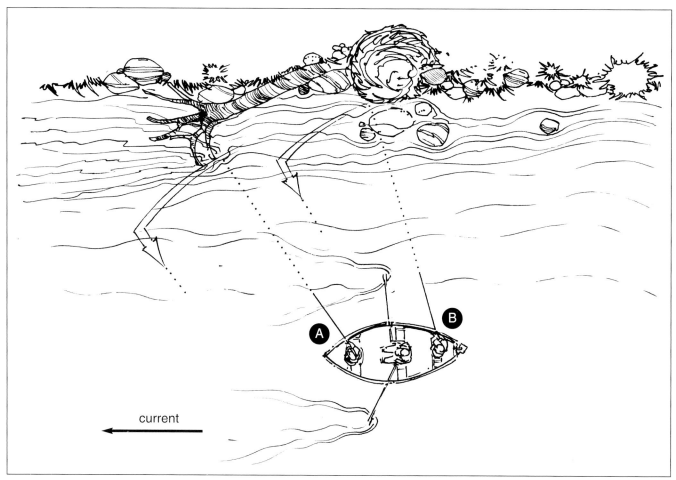

Streamer fishing from a boat is simple and highly effective. Because you are drifting at the same rate as the current, you can easily get a good retrieve without much mending. Both the bow angler (A) and the stern angler (B) should cast in a straight line or a little downstream for the best retrieve. Drift boats are ideal for streamer fishing because you can backrow to slow down your drift. Johnboat anglers often use drag chains or other methods to slow the boat's drift.

SURFACE PRESENTATIONS

Casting a floating fly and watching the take, whether it's a busting strike or a simple gentle sip, still gives me goosebumps. Smallmouth are a great gamefish because they attack flies on the surface, and nothing beats the visual excitement of fishing a floating fly for smallmouth in clear water where you can watch the fish follow and swallow your fly. Surface flies are such an important part of fishing for smallmouth that fly fishing for smallmouth bass used to be called popping bug fishing. Most people never bothered with sunken flies for bass.

Surface flies can be used to match the hatch when aquatic insects such as mayflies and caddis or terrestrials such as hoppers and ants are on the water. They can also be used to match minnows swimming close to the surface because they are crippled or perhaps feeding on the surface on emerging bugs. But surface flies can also be used when nothing is going on. Few things in nature that move across the surface of the water can't be eaten by bass. Who knows what the bass takes your popper for, but one thing is true: A lure chugging across the surface is often hard for a bass to resist, and even when you aren't catching fish, casting and watching a popper chug along the surface of the water is fun.

Many different styles of surface flies have been designed to be fished in a certain way, at a specific water depth, or to present a different characteristic. Each style of fly is best suited to match particular water conditions, the mood of the fish, and the way in which the fly is retrieved. As with many other things, however, there are no hard-and-fast rules; flies designed as streamers, such as the Muddler Minnow, can be fished on the surface, and flies designed for the surface can be fished on sinking lines. I'll talk about poppers, divers, floating minnows and sliders, and trout-style dry flies. These are the styles of flies that have been effective for me over the years. Other anglers have good luck with surface flies with small propellers added, like the Jitterbug bass fly; blades

Above: Smallmouth take a wide range of surface patterns— from trout dry flies to deer-hair divers to foam poppers such as this Pencil Popper.
JACK HANRAHAN

Left: For my smallmouth fishing, I switch between an EZ Popper (shown here) and a Floating Minnow, depending on how the fish react to the flies. An EZ Popper creates a lot of disturbance; the Floating Minnow is more subtle.
BOB CLOUSER

FORM AND FUNCTION

The design of the front of a floating fly determines its action. A flat or dished-out face makes the bug pop; a sleek, narrow taper starting at the hook eye and increasing near the back of the hook causes the fly to move and dive quietly through the water's surface. Poppers, such as the EZ Popper and Lefty's Bug, are designed to draw strikes from fish attracted to a lot of commotion on the surface. Lefty Kreh has pointed out that one reason poppers catch some of the largest specimens of many fish species is that a relatively small popper can imitate something large because of all the

disturbance it makes, yet unlike a large fly, it can be cast relatively easily. Because most bass are attracted to a disturbance on the surface of the water, poppers are an extremely effective means to catch them. However, sometimes bass shy away from the noise of poppers in low, clear water or if they have been heavily pressured. When noise spooks the bass, choosing a smaller popper or switching to a quieter style of surface fly is often more effective. Divers are good choices to try when fish don't want to commit to a popper or are spooked by it. Divers float on the surface like poppers,

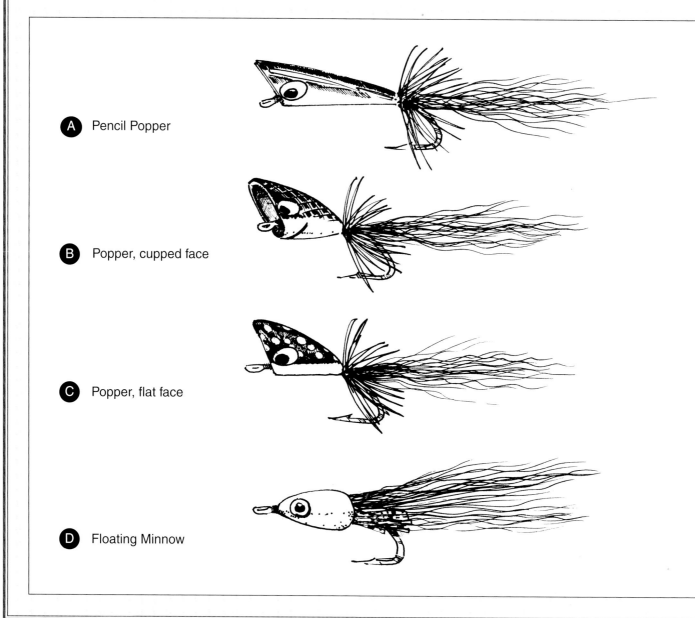

A Pencil Popper

B Popper, cupped face

C Popper, flat face

D Floating Minnow

but when they are retrieved, they dive under the surface of the water and then float back to the top. They are designed to imitate the actions of injured or surface-feeding minnows.

Larry Dahlberg's Diver popularized this style of fly. The head of the fly is trimmed flat on the bottom. A collar encircles the rounded top portion of the back of the head. This design allows the fly to pop and dive during the retrieve. When you retrieve this fly, it not only causes commotion on the surface, but it also leaves a trail of air bubbles behind it. My Crippled

Minnow (see page 98) borrows from Larry Dahlberg's influential design.

Floating Minnows and sliders are more subtle than poppers and divers, and some, such as the Floating Minnow and Bright Sides Minnow, have a more realistic profile. My favorite surface fly is the Floating Minnow. It moves across the surface with only a little disturbance, but the back end hangs below the water. This pattern is deadly for bass that are spooky or aren't aggressive enough to take poppers. Conventional sliders like the Sneaky Pete, a super surface fly, have a bullet-shaped head. The movements and ripples created by these flies represent numerous movements of baitfish, animals, or insects.

Trout flies and skaters come in numerous styles. They are the most subtle of all the bass surface flies, and I use them to imitate the adult mayflies on the Susquehanna River. When I'm not interested in seeking out large smallmouth, I go to light tackle and catch numbers of average-size bass. It's hard to cast a large popper on a small rod, but a 4- or 5-weight can easily handle a size 10 White Wulff. Many of the large deer-hair and foam pattern with rubber legs popular on western trout streams make excellent smallmouth bass flies, though you will usually catch smaller fish with small dry flies.

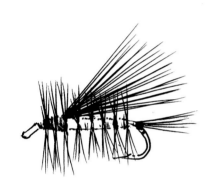

E Stimulator

F Dahlberg Diver

The design of different floating flies affects the amount of disturbance they create and how they swim in the water. Generally, in low light or dirty water, flies that create a lot of disturbance on the water are a good choice because bass feed by sound and vibrations more than by sight. In clear, low water, flies like Floating Minnows, sliders, or heavily dressed trout-type flies are better choices for spooky fish. Of course, there are many times and circumstances where poppers work well for bass in low, clear water.

Poppers (A, B, C) are noise makers designed to attract bass; Floating Minnows (D) create little disturbance on the water; divers such as the Dahlberg Diver (F) are a compromise between a popper and a low profile Floating Minnow. The head is designed to help the fly dive under the water when stripped. Stimulators (E), damselflies, and other trout-style patterns are good for small fish or for fish feeding on specific insects.

to make them dive, like the Rapala lures; or the Crease Flies designed by Joe Blados. These flies work, and as with all things in fly fishing, fly selection has as much to do with the angler's preferences as it does with the fish. I like to keep my fly selection as simple as possible.

Smallmouth, like trout, rise selectively to insects on the surface, but more often than not, they can be induced to take most any fly. For smallmouth bass, flies designed to look like the natural usually do not work as well as the ones that mimic their movements. Surface flies that imitate struggling insects or crippled baitfish disturb the water's surface, and they provoke strikes even though they really do not look like baitfish. Bass respond well to movement, so a fly skittered or twitched on the surface often gets the fish to bite. But the type of movement often can make a difference. At times, noisy surface activity spooks smallmouth, whereas quiet presentations entice a hit. You can control the way the surface fly moves through a combination of retrieves and fly design.

RETRIEVES

Presentation, accuracy, and action are important factors in successful bug fishing. Just because a particular technique worked one time doesn't mean it will be productive the next. Sometimes bass like a bug chugged across the water's surface. Other times they only take a dead-drifting fly that is twitched periodically. Once I was pulling a boat with some clients into a cove between a series of rock ledges when I spotted bass busting up a school of baitfish. After I had brought the boat into casting distance, the angler in the bow cast his topwater bug toward the commotion caused by the feeding bass. The bug hit the water, and the angler stripped it once and let it sit, but nothing happened. He picked the bug up off the water and cast again. This time, as soon as the bug fell to the water, he started a steady stripping retrieve. Two large smallmouth moved toward the bug, and one of them inhaled it.

This experience—and many others like it—taught me to experiment if a particular retrieve doesn't work.

Bob Popovics, an angler experienced with the fickle moods of striped bass on the New Jersey coast, changed up his popper retrieve and was rewarded with a nice bass. BOB CLOUSER

Good anglers constantly modify subtle things, such as the length of strip, length of pause, or the frequency with which they strip the fly back before pausing. Sometimes getting a fish to strike is as simple as knowing when to stop retrieving your fly and let the fish take it, or gently twitching your popper instead of stripping it back hard. Though I describe some general retrieving styles below, there isn't a simple formula for catching bass.

Many of the best anglers learn by experimenting with different retrieves *after* they have found one that works. How do you know the bass only wanted a fly stripped quickly if you don't try anything other than stripping the fly quickly? This is one lesson you can learn from inquisitive anglers who experiment even if it means catching less fish. If all you do is fish a popper with a steady retrieve and you are catching fish, how do you know that it is the best technique?

One important thing to remember is that in most circumstances, the action you impart to the surface fly comes from the design of the fly and your stripping hand. Although there are exceptions, for the most part you should not use your rod tip to manipulate a fly you are retrieving. Waving the fly rod tip up and down or back and forth creates slack in your line that will prevent you from quickly and firmly setting the hook on a fish.

Strip and Pause

This method is possibly the most common retrieve. Begin with the tip of the rod just above the water's surface, with the tip pointing down the fly line and in line with the popper. Pull or strip the fly line, forcing the popper to move toward the rod tip. Usually the length of the strip or pull can vary, but the popper should move about six inches at a time. Pause before stripping again. Smallmouth strike during the pause, so stay alert. This method portrays an injured or dying baitfish.

Steady Retrieve

In this retrieve, do not allow time for the fly to pause in between strips. This can be the most exciting of all retrieves. It portrays an escaping baitfish or even a land animal scurrying, panic-stricken, across the water's surface. I have seen some large smallmouth attack the popper with vengeance when this technique was applied. Lefty Kreh favors this method when using his famous Lefty's Bug. This retrieve can be deadly when stripped across stream.

Pop and Stop

The pop and stop can be very effective in slow-moving, clear water. This retrieve varies from the strip and stop by only popping the popper and not allowing it to be stripped forward. This takes a little practice but can make up for the many strikes that otherwise would not occur. The time between the pop and stop can be adjusted and should be varied until the strikes start. Anglers who use this technique should be aware of subtle takes by large smallmouth that will, at times, inhale the popper without leaving any sign on the water's surface.

Pop and Drift

The pop and drift is used mainly in clear water with wary smallmouth. At times, smallmouth spook when anything hits the water's surface and scurry for cover. The angler should be aware that noise sometimes deters strikes and should not move the popper until it drifts undisturbed over the water's surface. These long drifts from at least three through ten feet will usually bring up a wary smallmouth. If no strike occurs during the drift, try moving the popper with a subtle pop or twitch.

Dead Drift

The dead drift can be employed during a hatch of insects or just used randomly. You can apply this technique by casting up or across stream. After the popper hits the water, let it drift motionless downstream. I like to use this dead drift method over boulder-strewn bottoms or through current seams. I recall an instance where smallmouth would rise from behind a submerged boulder and take the popper as it drifted over the rear portion of the boulder. Large smallmouth often rise slowly to inspect the popper and then follow it as it drifts. At times, smallmouth will follow a drifting popping bug some distance before inhaling it. Smallmouth take drifting poppers subtly; in fact, some anglers take their eye off the bug for an instance and wonder where it got to when they try to find it. I have seen large bass look as if they are standing on their tails, with their noses directly under a drifting popper or Floating Minnow, for as long as five feet, and then without any disturbance, they inhale the fly.

A variation on this technique is to cast the fly and, when all the rings have dissipated after it lands, give it a subtle twitch. Sometimes bass are too spooked to take a popper immediately after it lands on the water, and letting it sit for a moment before twitching it can work well.

Many times, especially on windless days and super-calm, clear water, a bug that is left still for a few seconds and then twitched accounts for more strikes. Another trick is to cast the bug onto the water's surface, especially where slow-moving current is noticeable, and let it naturally drift without imparting any action. These methods seem to tantalize bass that are found around many types of cover. Rock piles, lily pads, heavy surface

Bob Clouser Jr. caught this hefty bass on a popper fished dead drift. When a big fish takes a popper, it often just sucks it in. Be ready to strike. BOB CLOUSER

grass, and downed trees usually call for a slow, quiet, tantalizing retrieve. When fishing this type of structure with a bug, adding a weedguard made from mono or wire is necessary in order to prevent hangups.

Skating Retrieve

The skating retrieve is popular with traditional trout dry-fly fishers of the East, who designed heavily hackled flies that would skate across the water's surface, as well as steelhead and Atlantic salmon anglers. Skating a dry fly on the surface of the water is an exciting way to catch fish and a deadly and overlooked technique for bass.

Heavily hackled flies lend themselves to this presentation, but anglers have reported great success with a Floating Minnow fished in this manner. It's really very simple. Cast across and downstream at about a 45-degree angle to start. Follow the fly with your rod tip as it skates across the surface. When it reaches a point directly below you, twitch it a few times in case a bass has been following it, and then pick it up and cast it again. You can control the speed at which the fly travels across the surface of the water with mends. Mend upstream to slow the fly down, downstream to speed it up.

CHANGING UP YOUR TACTICS

What do you do when the standard tactics you are using do not work? There are times when the typical strip and retrieve, dead drift, and pop and stop simply do not attract strikes. Nothing seems to be out of the ordinary, the water level is fine, the clarity is good, and the smallmouth are where they usually are. But for a reason known only to the smallmouth, they are not being cooperative.

Many anglers get caught up in an automatic stripping mode that never changes. Some strip a fly back using the same speed and stroke length on every consecutive cast, never changing the rhythm. You can be more successful just by varying the speed, pauses of the fly, and length of the strip. This is equally true when fishing flies dead drift. If the fish seem not to be interested in your free-floating nymph or crayfish, try twitching it a little bit.

If a smallmouth refuses your fly, change your approach and offer it from a new position. If, after you have changed your presentations a few times, you're still not having any luck, rest the fish and go back later. Allow some time to pass so the fish settles down, and then go back and make a complete fly change to something different in size and color. Sometimes a surface fly works if you got a short strike on an underwater fly.

A simple tactic that's not used by anglers as much as it should be is using sinking fly lines with floating flies. Sometimes smallmouth take a floating minnow only when it is rising toward the surface. An angler can apply this tactic by using a density-compensated or uniform sinking type 2 or 3 full-sinking fly line. One bright, sunny afternoon in five-foot-deep clear water, I watched a client make a sixty-foot cast with a sinking line and Floating Minnow toward submerged ledge rock. We could clearly see the floating fly as it was being pulled down to the depths by the sinking fly line. The angler started to strip the fly back, and as he did, we witnessed a new type of presentation in which the fly would rise toward the surface between pauses of the strip. This rising action of the fly brought on strikes from large, wary smallmouth that would have ignored a standard presentation.

CHAPTER 8

Ten Tips to Catch a Trophy

JACK HANRAHAN

Maybe you skipped the rest of the book and went right to this chapter. If you did, that might be okay, because this chapter is basically a crash course in fishing for big bass. Please read the rest of the book, but I hope this chapter helps you catch a big one.

What is a trophy? Size is relative, and on a small stream with a 3-weight, a two-pound bass is a monster. On larger water such as the Susquehanna, anything over four pounds is a trophy bass. The objective is not so much to get bragging rights, but to develop the skill, patience, and understanding to catch the least common and most difficult bass. Catching a large, seasoned bass like this is the ultimate recognition that you have studied hard.

When I caught my first five-pound smallmouth on a fly, at that time I was most interested in just learning about smallmouth and the flies to catch them. My favorite flies at that time were poppers and deer-hair bugs. I used many standard subsurface flies with some success, but not with the consistency of fishing the surface in the clear water of the summer. In those early years, I also found that I could catch larger smallmouth

To consistently catch large smallmouth bass—ones from three to five pounds—you need to know where to hunt these large fish, your skills must be honed, and you must use large flies.

Though size is relative and a fourteen-inch bass from a small creek is a trophy, bass over eighteen inches, wherever they are caught, are fish to be proud of. STEVE MAY

on the surface than I could on the bottom. During the 1960s, there were great numbers of smallmouth in the Susquehanna averaging from six to fourteen inches but relatively few large ones from nineteen to twenty-three inches in length. At that time, I had not caught one over eighteen inches.

On the evening of July Fourth one year in the late 1960s, I decided to put the boat in the river and take a shot at some popper fishing for smallmouth. I had a favorite section with some gravel bars surrounded by deep water that had a few large rocks about the size of

Volkswagen Beetles strewn around. One particular rock was named Snapper Rock, and it sat about seventy-five yards off the west shore of the river. Its rough, broken top rose about two feet above the water's surface, creating an eddy on its downriver side. My plan was to take the boat upstream of the rock and off to its left side and to make a few drifts past it and get closer each time, eventually drifting close enough to make a cast right into the eddy. My fly was a size 2 yellow popper with red streaks painted on it and yellow feathers protruding from the hook bend. I sent the popper to the small eddy at the downstream area of the rock, but it missed the mark, hit the rock, and rolled off it into the water. With amazement, I saw the popper disappear in a small swirl, and I set the hook on a twenty-one-inch smallmouth that was soon tail-dancing across the surface. I can still see that bass leaping at Snapper Rock with a yellow popper shaking in its jaw that July Fourth evening.

It has taken me many years to figure out some of the skills and techniques necessary to consistently catch large fish, and I'm still learning. Though the following ten tips are not all-inclusive—there are and there will be exceptions to every rule—they should help you catch a trophy smallmouth.

1. IMPROVE YOUR CASTING

For some reason, fly fishers often do not practice casting as much as they should. Though many times you do not need to cast more than thirty feet to catch some fish, being able to cast far is essential in low, clear water or when fishing to large, wary bass.

As important as distance—possibly more important—is accuracy. Not only should you be able to hit the target you are aiming for, but you should also be able to cast under control so that your fly, leader, and line land in a straight line (if that is what you intend) so you can begin your retrieve immediately.

Another element of casting efficiently is being able to make long casts without many backcasts. Most anglers spend far too much time false-casting line. Not only does this increase the likelihood of spooking fish, but it also wastes valuable fishing time. To help load the rod quickly, I sometimes shoot a little bit of line on my backcast. Also, the line that I use for bass—one that I helped design—has an aggressive front taper that helps load the road with a minimal amount of false casting.

Right: To catch trophy bass, you need to work on your casting skills so that you can quickly and accurately cast at least sixty feet with only one or two false casts. JAY NICHOLS

The larger and more wary the bass, the fewer chances you generally will have to catch them. Your first cast needs to be on the mark.
KEN COLLINS

2. PLAN TO CATCH BIG FISH

This tip is about thinking positively and focusing on results. If you want to catch large fish, you need to be prepared—mentally and physically—to catch them. That means always fishing at the top of your game. For starters, you need to stay healthy on the stream, drinking a lot of water and eating nutritious snacks—especially if you're on the water for the entire day. Some anglers make the mistake of fishing so hard on the first day of a weeklong trip, neglecting to rest, eat, drink fluids, that they suffer the rest of the week. Along these same lines, it's important to dress properly so that you will be comfortable in hot conditions or wet, cold weather, and to apply sunscreen throughout the day. In addition to keeping your body in working order, you must also take care of your fishing gear. Preventive maintenance and care are important, and this is an ongoing process year-round.

Throughout the day, you should check your hook points frequently, replace any frayed tippet, and be careful with your rods and reels.

Another important thing in your planning is related to the next tip: If you want to catch a big fish, you need to fish big flies. This means you may have to give up the large numbers of fish that you might catch with smaller flies, focusing your efforts on catching a few quality bass each day when other anglers are catching many smaller fish. Plan on using large flies, such as Half and Halfs on size 1/0 hooks from 4 to 6 inches long. You might catch only one to four big smallmouth during a day's outing, but they will be bragging size.

Along with large flies, use tippet stout enough to fight large bass. Under most circumstances, you can fish 10-pound-test monofilament or fluorocarbon tippet for bass without spooking them.

To catch and land big fish, you need to use tackle that can handle them. Inspect your hooks and tippets frequently. BOB CLOUSER

3. GIVE THEM THE GROCERIES

Smallmouth do not reach adulthood until their fourth year. At this age, they usually attain a length of twelve inches or more. Immature bass feed constantly on small items near the bottom of the food chain. Many species of nymphs, small crayfish, minnows, and other insects provide the protein needed for growth, and small bass need to eat continually to nourish this growth.

Large smallmouth bass rely on larger forms of food for their growth and survival. When a large smallmouth feeds, it must replace its energy expended with a greater energy source. Because of their size and weight, feeding constantly on smaller foods would not replace the energy they expend while feeding. After a large meal, big smallmouth usually rest for hours while their bodies absorb the energy needed to resume life. Big bass also become vulnerable to anglers during these feeding binges. Smaller bass are easier to catch because they need to constantly feed.

Fly size usually determines, at least a good percentage of the time, the size of the smallmouth you catch. One of the many reasons why fly fishers do not catch large fish is because the flies they use are too small. Standard conventional bass lures are much larger than most of the flies we use—plastic worms are 6 inches, jerk baits 5 inches. It's a proven fact that big bass eat big baits.

Of course, there are exceptions. Large smallmouth are occasionally caught on flies less than 2 inches long, and small bass are sometimes caught on large flies, but streamers from 3 to 8 inches long will entice the most trophy smallmouth. Lefty Kreh once said to me, "If you want to consistently catch big bass, don't give them a snack. Give them groceries." That advice has increased the number of big bass I have caught over the years.

To hook those big fish, your flies should look like a meal to bass, not just a snack. Large sculpins and other minnows, imitations that have bulk and a broad profile, often entice the biggest bass.
STEVE MAY

One of the advantages of tying flies with fur and feathers is that the proper materials expand in the water, creating the illusion of bulk. The best large flies are those that are easy to cast and do not foul, but look large and full of life in the water. Following this same principle of illusion, the best big flies for bass are not always sub-surface patterns. Lefty Kreh has long advocated using poppers to catch bigger fish, because they create a lot of movement on the surface of the water, suggesting a food form larger than the popper. This has also been my experience when fishing for smallmouth bass.

Before there were Clouser Minnows, I took to fishing poppers of all sizes and colors when I wanted to catch a trophy smallmouth. I found that by using all sizes including some very large poppers, I caught about the same number of big smallmouth bass each season regardless of the size of popper. I also learned that the larger poppers did not attract as many smaller bass. I have caught big smallmouth on poppers during all times of the day and seasons as long as clear water was available.

Lefty and I are smallmouth addicts and love to catch big bass on the surface. We prefer clear water in the fall when water temperatures are in the low fifties. At this time, the big boys rise to Floating Minnows and poppers. Big bass usually rise to the surface slowly and inhale the poppers, leaving only a small rise ring on the surface.

Do bass have a limit to the size of the prey item they will feed on? They do, but for the most part, anglers don't have to worry about their flies being too large. The limiting factor is often our casting ability and not the bass's willingness to eat the fly. I have seen smallmouth sometimes try to eat prey too large to swallow easily, and it can sometimes get them into trouble or even kill them. I have found dead smallmouth of all sizes with minnows, chubs, or suckers wedged in their mouths that killed them.

4. FISH IN BIG-BASS WATER AND FOCUS ON BIG-BASS HABITAT

Larger bass are more selective in choosing territorial habitat than small bass. Habitat that holds big bass continues to do so year after year.

Many waterways have limited habitat that will support large smallmouth. You should spend time on the water learning where the biggest bass live. Experience is still the best teacher.

I have found that big smallmouth prefer areas with deep water, moving currents, and structure that consists of large rocks, sunken trees, large logs, or some other type of debris into or under which the bass can escape. This habitat provides not only protection, but also ideal feeding stations and ambush points. Big smallmouth will

Poppers are very effective for large bass because they create a lot of disturbance on the water, providing the illusion of something large. BOB CLOUSER

lie in wait around structure, ready to pounce on an unsuspecting fish that enters its realm. They also will venture out of the deep water and move up onto shallow gravel bars or around grass beds in search of food. I have seen those large bass feeding in these shallow areas at dusk, on overcast days, at night, and in the early morning around daybreak. In some instances, my clients caught big smallmouth during midday on gravel bars with one to two feet of water over them. This can be a common experience if the gravel bar contains spots with deeper holes and a few large rocks in them. Big smallmouth lie in these deeper cut-out areas and use them for ambush points. These deep gouges in the bottom structure can be found scattered throughout the gravel bar system.

Big bass prefer water that provides a combination of food, shelter from currents, shade, and safety from predators. Here, Lefty casts behind a series of rocks that is a known home for big bass.
BOB CLOUSER

Big bass tend to be scarce near commonly used public-access areas. To find fish, sometimes you need to get away from the crowds. Floating a river can get you to lightly pressured areas of a stream.
JACK HANRAHAN

The Great Lakes tributaries are known for their enormous resident and migratory bass. If you want to catch a trophy bass in a river, these tributaries are good places to look.
STEVE MAY

Shade-covered pools along shorelines are good places to look for bass during the day when the sun is high. Look for ones that also have structure such as large rocks, sunken logs, or fallen trees. I have had clients cast surface poppers between the shoreline and a log, with only one foot of clearance, and get strikes from big bass.

When hunting for trophy bass, you should generally stay away from heavily pressured areas such as those found around boat launches and in the immediate vicin-ity of public-access areas. The best way to find unpres-sured water is to float in a boat or walk. Many fishermen tend to stay close to their cars, and a fifteen-minute walk can bring you some solitude—and undisturbed fish.

Another thing to consider when looking for large fish is to focus on tributaries where bass make spawning runs in from large rivers and lakes. The Great Lakes trib-utaries get runs of enormous bass and have resident smallmouth that also grow large.

5. HUNT HEADS AND CAST TO THE LARGEST FISH

At times, hatches of mayflies will start smallmouth feeding on the surface, allowing you to sight-cast to rising smallmouth and pick out the biggest bass. If you are hunting big bass, learning how to read riseforms will allow you to locate a large bass.

Riseforms can tell you the sizes of the bass making them. For instance, during a whitefly hatch, small bass often break through the surface while feeding. This leaping behavior is indicative of enthusiastic immature bass that haven't yet learned to feed efficiently. Medium-size bass usually cause a moderate swell or swirl in their riseform as they suck in the whiteflies. Larger smallmouth tend to sip or suck the fly under, causing a smaller, less noticeable ring on the water. They still show their size, though, because when a large smallmouth takes a fly from the surface, it makes an impression with its upper jaw as it breaks the surface, and after taking in the insect, it usually marks the water with the tip of its dorsal fin or its tail. This type of rise allows you to estimate the size of the bass by judging the distance between the snout and dorsal fin or tail. In many instances, a big smallmouth will ignore a small mayfly and rise to the smaller bass that are busy eating the insects. The riseform in this case is also very delicate, but a larger swirl will be visible as the big smallmouth sucks in the unsuspecting prey.

In clear water when you are sight-fishing, going after big fish also means floating or wading past smaller smallmouth or even groups of small fish. A true headhunter walks right past fourteen- and sixteen-inch smallmouth in order to maximize the time spent fishing for trophy bass. If you really want a five-pound fish, don't be distracted by all those little ones!

An effective way to hunt the largest bass is to float the river in a boat—a johnboat, canoe, or pontoon boat. Instead of casting to every fish you see, save yourself for the largest fish. KEN COLLINS

Patience often pays off. This bass was holding in a side channel and spooked when the angler approached it unaware. But after the spot was rested for fifteen minutes, the bass took the fly without hesitation.
JAY NICHOLS

6. BE PATIENT

One of the tricks to catching big fish is to wait for them. Many times smaller fish will start to feed first, and big fish will feed a little later. If you immediately start casting to the smaller fish, you may spook the larger fish and never get a shot at them. Also, if you see a big fish but it looks spooked, don't start casting to it. Let it settle down and resume feeding before you make a cast.

Large smallmouth will come to an area and establish a feeding pattern only if the natural sounds and activities of other fish in the area remain undisturbed. On one fishing trip, an Ohio angler wanted to catch a large smallmouth on a dry fly. I had seen a large smallmouth feeding fifty or sixty feet below a submerged rock ledge on a previous evening, so prior to the hatch, we tied on a fresh 6-pound tippet and a size 10 White Wulff, dressing the fly with floatant. We made sure everything in the boat was secured out of the way, as we did not want to bump or upset something that would make noise and spook the fish. The angler was in casting position as the hatch started. We waited as riseforms began to appear, and our eyes scanned the surface just above the submerged rock ledge for telltale signs of the big bass feeding. I could tell the angler was getting impatient and wanted to cast to the many other feeding bass that were in casting range, but he knew that if we disturbed the area and alarmed any smaller fish, the large bass would not feed.

Twenty minutes later, the large smallmouth finally appeared. It held in the same spot as on previous nights, feeding four feet behind three other smaller bass. This position did not leave much room for casting error, and the angler knew he had only one chance. He made the range adjustments with two false casts, and then sent the fly three feet above the large bass. The fly disappeared in a swirl. The angler lifted the rod to set the hook, and a smallmouth of four and a half pounds jumped into the air with the Wulff embedded in its jaw.

7. BE STEALTHY

Trophy bass live a long time by being careful. They do occasionally feed with reckless abandon, but usually they are extremely wary. Many wise old fish don't swim away when spooked; they just hunker down and refuse to feed.

Here are some basic rules for stealth fishing:

• Don't create unnecessary disturbances in the water when wading, and when possible, approach from downstream. If in a boat, be careful not to drop things on the deck.

• Be mindful of the direction of the sun and where you are casting a shadow. Keep the sun in front of you or to the side to avoid spooking the bass with your shadow.

• Stay low when approaching a fish, and cast sidearm and low to the water.

• Make long casts and use as long a leader as possible.

• Know where the bass you want is holding, and make your cast to that spot.

• Learn to cast so that your fly lands gently.

A 10- to 12-foot leader with a 6- to 10-pound tippet is a good choice when you have a combination of big, spooky smallmouth and low, clear water conditions.

Early season, when bass are awakening from winter and starting to feed to prepare for spawning, is an excellent period to target large bass. Similarly, fall—as bass feed before the onset of winter—is also a good time.
KING MONTGOMERY

Below: Large bass can be easy to catch at night, because they feed voraciously under cover of darkness. STEVE MAY

8. TAKE ADVANTAGE OF THE PROPER TIMING AND TEMPERATURE

Early spring, when bass are spawning, and late fall are often the best times to catch the largest fish. In the spring, large bass are aggressive and attack flies, and you can often sight-fish to the biggest ones when they are on or near their nests, but I don't like to interfere with the important spawning process. Sometimes when male bass are defending their nests after spawning, they will grab almost any fly you throw at them, giving you an unfair advantage that makes it almost too easy. My favorite times of the year to fish for big bass are when the water temperatures rise above 85 degrees and when they fall below 55. Big bass feed during the high water temperatures of midsummer because their metabolism is at its highest point of the year. When the water temperatures drop below 55 degrees in the fall, the bass also feed heavily to store up energy for the winter. In high water temperatures, smallmouth tend to seek out larger prey and feed both day and night. In the fall, bass are most active at midday, when water temperatures rise to their daytime highs, and small flies become more effective than in the summer.

Night can be an excellent time to hunt large smallmouth. Fewer anglers are disturbing the water, so the bass feed with more confidence, and you are less likely to spook larger bass fishing under the cover of darkness. Big

Morning is also a great time to find big fish. Though bass can feed all day, if you get on the water before other anglers, you have a better chance of finding fish that haven't been spooked. LEFTY KREH

bass lose their daytime shyness and become much more aggressive at night, boldly roaming into shallow water to feed where they may not go in the daytime. They also tend to be less selective at night and hit anything that disturbs the water's surface, such as a popper, slider, or heavily dressed fly that pushes a wake or moves water. If it moves, they want it. Fishing at night requires a great deal of familiarity with the water. You don't want to try it on new water, but if you have a favorite gravel bar or riffle you like to wade, or are confident in your boating skills and knowledge of a certain area of the river, night fishing can produce big bass. It's an important card to play if you frequently fish in an area where you know there are big bass but have a hard time hooking them in the daytime. Go back at night, and it may be a totally different experience.

Rising water can force baitfish closer to shore where large bass ambush them. A chartreuse Clouser Minnow stripped through the shallows took this trophy bass after a heavy rain.
JACK HANRAHAN

9. FISH THE RISE

Timing doesn't just mean fishing during the best part of the day or the best seasons for big bass—it also means fishing when the water conditions promote catching bigger bass. I have found that the best water conditions for catching large bass are during a rise. When the water is rising as a result of rain, big fish go on the prowl. More food becomes available as water disturbs the bottom debris and knocks insects and crayfish loose from their crevices. High water pushes baitfish out of the heavy current in the center of a river and toward the margins along the shore. When the bait are concentrated along these areas, the bass move in to feed, and just as at night, they feel more protected in murky water and are less wary. Once the water level peaks, the catch rate also peaks.

The best information can be had from other anglers who are on the water. The second best is from U.S. Geological Survey (USGS) stream gauge data. USGS stream gauges are positioned along many streams, and that data is available at www.usgs.gov. If you learn to read the data and understand how these numbers relate to conditions in the stream, careful reading and experience can help provide a picture of the water levels and whether they are rising or falling. If the river is dam controlled, the dam also may have this information posted on a website or available by phone. An experienced understanding of the drainage—whether it muddies quickly or takes a long time to muddy and a long time to clear—can also provide this same kind of information. Some old-timers need only to look at a rain gauge to know whether the river is rising or falling and what the conditions may be like.

10. LOOK FOR MUD STREAKS FROM FEEDING CARP

The mud streaks created by bottom-feeding fish such as carp are bass magnets. Even more interesting to trophy seekers is that mud streaks tend to attract larger-than-average smallmouth. Maybe small bass feel insecure in the mud streaks because they can't see approaching predators, maybe the big bass chase the smaller bass away, or maybe small bass just haven't learned that the muddy water stirred up by carp rooting along the bottom is an awaiting banquet. Whatever the case, I've found that fishing mud streaks in the hot summer months is the best way to catch large bass consistently when the sun is high and the river is generally clear.

Casting to carp not only is exciting fly fishing in and of itself, but it is also a great way to find a trophy bass. MIKE O'BRIEN

If you are wading, you'll count yourself lucky if you find a mud streak where you happen to be fishing. In a boat, you can cover a lot of water searching for mud streaks or just keep a lookout for them as you move from spot to spot. A long way downstream from its source, you may notice only a faint tinge of color over a wide swath of water. As you progress toward the source of the mud, the streak will become more defined, until you finally see its origin, which is usually one or more carp using the tops of their foreheads to turn over small rocks in a silty section of the riverbed.

A single carp misses much of the food it manages to stir up from the bottom. A group of carp stirs up the river quite a bit more, and each benefits from what the other carp are scaring up off the bottom, but plenty of food is always left over for the smallmouth bass that are attracted to the muddied water. A large mud streak created by a group of carp may hold half a dozen or more good-size bass, which may be hovering directly over the carp, just a few feet behind, or several yards downstream.

Smallmouth often take on a dark color when they are feeding in a mud streak, and you can see them drifting in and out of the mud, waiting to pounce on whatever may come to them. Even if you can't see a smallmouth, one may be on the bottom in the mud where you can't see it or directly in the mud cloud behind the carp. Take a few casts to see if anyone is home, but be careful not to disturb or spook the carp. They may

Bass follow carp around because the feeding carp root in the mud and overturn rocks, disturbing the water and kicking up aquatic insects and crayfish. MIKE O'BRIEN

feed like this for quite a while, and it may take some time for the mud streak to reach a bass. When it does, the smallmouth will travel to the source of the mud streak. This is a good time to observe rule 6, be patient. If there are no bass in a mud streak you just found, go fishing somewhere else and come back later, or have a sandwich and then see if any big bass have moved into the streak.

You may think that bass feeding in a mud streak would take flies only on the bottom, and this isn't a bad premise. If the smallmouth are cruising along the bottom in and out of the mud streak created by feeding bottom fish, a Purple Darter, Foxee Redd Clouser Minnow, crayfish imitation, or big weighted Woolly Bugger should provoke a strike. If you see smallmouth on the back of or cruising near the bottom fish, they will hit a surface popper or Floating Minnow. Sometimes the bass can't see the fly well in muddy water. If, for some reason, you are having trouble getting your weighted fly near the bass, the disturbance created by a popper can sometimes bring the fish to your fly.

To find mud streaks, look in the back bays, coves, side channels, and sections between protruding rock ledges. Bottom-feeding fish prefer silt-covered river bot-

Mud streaks created by bottom-feeding fish such as carp are big-bass magnets and provide the best opportunities to consistently catch large bass when the sun is high and the river is clear. A large mud streak created by a group of carp may hold half a dozen or more good-size bass either hovering directly over the carp, just a few feet behind the carp, or several yards downstream.

This nice bass was caught by casting immediately behind a mudding carp. Though the angler couldn't see the bass in the mud, the gamble paid off. MIKE O'BRIEN

toms or areas with slow water over a bottom of broken rubble. You will also find smallmouth and bottom-feeding fish together in weedy areas protected from strong currents.

I would like to leave you with an experience of the kind that anglers will store in their memories for a lifetime. The nose of the boat was approaching a feeding carp that was escorted by two big, four-pounds-plus smallmouth, at a range of about sixty feet. I dug the end of the push pole into the hard bottom of the river, stopping the boat and turning it into position for the cast. The angler gently cast a Floating Minnow toward the prowling bass. The big smallmouth that was closest to the fly inhaled it first. When the angler struck, the bass jumped and threw the fly. As soon as the fly landed on the water again, the second smallmouth took it. The fish jumped and the fly fell out of its mouth, leaving us in total awe.

CHAPTER 9

Equipment

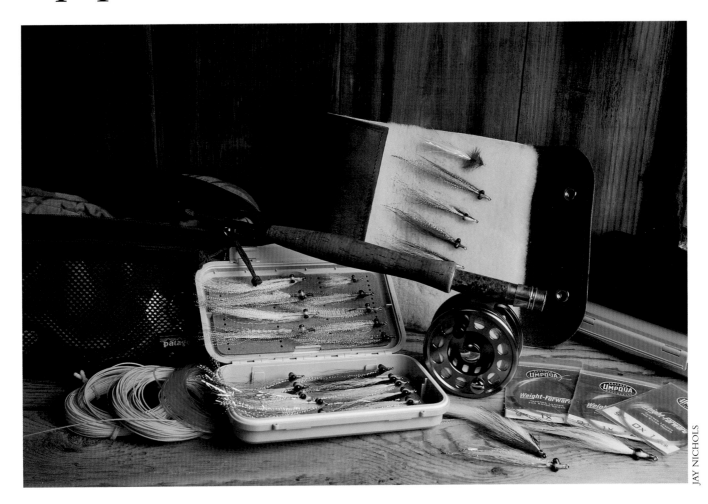

Compared with trout fishing, fishing for small-mouth bass doesn't require a lot of tackle. You don't need to carry five diameters of tippet or eight fly boxes. In fact, on most smallmouth streams, you don't even need waders. But to effectively fish for smallmouth bass, there are a few important equipment considerations.

This chapter addresses issues with tackle that I think are important to be aware of in order to be a good smallmouth bass angler. I'm not going to cover complete rigging techniques or go over the inner workings of a large-arbor reel, because many others have done that in detail in books and magazines. Instead, I will talk about the gear I use and why I use it for bass.

FLIES

The fly's size and weight help determine line size, leader length, and rod weight, so they should not be an afterthought. Many anglers buy their rods, reels, and lines and then ask what flies they should use. A better approach is to think about the flies that you will be using, and then buy the appropriate fly line and a rod to match that line.

When buying or tying flies, you don't need to go overboard. It's better to have several sizes of a few

Fly-fishing for bass doesn't require a lot of specialized equipment, but I recommend using a 7- or 8-weight rod to cast the larger flies needed to catch bigger bass.

Here, I am discussing fly choices with Lefty Kreh. On the boat, I like to carry my flies in large plastic boxes or lure bags.
KING MONTGOMERY

patterns than to have only one of a wide range of patterns. That's because you can often fool a bass by changing sizes first, instead of switching patterns. Having only a few trusted patterns makes things simple, allows you to stay organized, and keeps you from wasting time thinking about which fly to choose when you could be fishing. Though I carry a wide range of flies on my boat, I take only one or two fly boxes with me when I'm wading. You need fewer of each style of fly than with trout dry flies, because a well-constructed bass fly such as a popper or Floating Minnow lasts a lot longer.

It's a good idea to debarb all of your flies at the bench, but for those times when you forget, you should carry hemostats or pliers as part of your essential gear to crimp down the barbs and pull hooks from fish's mouths. Crimping down the barb on a fly is important. Not only does it do less damage to the fish's mouth and allow you to unhook it easily, but it also makes the fly a lot easier to get out of your clothing or skin if you hit yourself with it, which can happen to the best of us.

Test the hook points of your flies at the vise, and if they are too dull, sharpen them in the vise so they are ready when you hit the river. In case you forget to do this or the hook point dulls when fishing, such as when bottom-bouncing crayfish, carry a hook sharpener with you in your vest or on the boat at all times. Whenever

Above: At home, I store my flies in plastic compartment boxes that I label. I also bring these on my boat when I fish, and I stock up my fly boxes from this supply when I wade-fish. I organize the individual flies in clear plastic sleeves.

JAY NICHOLS

Left: The plastic boxes in which I organize my flies fit inside my large tackle bag that I use for other gear, such as tippets, sunglasses, and pliers.

BOB CLOUSER

you feel your fly tap bottom, free your fly from a snag, or hit the boat, check your fly point and leader. Also check your point after hooking a few fish or if you have more than two fish strike your fly and you don't hook up. Dull hook points catch fewer fish. A little preventive maintenance will help you catch more fish.

You can store your flies in a wide variety of things. If you use foam-lined fly boxes or fleece-lined wallets, choose ones long enough to fit streamers with long hair and deep enough to fit wide-bodied poppers. I like to use small, clear plastic envelopes purchased from a bag supply company, especially for slimmer flies like Floating Minnows and Clouser Deep Minnows. I use large Ziploc bags to hold the smaller bags, but some anglers store them in large plastic tackle boxes. A system like this keeps the flies organized and makes it easy to grab the ones you need.

It's important to take care of your flies. Quality flies are expensive to buy and time-consuming to tie, so either way, it pays to take care of them. A well-tied popper or Clouser Minnow will last for many bass. One customer who came into my shop claimed he caught fifty-three smallmouth on one Clouser Minnow before it was destroyed. When I change a fly, I put the one I took off on a drying patch on my vest or a patch of foam or other material on my boat. Don't put the wet fly back in your fly box, because that introduces moisture into the box that can rust your flies if you do not use stainless-steel hooks. At the end of the fishing day, you can gather all the flies that you've used and put them back after they have dried. You can rejuvenate water-soaked or matted flies by holding them with tweezers over steam. After the steaming is completed, let them dry before storing.

LEADERS

Leader design can make the difference between a good day and a bad one. Wind, casting style, and the size and weight of the fly all affect leader performance. The most important consideration in leader design for smallmouth bass fishing is the length and diameter of the butt section.

Most anglers divide leaders into three different sections. The heaviest part of the leader is the butt section, which joins to the fly line and helps transfer the energy of the unrolling line to the rest of the leader and the fly. The middle section of the leader is basically a transition from the butt section to the tippet section, which is attached to the fly. In trout fishing, long tippets are sometimes necessary, but in bass fishing, the most important considerations are matching the tippet size

to the fly and making sure the butt section is long and heavy enough to turn the rest of the leader and the fly over.

Hair bugs and poppers are air-resistant and act like parachutes, trapping air and preventing leaders without backbone from turning over. Leaders for large or air-resistant flies should have a heavy butt section of .020- to .028-inch diameter that is at least 50 or 60 percent of the leader length. You can use this same construction for weighted flies, but turning a weighted fly is not as much of an issue, because the extra weight helps them turn the leader over, provided the cast was made properly.

In some instances, long leaders are necessary to catch bass in low, clear water. The main purpose of a long leader is to distance the fly from the line. Some anglers I know use 15-foot leaders, but I think a 10- to 12-foot leader with a 4-foot-long tippet is long enough in low, clear water. Lengthening the tippet allows the fly to move more during the presentation and is often the key to catching difficult bass.

Determine the length and pound-test of the tippet by the size of bass you expect to catch and the weight of the fly you are casting. If you tie your own leaders, you can make them as long as you like, but most store-bought leaders come in sizes between 7 and 9 feet, which is fine for most presentations with floating flies and floating fly lines. These types of leaders may be identified on the package for use with streamers or bass flies in particular.

I tie my own leaders. Not only is it economical, but it also allows me to construct them specifically to turn over the flies that I use the most. Most leaders made today are designed for 2-foot tippets, but my leader design provides enough forward energy to turn over several different leader tippets lengths, from 2 to 4 feet, and diameters, from 6- to 12-pound-test, so it is a good all-purpose design that works for different flies and conditions. When fishing sinking lines, you don't need a tapered leader; instead, you can use a single 4-foot piece of 10- or 12-pound-test attached directly to the sinking line with a nail knot or loop-to-loop.

When fishing dry flies, you can tell that the tippet is the right length if it lies on the water in snakelike curves. If the tippet has excessive coils, it's probably too long. If it's completely straight, make it longer.

Check your leader often during a day of fishing for abrasions, twisting, or kinking, which can all cause failure. Leaders can become dirty and should be wiped down with soapy water and rinsed clean along with your fly line. Do not store or leave leaders or leader material for any length of time in direct natural or artificial light.

I use floating lines most of the time for bass. The line I like the most is one I helped design specifically for casting heavy flies. It has an aggressive front taper that turns over the leader and fly. I mark my lines with bars to designate the weight—a long bar equals five, and a short bar equals one. BOB CLOUSER

LINES

Most line manufacturers have diagrams on the backs of their boxes or can provide you with information about the taper and what types of flies their lines are designed for.

Floating Fly Lines

For bass fishing, a standard weight-forward floating line is the best all-around choice that will allow you to fish floating flies and nymphs. Weight-forward means that the line has a relatively thin running line that tapers to a head of about 30 feet or so, depending on the manufacturer. The taper of this head helps determine how it turns flies over. Because there are so many specialized lines on the market, lines designed for large flies that have shorter front tapers generally are best, though a standard floating line with a properly designed leader will also work if you have good casting skills.

If you fish mostly nymphs and streamers, you may want to try one of the lines on the market with an aggressive front taper. These are often marketed as nymphing lines or bass, pike, and muskie tapers. I helped design a floating fly line for RIO Products with an aggressive front taper, called the Clouser Taper. This line excels at casting a wide range of weighted flies and poppers and has become my favorite line.

Sinking Lines

Sinking lines are useful primarily for swimming your fly deep in high, fast-moving water or through deep pools. If you have already purchased a floating fly line, the next line you purchase should be a sinking line. You have many choices. Sinking lines are loosely classified by their sink rate—slow or intermediate, medium, or fast—and whether they are full-sinking lines or only a sinking tip attached to a floating running line.

QUICK TURNOVER BASS LEADER FOR ROD WEIGHTS 8 AND 9

Each of these formulas builds a 7-foot leader butt to which you can attach from 2 to 4 feet of tippet, giving you a leader that can range from 9 to 11 feet. The first leader formula works with tippet sizes ranging from 6- to 10-pound-test. The second matches tippet sizes of 6- to 12-pound-test, and I use it for my heavy work; it's great for air-resistant flies and heavy Clousers. For a longer leader, simply add to or reduce each section, keeping the same proportions. To turn certain flies over faster, shorten the three 10-inch sections and the length of the tippet.

Whether you prefer fluorocarbon or nylon monofilament, any quality material works for this leader. I use either Maxima Clear or Berkley Big Game monofilament. I tie all the sections together with blood knots. Tighten each knot with saliva or a little Chapstick from your lips so the knot slides together snugly without damaging the line. I tie loops on each end of the leader, and I whip a loop on the end of the fly line so that I can easily loop the leader to the butt of the fly line and the tippet I need to the end of the leader butt to quickly change leaders depending on conditions.

Rod weights 6 to 8	Rod weights 8 and 9
36 inches of 40-pound-test (.024-inch diameter)	36 inches of 50-pound-test (.028-inch diameter)
18 inches of 30-pound-test (.022-inch diameter)	18 inches of 40-pound-test (.024-inch diameter)
10 inches of 25-pound-test (.020-inch diameter)	10 inches of 30-pound-test (.022-inch diameter)
10 inches of 20-pound-test (.017-inch diameter)	10 inches of 20-pound-test (.017-inch diameter)
10 inches of 12-pound-test (.013-inch diameter)	10 inches of 15-pound-test (.015-inch diameter)

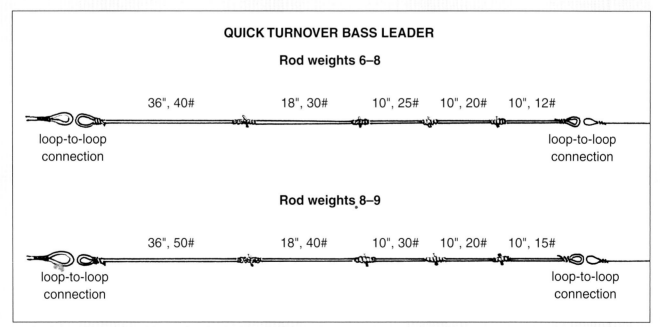

QUICK TURNOVER BASS LEADER

Rod weights 6–8

36", 40#   18", 30#   10", 25#   10", 20#   10", 12#

loop-to-loop connection   loop-to-loop connection

Rod weights 8–9

36", 50#   18", 40#   10", 30#   10", 20#   10", 15#

loop-to-loop connection   loop-to-loop connection

Each of these formulas builds a 7-foot leader butt to which you can attach 2 to 4 feet of tippet, giving you a leader that can range from 9 to 11 feet. For a longer leader, simply add to or reduce each section, keeping the same proportions. To turn certain flies over faster, shorten the three 10-inch sections and the length of the tippet. Tie perfection loops at the end of each leader for attaching tippets and a loop on the butt end for attaching to whipped loop on fly line.

The leader designed for rod weights 6 through 8 (top) works with tippet sizes 6- to 10-pound-test. The one designed for rod weights 8 and 9 works with tippet sizes 6- to 15-pound-test.

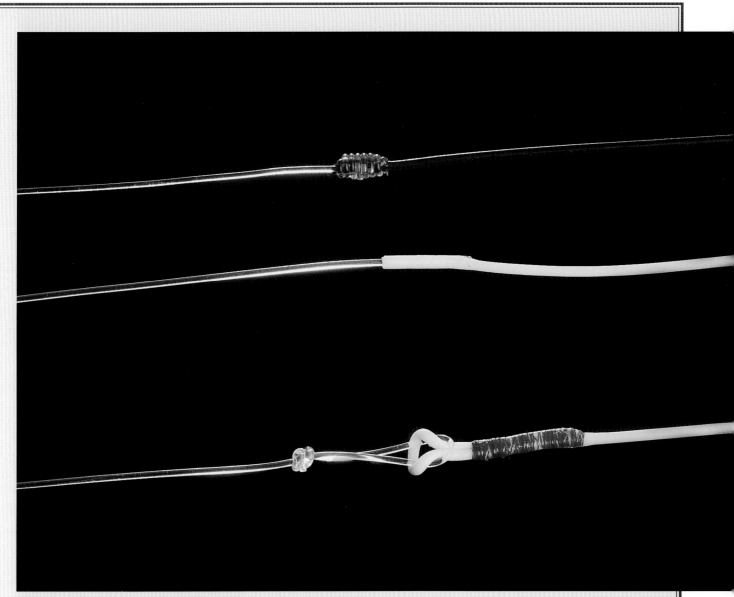

To connect leader butt with fly line, you can use a nail knot, Zap-A-Gap splice, or loop-to-loop connection. I prefer the loop-to-loop connection because it allows me to easily and quickly change leaders. JAY NICHOLS

A properly connected loop-to-loop connection forms a square knot.

From left to right, sinking, intermediate, and floating fly lines will cover the range of water conditions you encounter. BOB CLOUSER

Full-sinking fly lines are the most underused lines on the market. They have a permanent place in my boat and have accounted for more smallmouth than any other line my clients or I use. They are available in many sink rates, and on my home waters, a type 2 or 3 gets the job done.

A uniform full-sinking fly line, sometimes called density-compensated, sinks first at the tip where the fly is attached, then the remainder follows suit, so that the line and leader are straight. Some full-sinking fly lines sink belly first and tip last, creating a sag in the line. Most people prefer to fish the uniform-sinking fly lines because they sink evenly and create less sag in the belly of the line, which helps you stay in touch with your fly better and makes it easier to set the hook.

Many anglers prefer to use sinking-tip lines or a shooting-head system. Sinking tips most often are short tips of 6 to 12 feet attached to floating running line. Their main advantage is that they are easy to cast. Sinking-tip lines can be the ideal choice for wade-fishing in streams or rivers. I prefer a short sinking-tip from 5 to 10 feet in length for use on my home river. These lines also have a place when you are streamer fish-

ing from a boat. The short head and floating running line make it easy to quickly pick up the fly and line after the retrieve, whereas with a shooting taper or full-sinking line, you need to retrieve more line.

Shooting heads are available as either integrated into the running line or as interchangeable heads that are connected to the running line loop-to-loop. Both integrated and interchangeable shooting heads come in different lengths and sink rates (grain weights). The advantage of having an interchangeable shooting-head system is that you can easily and quickly change heads depending on water conditions. In many instances on my home waters, a 250-grain head gets the fly deep enough and is just the right weight to load an 8-weight rod, so an integrated, 250-grain head anywhere from 24- to 30-feet long is fine for me. However, if I was traveling and didn't know what kind of water conditions I would have to deal with, I'd probably bring an interchangeable shooting-head system with intermediate to fast sinking heads (600 grain or more).

With a long leader and many types of fast-sinking lines, the line sinks faster than the leader. The fly rides higher in the water column than the line and puts a sag in the leader. I use short leaders with sinking lines to limit this sag effect and help the fly sink faster.

Slow or intermediate lines are slightly heavier than water and sink your fly at a rate of about one or two inches per second, depending on the manufacturer. Since the line sinks in addition to the leader, the line doesn't pull your fly up through the water column on the retrieve like a floating line does, keeping your fly at the level where the fish are feeding longer.

Intermediate lines are useful in windy situations, because their narrow diameter cuts through the wind like a knife in conditions that would make it difficult to cast a floating line. Also with an intermediate line, the shooting portion that usually lies on the boat deck or at your feet doesn't blow around and tangle as much as with a floating line. And the intermediate line will not wash around on the water's surface when it's choppy, which aids in fly control and strike detection.

You can use floating flies such as Dahlberg Divers, Clouser Crippled Minnows, or poppers with intermediate lines for an action fish sometimes find irresistible. In a pinch, you can add fly floatant to your line and fish it like a floating line.

A big advantage of many intermediate lines is that because they have neither tungsten powder to make them sink or hollow glass microspheres to make them float, manufacturers can make them completely clear or with a clear tip. This allows you greater stealth and more accuracy with easier casting, because you don't have to fish a long leader. You still must be careful not to throw a shadow overhead with these lines, but submerged they are less obtrusive.

Intermediate or very slow-sinking fly lines are also good for fishing a fly deep, but not right on the bottom where you will snag your fly. I've found that a fast-sinking fly line of type 5 or more drags a fly across the bottom regardless of the fly's weight, causing the line and fly to snag in the crevices of rocks and other debris. Lightly weighted flies fished with an intermediate or a type 3 sinking line sink or fall slowly toward the bottom. Many species, especially smallmouth bass, take a fly as it descends toward the bottom. The combination of the slow descent of the intermediate or type 3 sinking line and the fly allows the angler to take advantage of this type of feeding activity.

CARE AND STORAGE OF LINES

Fly lines aren't cheap, so it's important to take care of yours to get as much use as possible out of it and so that it performs well for you. Cracked or dirty fly lines don't cast as far as new lines, nor do floating lines in poor condition float as well. Cleaning your line on a continual basis adds to its life.

Many bass waters have fine particles of dirt in them that stick to fly lines. After each use, you should wipe down the portion that was being used with mild soap and water or according to the manufacturer's recommendations for the line. It's important to follow the manufacturer's recommendations, because not all lines are constructed the same way. If you use a cleaner, wipe the excess from the line after you apply it; if using soap and water, be sure to rinse all the soap from the line.

When you store a line on the reel, load it with moderate tension. Loose line can cause problems, allowing the outside coils to intermingle with the inside coils and leading to a tangled fly line. When storing the line in a vehicle, never expose it to the rays of the sun. Heat from any source can destroy a fly line. When storing fly line in the home, even when left on the reel, it need only be put in a Ziploc bag and placed in a dark area such as a drawer. If the fly line is not wound tightly on the spool, it's not necessary to remove it for storage in larger coils. A fly line left hanging over the winter months exposed to the heating of a home can become dried out and shorten its life.

It's always a challenge to store lines to prevent tangles and keep them organized. I simply coil the head and running line, secure the coil with bag twisters, and drop them into a Ziploc bag labeled with the contents for future reference. I also store my sections of lead-core and T-14 in Ziploc bags.

One area especially prone to cracking over time is the portion of the line where the leader is attached. To repair this, clip off the worn section and reattach the leader. On most fly lines, you can remove at least 2 feet from the front of the taper before there is any noticeable change in casting or fly presentation.

FLY RODS

You can fish for smallmouth with rods ranging from 2- to 10-weights. The most important thing is to match the rod with the flies and lines you will be using rather than the quarry. Lee Wulff proved many years ago that you can land large fish on light rods, but that doesn't mean that casting a heavily weighted Clouser Minnow or a sinking line on a 2- or 3-weight rod is effective or any fun.

If you are fishing dry flies, small poppers, or small minnow imitations and nymphs, a 5- to 6-weight rod works fine. One reason why it's so fun and easy to make the transition from trout to smallmouth fly fishing is that most of your trout equipment works for bass. Light-weight rods are good for days with relatively no wind, when you are fishing small dry flies or poppers to bass,

You can fish for bass with rods as light as 3- or 4-weights, but to fish large flies for long periods of time, an 8-weight is most efficient.
BOB CLOUSER

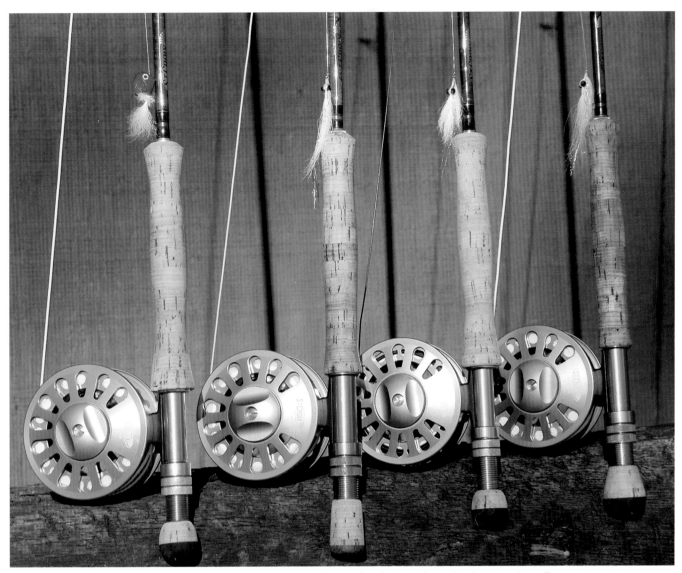

It's important to first select the flies you are going to use, and then pick a line weight and rod to cast those flies. BOB CLOUSER

streams with small bass, or small streams where the fishing often does not require large fly patterns or heavy hooks. As you progress and learn to target larger bass, a 7- or 8-weight rod is the best tool for casting large flies, fighting fish in the three- to five-pound range, and dealing with wind. After you've mastered proper casting technique, a larger rod makes a day of casting these large flies enjoyable and lets you get the distance you sometimes need to fool fish.

A 7- or 8-weight rod also subdues fish quickly, which is important, especially when the water temperatures hover in the high seventies or eighties. Landing a fighting smallmouth with a rod is different from a smallmouth landing itself from exhaustion. Tackle heavy enough to fight and land the bass quickly allows the catch-and-release practice to better ensure the survival of a released fish. Another reason I like to use 8-weights

is because where I fish, we often have shots at carp, which require a heavy rod. Many smallmouth waters also have carp, muskie, freshwater drum, or other larger species you may want to cast your fly at.

I like 8½- to 9-foot rods. Short rods are fun, but they aren't the most efficient tools for casting flies all day or high-stick nymphing. A long rod allows you to mend your line more efficiently than a short rod, and that's important. The rod designers at the St. Croix Rod Company built me what I think is the ultimate in a bass fly rod. It has the feel and flex of a 6-weight, yet has the power to fight large 10-pound-plus striped bass. It is 8 feet, 9 inches and has good balance that enables me to cast all day long without getting tired. It handles large and small flies, plus air-resistant flies of any size. It is my favorite rod, but when you choose yours, make sure it meets your needs.

Left: Another reason using an 8-weight is a good idea is that you never know what else you might encounter on a bass stream. Carp and muskies are two enormous fish that can share the same water as bass. BOB CLOUSER

REELS

Just about any reel that holds the fly line rated for your rod, plus 50 yards of 20- or 30-pound braided backing, and has a smooth drag that will not allow the reel spool to overrun when you strip off line or the fish runs will do the job. On many bass streams, however, you might encounter other, larger fish that you might want to cast to, such as carp. These fish make long, fast runs, so if you also want to fish for this species, it pays to have a good-quality reel with the capacity for at least 100 yards of backing.

If your reel is undersize and you can't seem to fit 100 yards of backing plus a full weight-forward floating line, try cutting off the rear 20 feet of running line. Most anglers rarely cast the full 90 feet of fly line, and 20 feet of floating line could be replaced by 50 yards of backing.

It's important when winding backing and line on the reel not to overfill the spool. A properly filled spool should not jam the line under the reel's frame just as the last portion of line is wound on the spool. A full spool aids in faster pickup of the line when you are reeling it back on the spool, but an overfull reel causes you to wind the line on too tightly for storage purposes, which leads to excessive coiling and may damage the line.

BOATS

This is a broad topic and one that deserves a book of its own. As with fly rods, there is no one perfect boat; each has its advantages and disadvantages. Some factors to consider when thinking about a boat are purchase price and maintenance costs, storage, ability to transport it, number of people you want to be able to carry in it, stability, space, type of motor you wish to mount on it, and its draft, how shallow it will run.

Pontoon boats rated for use on rivers are an economical way to float a river with a minimal amount of storage. They are easy to store, many assemble easily, and you can get them to the river without a trailer. Some models are packable enough to take on a plane with you when you travel. These craft are good for shallow water or as a way to get from one fishing spot to another on your way downriver. Most models have anchor systems, rod holders, enough storage space to make fishing out of them a pleasure, and oars for when you want to move quickly or navigate difficult water. When you are fishing, you stow the oars and position the boat with flippers so your hands are free to fish. Some models are stable

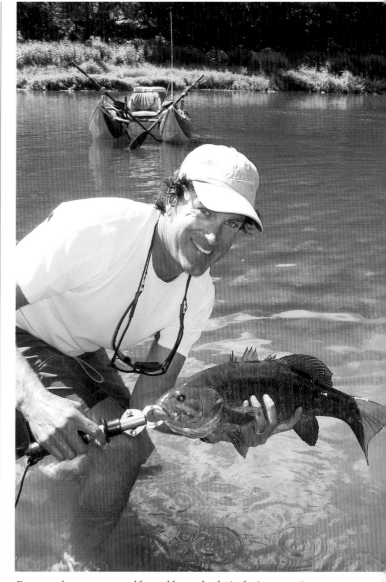

Pontoon boats are portable, stable, and relatively inexpensive, and they are easy to fish from while floating. Most accommodate only one person. STEVE MAY

enough to navigate some serious whitewater or allow you to stand up and spot fish in flat water. You can pole some pontoon boats, and others let you attach a trolling motor. Some models can carry two people and are set up so that one person rows while the other fishes.

Many canoes are lightweight, and one person can load them on a car roof rack or in the bed of a pickup. They are large enough to carry a day's worth of fishing gear, and you can put a trolling motor on them—right on the back if the canoe has a square stern or to the side with a motor mount. Some manufacturers make stabilizers that fit to the canoe to increase stability and allow you to stand up and fish. This is an advantage in slow-moving rivers without risk of hitting rocks while you are standing up. Some canoes are rigged with oarlocks so

Canoes can fit more than one angler and are great for getting from one point to another on a smallmouth stream. They are hard to fish from if you are alone. STEVE MAY

you can row them. They are much better than pontoon boats at moving rapidly over great distances, but you can't maneuver a canoe or kayak with feet and flippers, so it's difficult to position the boat for fishing while alone. A canoe is best if you have a buddy with whom you can take turns paddling while the other person fishes, or if you use the craft mostly to get from one fishing spot to the next.

More and more anglers are using western-style drift boats on smallmouth rivers across the country. If you have a shuttle from one point to another, this is an excellent way for several anglers to fish a smallmouth river. Though I haven't done it, more and more guides are fishing from drift boats on bass rivers across the country. The oarsman can maneuver these craft over shallow water where some other types of boats cannot go. The only disadvantage to using a drift boat is that on

wide rivers, it can be a lot of work to row back and forth to hit all the hot spots. With a drift boat, you need to float down one side of the river or the other and take what comes to you. Rafts are popular options on rivers that get shallow in the summer or have unimproved boat launches.

On many smallmouth rivers across the country, johnboats are the preferred fishing craft. Made from aluminum, they are durable enough to withstand dings from the many rocks typical in good smallmouth habitat. Johnboats come in many sizes and are available with many hull designs. I prefer a flat bottom because it provides a shallower draft. I've also found that the longer and wider the boat, the shallower it will run. The boat I use for guiding is twenty feet long and has a five-foot-wide bottom. It floats in eight to ten inches of water with a guide and two clients on board. It will plane off

Above: More and more smallmouth anglers are using western-style drift boats for their fishing.
KEN COLLINS

Left: Rafts are great for low water or where you may need to portage around a dam or other structure.
KING MONTGOMERY

I think the johnboat is the perfect craft for smallmouth bass. An engine is important for traveling on some of the larger river systems.
JACK HANRAHAN

and go over five inches of water when powered by a sixty-five-horsepower jet prop engine.

When I first started my guide business, I had a fourteen-foot double-wide johnboat with a fifteen-horsepower prop motor. It was too small for two fishermen plus a guide, and I soon changed to a sixteen-foot flat-bottom. The sixteen-footer needed less water to float it in. I found one disadvantage with the sixteen-foot craft, however: When I had two clients as big as a football lineman in the boat, I would not have much freeboard left, and the boat was not as manageable. A friend at the marina where I purchased my boats told me about a new twenty-footer, and I decided to give it a try. It was the best decision I ever made on purchasing a boat. The first time Lefty Kreh went out with me on this new boat, he remarked that you could make a helicopter landing pad out of the front deck. I never did, though. The new rig got me into areas that were impossible to fish with my other boats.

When operating any boat, especially those with motors, be extremely careful. If you are new to a river, take it easy and slow.

GENERAL TACKLE CARE

The most important thing you can do for your fishing tackle is to keep it clean and in good working order to ensure trouble-free days on the water. Broken equipment should be properly cared for as soon as possible. It's frustrating when you're invited on a spur-of-the-moment trip with a buddy but your reel isn't working properly or you can't find your tackle.

Rinse and wipe your fly rod dry after each use, especially before storing it in the rod sock and tube. Glass or vinyl cleaners or a product called Dyna-Glide can be used to not only clean the rod, but also add a protective coating. Putting a wet rod in a sock and tube causes both the cork grip and the cloth to become mildewed and stink, and moisture can even penetrate the epoxy over the thread wraps on the rod.

Worn line guides can shorten the life of a fly line. Check all guides for cracking and wear, and replace

Right: You should keep your tackle in top condition. You never know when you'll catch the fish of a lifetime that will test your rod, reel, line, and tippets. JACK HANRAHAN

Forceps or pliers are necessary for crimping down the barbs on hooks and help take the hook out of a fish's mouth.
KING MONTGOMERY

A net helps you land larger fish and keep them under control while you take the hook out. Use either a rubber-mesh or soft nylon net to prevent damage to the fish. KING MONTGOMERY

them if necessary. Loose or frayed threads that hold the guides in place should be covered with a rod-wrapping finish. Many fly rods consist of two to four pieces that fit together with a ferrule system. Constant flexing and removal of pieces can cause wear to the ferrules. Using a thin film of soft fly-tying wax on the male ferrule before joining the pieces together prevents wear and slippage.

I prefer to assemble multipiece rods by inserting the male section into the hollow female end, aligning the two sections off-center about 45 degrees and slowly turning them clockwise while pushing them together. This method usually prevents the rod from coming apart

while using it. It also prevents wear on the male and female ends of the rod sections. Sections have to be twisted in the other direction to take them apart.

Fly reels especially need attention when exposed to mud, silt, or sand. Always be careful where you set your reel down. Often when anglers are stringing up their rods to begin fishing, they put the reel on the rod and then set the rod on the ground to pull the line through the guides. Reels also get dirty after you catch a fish and in the excitement of releasing it, you place the rod in the water. Learn to reverse the rod and tuck the butt up under your arm; this gives you a free hand to release the fish, and your reel won't fall in mud or sand and get grit in the moving parts.

To clean your reel, first remove the spool, and then submerge your reel in a solution of warm, soapy water and vigorously move it back and forth. Rinse with clear water and apply a light grease, oil, or dry lubricant to the reel. A dry lubricant like Dyna-Glide not only lubricates the reel, but also cleans and protects it, and you should coat all moving parts on new reels if needed. Keep the parts and instruction sheet provided with the reel so you can easily get replacement parts from the manufacturer. If you want to keep your reel looking shiny and new, keep the reel cover on the rod at all times, especially when the reel is on the rod and banging around in the bottom of the boat.

Your waders also need care and an occasional washing with a mild soap and water. This goes for neoprene and breathable waders. All waders should be dry on both sides before storage. They will dry quickly if you hang them upside down by the feet or boots, allowing air to circulate throughout the inside of the wader. You can also tumble dry many brands of breathable waders on low heat, but it's important that you read the manufac-

turer's care instructions and follow them closely. They should have detailed directions on how to wash and re-treat the waders. Don't leave your waders exposed to the sun or the heat inside your car. Not only will the light rays and heat break down your waders, but the stink of wet waders baking in your car is a bad one. Don't fold your breathable waders for storage. Roll them instead.

Felt soles that are worn thin should be replaced. It's not necessary to remove the old felt soles before adding new ones. In many instances, if the felt is securely attached to the boot bottoms, leaving the old felt, cleaning it with a stiff-bristled brush and then applying glue, will allow a stronger adhesion of the new soles.

Fishing vests last longer if cleaned periodically. Cleaning should be done as soon as possible after being stained by floatants, oils, or dirt. Vest and hats treated with a water-repelling solution such as Scotchgard remain cleaner and wear longer. Repair areas that have separating seams and loose threads. Never store wet fishing clothes where they cannot dry properly.

Remember, an ounce of prevention is worth a pound of cure. I have made a habit of checking everything I use to make sure it's in the best shape before

A Boga Grip is another good tool for handling large bass and carp. As an added bonus, it also has a scale. KEN COLLINS

Above: A wading staff is a critical item when wading in fast water or over slippery rocks. JAY NICHOLS

Right: Good nymph anglers change weight more than they change flies. I carry split shot in assorted sizes as well as twist-on lead strips.
JAY NICHOLS

every fishing outing. This includes all tackle, gear, clothing, food, drinks, boat, motor, trailer, and the truck or automobile.

Even more important than your tackle is your physical condition. I've seen too many anglers not able to fish well because they had become dehydrated or tired. A month before every guiding season, I start exercising to shape up for the ordeal. To fish effectively, you need to take care of yourself as much as you do your equipment. During the day, especially in the summer, drink lots of water, eat nutritious foods, and wear sunscreen. A break every now and then will help keep you focused on the task at hand. Fish smarter. Take breaks and eat or drink when the fishing is slow. Fish hard when the bass are on the bite.

MY TACKLE CHECKLIST

Here's a list of all the things that I carry with me when I go bass fishing or guiding anglers for the day. No matter what we carry along with us, it often seems as if we've forgotten something. If so, add it to your list for next time. The tackle bag we thought was big enough only seems to get smaller the longer we own it. In addition to the following list, if I am using a boat, I make sure all the required safety devices are aboard.

TACKLE CHECKLIST

tackle bag	extra clothing
flies	hat
leaders	sunglasses
tippet material	boots or waders
clippers	wading staff
pliers	first-aid kit
pocketknife	rods
hot-melt glue	reels
tip-tops	fly lines
split shot	insect repellent
twist-on lead strips	food
hook sharpener	water and other
compass	healthy drinks
binoculars	Ziploc bags in one-
sunscreen	and two-gallon
lip balm with	sizes
sunscreen	trash bag
camera	cleaning towel or
clothing to protect	napkins
you from	cell phone in case of
sunburn	an injury

CHAPTER 10

Bass Waters

JOHN RANDOLPH

Whenever you go to a new river to fish, one of the most helpful things you can do is to ask a local angler who understands the fishery for some tips. Though I have fished around the country for smallmouth bass, most of my experience has been gleaned from days spent on Mid-Atlantic rivers. Even though bass in this part of the world behave like those in other rivers across the country, I have asked a few friends to write about their local smallmouth rivers. There's always more to learn, and there is no substitute for local knowledge.

I have heard from smallmouth anglers all across the country about the great fishing they have nearby. Wherever bass are introduced, they thrive, from California's Feather River to Montana's Musselshell to Maine's Penobscot. Chances are if you live in or are traveling to any state, other than Florida, Louisiana, or Alaska, bass fishing can be had nearby. A simple search online or calls to local fly shops or fish and game departments for each state should give you a good place to start your search.

It's impossible to list all the great bass waters in one chapter, let alone a library of books. So I have asked a

The Susquehanna River in Pennsylvania has all the traits of a quality smallmouth stream, with plenty of structure and lots of food.

191

A good guide can help put you on fish, and most can teach you more in one day on their home waters than you could learn in a year. KEN COLLINS

few friends and smallmouth enthusiasts to write about the rivers they like the most and share some of their thoughts and techniques for bass. These short write-ups provide insight not only into various rivers, but also into other anglers' approaches to catching bass. In some cases, a particular river is mentioned more than once. Instead of leaving out one angler's description, I thought that reading different anglers' insights into the same fishery might be valuable.

As any reader from New England, Arkansas, or Michigan will point out, there are some serious omissions in this chapter regarding great bass waters. Some extraordinary smallmouth fisheries in the East are not discussed, including Maine's Androscoggin and Kennebec; Vermont's Lake Champlain tributaries; Massachusett's Merrimack River; Housatonic River in Massachusetts and Connecticut; the Connecticut River near Enfield, Connecticut; and New York's Hudson near Corinth and its tributary, the Mohawk.

Roger Lapentor's descriptions of Wisconsin rivers might provide insight into other upper Midwest streams, such as Michigan's Muskegon, Grand, and Huron Rivers. The upper Mississippi and Root in Minnesota are well-known bass fisheries. Traveling much farther south, Crooked Creek and Buffalo River in Arkansas are must places to fish if you are interested in sampling the country's best bass water. Out west, we take a look at the fine smallmouth angling in California and Oregon but skip over the fantastic and little-known fishery on the Columbia River in Washington. Smallmouth bass are almost everywhere.

In many instances, the people I contacted also recommended guide services, fly shops, and accommodations. Because of the ever-changing nature of the fishing business, I thought that it was better to maintain an online directory of locations across the United States, including those rivers mentioned here, that I can update or add to as things change. For this listing, please visit www.clouserflyfishing.com.

RESEARCHING YOUR BASS WATER

The great amount of information on the Internet has made it simple to begin preliminary research on many smallmouth bass destinations. Online, you can look at maps, read fishing reports, and visit different websites with detailed information about destinations and techniques for stream smallmouth bass. You should take the reports with a grain of salt, however, and it's probably best to call a local fly shop for current information. A good fly shop will also be able to answer in-depth

Right: A DeLorme Atlas and Gazetteer can help you find developed access points. South Fork of the Shenandoah, Virginia. KING MONTGOMERY

questions about access information, flies to use, and water levels. Guidebooks can offer good advice and are fine places to start, but fisheries can change and the river information may become outdated. Current magazine articles are often better resources, but even they can become out-of-date quickly. Without current reports, you may make a long trip and wind up disappointed.

Though there are some exceptional and advanced mapping websites, a quality and detailed map such as the DeLorme Atlas and Gazetteer for the area in which you intend to fish is an indispensable research tool. You can easily take it on the road with you to your destination, and many of the best anglers I know make extensive notes on theirs as they accumulate information. Other excellent resources are the various states' fishing agencies. Not only do they often provide lists of which waters have smallmouth bass, but many also offer current fishing reports and even hotlines.

A good guide is invaluable, even in areas where smallmouth bass live in many rivers and average-size fish aren't that hard to catch. Not only can they help with the logistics of a quality smallmouth float down a river, but they also will run the boat while you and your partner relax and enjoy the day catching fish. And they have local knowledge that is indispensable for catching the river's larger fish. If you plan any trip to distant waters, I recommend getting a guide for at least one day.

RIVER PROFILES

Following are brief descriptions of some of the best and most well-known bass waters, grouped by region across the United States. This is not an all-inclusive list, but it could be a good start for you when planning a trip. Throughout this chapter, friends of mine have contributed information on the spots they most like to fish, as well as on fishing techniques and fly selections.

Angler: LEFTY KREH

I began my fly-fishing career in 1947 by fishing the Potomac River in Maryland, near where I lived. I have fished its more than 150 miles, from the headwaters in the Blue Ridge Mountains to the tidal waters near Chesapeake Bay. Upriver from Washington, D.C., the main species is smallmouth, but the tidal area is a large-mouth domain.

The Potomac is like so many other smallmouth rivers I have fished across the country. If a river begins in the mountains, the water is cooler and clearer, with little development in the watershed. I believe that because the water is so clear, the bass have little trouble seeing and catching their prey. Almost all smallmouth rivers running through and just out of the mountains do not produce on average as large a smallmouth bass. Once the rivers leave the mountains and meander through farmlands and past towns or cities, they gather nutrients, which causes the water to discolor only a little but adds food for the prey that smallmouth feed on. The lesson here is that if you are looking for larger smallmouth on average, spend your time out of the mountain's watersheds.

However, I might mention that the mountain portion of the rivers can be fun with a light fly rod and

Upstream of Washington, D.C., the Potomac is an excellent smallmouth fishery and deserves its place as one of the East's best smallmouth rivers. LEFTY KREH

smaller flies. Much of this resembles trout fishing, where dry and wet flies and surface patterns such as poppers dressed on size 6 and smaller hooks are most effective.

Most of the time, I prefer to catch smallmouth that range from ten to eighteen inches. My favorite rod is an 8-weight with a weight-forward floating line and a 9- to 10-foot leader tapered to 10- or 12-pound-test. I like to keep the tippet less than 18 inches; longer tippets tend to gather overhand knots. Where the rivers run a little deeper, I often switch to a number 3 sinking fly line, preferring to use a shooting taper rather than a full-sinking line. With sinking lines, I often shorten the leader to 7 feet.

My favorite flies are few. If limited to a single small-mouth pattern, I would opt for a Red and White Hackle fly. Next in choice would be a variety of Clouser Minnows in different lengths and color combinations, especially chartreuse and white and Baby Smallmouth (both with Mylar flash). I am never without a few Half and Halfs, especially when seeking larger smallmouth. These patterns have worked wherever I have fished rivers for smallmouth.

Potomac River, West Virginia and Maryland
When seeking larger smallmouth, my favorite stretch of the Potomac is from just downriver from Harpers Ferry, West Virginia, to Seneca, which is located a few miles upriver from Washington, D.C. In this portion of the Potomac, you stand a good chance of catching a trophy. This area also sees a nice hatch of white miller flies at

The Upper Potomac River has excellent public access because of the 184.5-mile Chesapeake and Ohio Canal National Historical Park, which begins in Washington, D.C., and runs up the Maryland side of the Potomac River all the way to Cumberland in Maryland's panhandle. Along its path, the river forms the boundaries between Maryland, Virginia, and West Virginia.

KING MONTGOMERY

For numbers and size of smallmouth bass, the James River in Virginia is hard to beat. BOB CLOUSER

dusk, usually in the first week of August. My favorite wading area in the Potomac is upstream from Brunswick, Maryland, a few miles below Harpers Ferry.

James River, Virginia

Virginia has a number of great smallmouth rivers, yet almost every year when I checked the listing, the James River led with the most catches. My favorite stretch of the James would be that portion running south and especially south-southeast of Charlottesville. There are lots of places to wade the James, but I prefer drifting in a boat and casting. You can cover more water and get to places a wader can't reach. I also like to carry cameras and other gear.

New River, Virginia and North Carolina

Chuck Kraft, legendary Virginia smallmouth guide, introduced me to the New River, which some say is the oldest river in America—how they know, I am not sure. I know this may sound like a fairy tale, but it is the only river I have fished where I was sure that I saw at least two smallmouth bass that exceeded seven pounds. Chuck Kraft used to guide regularly on the river and kept a photo album of the previous year's catches. Look-ing through the albums, you find an astonishing number of five-, six-, and even an occasional seven-pound small-mouth. These are really top-of-line smallmouth for rivers—anywhere in this country.

The New is located in the extreme southwestern portion of Virginia and runs into North Carolina. My favorite stretch of the river is in the very southern end of the state after it leaves the dam on Claytor Lake. The water from the dam is incredibly clear and calls for a slight change in fly-fishing tactics. A floating line and at least a 10-foot leader is necessary for working on or near the surface with flies. But a major food source for the husky smallmouth in this river is crayfish, and the best results and biggest fish are usually taken on flies presented well down in the water column. Because the water is so clear and in many places as much as eight or ten feet deep, the fish get a good look at offerings. Using con-ventional fly lines in these conditions often results in refusals. I rarely write about using a specific piece of fish-ing gear, but a line that I really like for presenting flies in very clear water, such as many lakes—and the New River—is the Scientific Anglers Streamer Express Clear Tip. This line has a twenty-five-foot clear front portion that sinks, with a faster-sinking line behind it. In front of

Also in Virginia, the Rappahanock above Fredericksburg is a fine smallmouth stream. KING MONTGOMERY

this, I tie a five-to seven-foot leader. What you really have is thirty to thirty-two feet of leader that gets the fly down in this air-clear water.

Because crayfish are a preferred food, drifting crayfish imitations is very effective. I try every crayfish pattern I can get my hands on, but none has been as effective for me as the Clouser Crayfish. Many anglers make the mistake of stripping a crayfish fly on the retrieve. But the best method is to allow it to tumble and drift naturally in the current, fishing it as you would a nymph for trout. There are times when a Half and Half or a weighted Red and White Hackle fly are also effective.

If a fly fisher is seeking trophy smallmouth, the New River may be the best choice.

Penobscot River, Maine

There is a certain mystery for me when I fish the small-mouth rivers in northern Maine. Having grown up fishing the limestone streams of the Mid-Atlantic and Midwest, I am used to rivers where the waters are clear. But northern Maine's rivers, while clear, have that diluted tea color that really charges my batteries.

Perhaps some of the best river smallmouth fishing in our country is in northeastern Maine. First, because of their rather remote location away from large numbers of anglers, the fish are not as pressured. This part of Maine is not heavily populated or industrialized, so the rivers are rather pristine and not as abused as rivers farther south. And without the heavier pressure, the fish tend to grow bigger, and your chances are better for catching bigger-than-average river smallmouth.

My favorite of all these rivers is the Penobscot, which I believe is the largest river in Maine. The area I prefer fishing is just downriver from the town of Bangor. This is a big, wide, but often shallow river that is filled with riffles, grass beds, rock ledges, and perfect habitat for smallmouth. My most favored fly is the Red and White Hackle, followed by the Half and Half, usually in white with a chartreuse overwing. Popping bugs are also deadly most of the time and often draw the larger bass. This is perhaps because a constantly moving bug makes such a disturbance that it creates an illusion that it is a much larger and helpless prey.

The Penobscot River is arguably the Northeast's finest smallmouth stream, with the chance to catch lots of fish in the fourteen-inch range and some trophy bass. KEVIN MCKAY/MAINEFLYFISH.COM

Angler: JOHN RANDOLPH

Umpqua River, Oregon

The Umpqua River is world famous for its steelhead, salmon, and shad, but smallmouth bass are another icing on its cake. Knowing where and when to find them can make for fifty- to seventy-fish days of angling with wets or drys.

Some of the best wade and drift fishing for smallmouth lie in the fifty-mile stretch of flats and river meanders between the towns of Roseburg and Elkton on the river's main stem. The fishing begins, for smaller fish, in May and June. Smallmouth spawning runs occur from May into June, concurrent with the arrival of an estimated 500,000 to 750,000 three- to five-pound spawning shad, a blast on fly-rod jigs. But the best fishing occurs in July and August, when water temperatures reach the 55- to 65-degree range. You'll need a boat to reach this fishing, since walk-in access can be limited. Most bass are in the eight- to twelve-inch range, but fish up to five pounds can be taken at the heads of pools and in the fast runs. The river has miles of ledge-rock pools and long sand-gravel runs ideal for wade, pontoon boat, or drift boat fishing.

Favorite flies include very sparsely tied size 6 Clouser Minnows in yellow and red or chartreuse and red, foam and pencil poppers, or size 6 Woolly Buggers in yellow and brown. Large fish lying in the deeper, faster water are taken on the deep-swimming wets fished on type 2 sinking lines

Guide Gary Lewis says the smallies will not take heavily dressed Clouser Minnows but will eagerly grab sparsely dressed offerings. He uses only a tiny amount of yellow deer hair and red Krystal Flash or yellow deer hair and chartreuse Krystal Flash tied on a size 6 long-shank hook.

Public accesses are available every six to eight miles from Roseburg to Kellog, but there are long stretches of seventeen and twenty miles between launches and take-outs from Kellog to Elkton. Wading is legal in Oregon to the natural high-water mark.

John Day River, Oregon

Oregon's John Day River has carved its meanders through the Pleistocene layers of rock laid down where three lava flows converged in a broad peneplain on the south side of the Columbia River. The John Day was named after a famed mountain man, who arrived in the area with the Astor-Hunt overland party in 1812 on a trapping exploration out of Jackson Hole in present-day Wyoming. Day and partner Ramsey Crooks win-

The thirty-four-mile Twickenham to Clarno Bridge section of the John Day River has exceptional smallmouth fishing from drift boats, fishing large wets and poppers to the banks. The river scenery is spectacular. JOHN RANDOLPH

tered with the northern Piute Indians in what is now John Day Canyon.

The river between Twickenham and Clarno may be the best place in the West to immerse yourself in smallmouth, basalt canyon walls, juniper, sagebrush, wildlife, wood smoke, swimming, campfire food and wine, and the peaceful sounds of moving water and silence. This river is a smallmouth factory, and you can take them like candy, two ways: easily, like a child catching and giggling over seventy-five small fish a day, or stalking big, solitary, and intelligent fish—some over twenty-four inches—hunting for crayfish quietly in the shallows in morning or evening low light.

The best rafting—and fishing—on the river is from mid-July through mid-August, but shallows necessitate a

Though crayfish are the main food of John Day bass, they rarely pass up the opportunity to crush a popper.
JOHN RANDOLPH

shallow-draft or inflatable drift boat. The John Day is a wide, relatively shallow river, ranging in flow from 600 (cubic feet per second) in September to 8,100 in January. Its clear water allows sight-fishing to the larger smallmouth, wary fish that hide in the deeper pools and runs in high daylight and forage into the shallows for baitfish and crayfish as the light falls.

The best stretches for smallmouth lie in the middle river, in the thirty-four-mile stretch from Twickenham to Clarno Bridge or the roughly seventy-mile stretch from Clarno Bridge to Cottonwood Bridge. In both cases, an outfitter is essential unless you outfit yourself with a drift boat, food, and camping and fishing gear. There are no take-outs, so you should plan on five or six days for fishing and rafting.

Crayfish are a main source of food for John Day smallmouth, so imitative flies such as size 6 sparse brown Clouser Minnows, Whitlock's NearNuf Crawfish, black Woolly Buggers, or conehead rubber-legged Buggers work well. For childlike fun, fish a popper-dropper rigged with a size 6 black popper followed by a size 10 Muddler in the shoreline shallows and pockets of back eddies while drifting. Small brown rubber-legged streamers, fished with short twitch retrieves, are eaten like easy candy by these smallmouth. For larger fish, use type 2 sinking lines and large rabbit-strip Muddlers on short leaders in the deeper pools and runs. Fish size 8 white or black rubber-legged Muddlers, dry and wet, from dusk into darkness for kahuna smallmouth. A medium-action 6-weight graphite rod with a strong butt matched with a hard-surfaced, bass-taper line for long casting is right for this fishing. Fasten your streamers to the fly with nonslip mono loop knots for enticing action.

The John Day surroundings make the trip, so don't hurry. You'll find easy bass every step of the way, along with a wealth of history, both geologic and cultural, so kick back, slow down, and look, listen, and reflect. Before taking this trip, read *John Day River: Drift and Historical Guide,* by Arthur Campbell. The high-desert air is clear and sun-drenched. Treat all exposed flesh liberally with sunblock rated at thirty SPF or higher to avoid the risk of skin cancer. Polaroid glasses are essential in this bright light, and sun gloves make good sense. Most fly fishers also wear rafting sandals.

The John Day has an unusually high drop for a meandering river, but it is relatively easy going for experienced river travelers, especially in July and August, except at the Burnt Ranch class 3 rapids and during spring runoff.

White River, Vermont

I like rivers where I can fish a hatch over large rising trout and sight-fish to large smallmouth in the same water. My favorite is the Vermont White River, which offers great trout fishing for rainbows and wild browns, as well as gentle excitement, fishing leisurely by canoe or pontoon craft or wading for feisty smallmouth.

In its upper reaches, the White's water looks distilled, and it remains clear below Bethel. It's one of those rare gems, an eye-candy stream where you can see the bass and trout below the surface as they take your fly. The lower White is a bass factory, with an abundance of three-pound smallmouth and fish over five pounds, but in a world where trout rule supreme, it is fished by few anglers. It's my kind of secret water.

The traditional way to fish the White is from a canoe, preferably flat-bottomed for fishing stability.

The high bluffs on the John Day cast dramatic shadows in the late-afternoon sun. On a float down the river, the fish come easily, allowing you to relax and enjoy the scenery. JOHN RANDOLPH

Though the river has no state boat launches, a main road runs along its length from Royalton to White River and there are many places to pull out, so three- to five-mile floats—Royalton to South, Royalton to Sharon, Sharon to West Hartford—or longer are easy. Floating allows you to fish deeper holding water, where the large bass (and brown trout) lie and feed, and stop and fish the long, gravelly flats in the river's lower reaches. The river is ideal for fishing by pontoon craft. Always pass behind wading fishers.

Two food items drive this fishery: crayfish and hellgrammites. The White is an exciting stream where you can flush dozens of crayfish while wading and turn flat-bottomed rocks to discover hellgrammite nymphs (careful, they pinch). This cornucopia of foods makes fly selection easy: Just fish weighted or unweighted black or brown Krystal Buggers in sizes 4 to 10, preferably dressed with white rubber legs. Other crayfish imitations

also work well, and when the evening hatches are on—spring mayflies, summer evening caddis, and fall flying ants—the dry-fly fishing can be spectacular.

A medium- or fast-action 9-foot, 5- or 6-weight rod will cast these flies while boat- or wade-fishing, and they will handle a 200-grain, 12- to 27-foot sinking-tip line, which is ideal for casting Woolly Buggers and slow-stripping them through runs, tailouts, and around boulders. Fishing black size 6 poppers trailed by a size 10 brown Muddler tied off the hook bend is the ultimate visual experience. The popper makes a surface commotion to attract the bass, often in schools, and the Muddler provides the food. This rig should be fished on a floating bass-taper line.

To catch the largest smallmouth, up to four pounds, fish at first light or in late-evening low light using black Krystal Buggers, Clouser Minnows, or black rabbit-strip Muddlers, weighted or unweighted, in tailouts or flats.

Anglers:
STEVE MAY and KEN COLLINS, Grand River Troutfitters, Fergus, Ontario

Ontario, Canada, is a high-quality smallmouth destination that is relatively unknown. Three major rivers flow into the Great Lakes from the north side, offering beautiful scenery, quiet waters, and trophy bass fishing. The Grand, Maitland, and Saugeen Rivers should be on any serious bass angler's must-fish list. Ontario's bass season opens the last Saturday in June and closes at the end of October, so fishing spawning fish is not legal here, but this has resulted in healthy populations of bass. Floating a scenic river on a beautiful summer day and sight-casting to large fish is what these rivers are all about.

Grand River, Ontario

The Grand River flows to the west of the Toronto area and through the towns of Kitchener, Waterloo, Cambridge, Brantford, and Caledonia. It is a medium-size river that is very easy to access by canoe or drift boat, and it has many walk and wade access points. From Kitchener to Caledonia, the river has a variety of habitats that hold good numbers of bass. The "exceptional waters" area from the town of Paris through Brantford is probably the most popular place for summer bass anglers. Steelhead and resident rainbow trout are found mixed with the bass at certain times of year, and catch-and-release regulations for all species of fish ensure good populations of bass.

These fish are especially susceptible to good minnow imitations in the 2- to 3-inch range. Clouser Min-

The Grand River has miles of big bass water. The "Exceptional Waters" area from the town of Paris through Brantford is probably the most popular area for summer bass anglers. STEVE MAY

The Maitland has air-clear water and the opportunity to sight-fish to trophy bass. JAY NICHOLS

nows, Redneck Rabbits, and Woolly Buggers are standby patterns, and other realistic minnow imitations such as Steve's Perchie and small Puglisi Minnows can be dynamite in the clear, low flows of summer. The Grand is a "numbers river": It has a lot of fish, but the maximum size is a bit smaller than in some other Ontario rivers. Catching dozens of ten- to thirteen-inch bass is common on this river. Bass of sixteen to nineteen inches are also regular catches, but a fish over twenty inches is a real trophy for even the most experienced Grand River bass angler.

"Pickup shoals" are hot spots for streamer fishing—areas that are deep enough to hold bass but shallow enough to get more current flowing over the rocky bottom. Bass sometimes feed on the top of these shoals, but look for more and bigger fish waiting in the shadows beside and behind this type of water. Swimming a streamer around the fringes will result in a lot of hookups. Deep, boulder-studded runs are also common throughout this reach of the Grand, and pods of quality fish roam this prime habitat looking for minnow, leech, or crayfish imitations.

To hook up with silly numbers of medium-size bass on the Grand, or the upper reaches of any Ontario bass river, try working a nymph rig in deep, boulder-strewn runs below riffles. On the longer glide pools, poppers come into their own. Clouser Floating Minnows worked slowly and erratically can also bring up some serious fish.

You can easily access the Grand River at Bean Park in Paris and fish it through to Brant Park Conservation Area. Another drift is from Brant Park Conservation Area to Cockshutt Bridge at the downstream end of Brantford. Fishing from Caledonia to the village of York is also a nice little drift, and from Cambridge to Glen Morris or Paris is a good float in a canoe. You can put a drift boat in at the launch in Cambridge, but you can't take it out at either Glen Morris or Paris.

Maitland River, Ontario

The Maitland River is a Great Lakes jewel. It is a well-known steelhead river as well as a bass mecca. The Maitland is a good-size river, about a hundred to two hundred feet wide in most places, with deep pools and long, expansive runs and riffles set in a heavily forested river valley. Its productive waters are home to good numbers of trophy-size smallmouth, although flow conditions and frequent rock ledges along the course of this river make it a challenge to float unless there is enough water. After a good rain, the river is usually driftable for a week or so. Extended dry periods make floating impractical. Dragging a drift boat over a couple miles of a six-

The Saugeen doesn't have as many fish as the Maitland, but they are, on average, larger. This river also has a good population of muskies. STEVE MAY

mile drift is no fun. In low-flow conditions, the river is much more conducive to walk-and-wade angling or fishing from a pontoon boat, as it is much easier to drag over long, shallow riffles. When the water is low, this also concentrates the fish in quality pools. The fish may be selective and spooky during these conditions, but once you find the right habitat, you will have a lot of quality fish in front of you. Because of the limited access, floating this water with a guide is a great way to get at these incredible fish.

The Maitland often has air-clear water during low-flow conditions. Stealthy approaches and realistic patterns that both look and act natural are keys to success on the Maitland. I have had good luck with crayfish patterns such as the Full Motion Crayfish and Clouser Turkey Crayfish fished slow and on the bottom in good fish-holding pools during low-flow conditions. Small min-

now patterns can also be effective when you need to cover water. This river has prolific insect life, and trouty tactics can be very effective, especially in early July when there are still good caddis and mayfly hatches. Nymphing with drab-colored Hare's Ears or other fuzzy nymphs with a bit of motion, like the Full Motion Hex, can produce surprising results.

Under good flow conditions, a wide assortment of techniques work on Maitland fish. Poppers, bold streamer presentations, and Clouser Floating Minnows are all very productive when the water is up on this beautiful river. During prime conditions, you can expect spectacular fishing for numbers of quality fish in a gorgeous river.

On the Maitland, bridge-hopping anywhere downstream of Wingham on foot or by boat can be excellent. Hot spots are from the road crossing just outside Holmsville to Ben Miller and from Ben Miller to Goderich, but upstream of this area are more drift and walk-and-wade options for those who snoop around.

Saugeen River, Ontario

The Saugeen is a larger river that is floatable throughout the summer, even in low-flow conditions. There are several drifts on this scenic river, but don't expect to see elaborate developments at put-in and take-out points. At many of the sites, it can be a challenge to get a drift boat to the water, and the local guide services have negotiated with private landowners to get at much of this water. As a result, though, you'll rarely see other anglers at places except bridge crossings and riverside campgrounds. This is not a great walk-and-wade river because of its size and average depth.

The Saugeen produces fewer numbers of bass than other top Ontario rivers, but your chances of landing a trophy are very good. One reason for the larger fish is that the river also has a healthy population of muskies, and small bass make great meals for these super predators. (Muskies also are fun to catch, and Grand River Troutfitters specializes in tackling these fish on the fly.) In many areas of the Saugeen, catching small fish is quite rare. Sometimes the smallest bass an angler lands is fifteen or sixteen inches long.

The tactics that work best for big bass on this river include searching for fish on "pickup shoals" and in deep, boulder-studded pools. We have had big bass bust our twelve-inch muskie flies, so a big streamer is a good item to throw if you are after a trophy bass. Deceivers of about 6 to 8 inches are good flies for aggressive Saugeen fish. Clouser Minnows, especially in olive and white, work well, as do Redneck Rabbits in olive, black, orange, or purple. Black Woolly Buggers are tough to beat, and popper fishing can be good, especially in the long, slow pools that are so common here. When things get tough in low-flow conditions, fishing slowly with crayfish or nymph patterns can make for a memorable day. However, the best fishing comes in late August, when the Hexes hatch on this river. Picture yourself enjoying the sunset on a beautiful still evening, watching a big, bushy dry fly lazily float over a large pool, when it disappears in a violent swirl. Big bass love Hexes, and both are abundant in many areas of the Saugeen.

The Saugeen has canoe launches all along the river, but focusing attention downstream of Walkerton is your best bet. The Grey Bruce Tourism Association offer recreational maps that include river access. All of the drifts from Walkerton to Port Elgin are good, though it would take you a week to fish all the way from Walkerton to Port Elgin!

River bass are a slow-growing lot. In Ontario, an eighteen-inch bass can be more than twenty years old. This is due to the limited growing season for bass in the area rivers, which warm slowly compared with the shallow bays of small to medium-size lakes. They also cool off quicker in the fall, and a good-quality river will have relatively cool water throughout the summer. So river bass have to take advantage of the short growing season in the heat of the summer. For this reason, it is even more important to practice catch-and-release with quality river bass. Lee Wulff's words still ring true that "a game fish is too valuable to be caught only once."

Angler: DAVE DUFFY

My favorite fishing for smallmouth is on the French Broad and Nolichucky Rivers. The rivers range from sixty to more than three hundred feet wide, with ledge, pool, and riffle structure and some weed and grass beds. The bottoms are primarily cobble and large rock. Both rivers are best fished from nonmotorized floating craft—a canoe, raft, or inflatable pontoon boat—and it takes some degree of skill to navigate the boulder gardens and faster riffles. Access, for the most part, is limited to roadside pullouts and bridges. You can wade the rivers if you take care. Big flies on these rivers will usually produce big fish.

French Broad River,
North Carolina and Tennessee
Nearly a hundred miles of the French Broad River flows between Asheville, North Carolina, and Newport, Tennessee. Fishing is good and the water exciting, with the

Section Nine rated as one of the better white-water gorges in the South. Smallmouth spawning starts around the first week in May. The fishing picks up in early June and continues through the end of October, with the best fishing in the summer months. The river is almost always fishable when the USGS gauge in Asheville reads around two feet.

River access has been developed around Asheville and down to Marshall. Hot Springs, North Carolina, has a canoe livery, campground, and a few white- and not-so-white-water outfitters. The Forest Service has a carry-in access just across the Tennessee border.

Nolichucky and Toe Rivers,
North Carolina and Tennessee
The sixty-plus miles of the Nolichucky River and its tributary the Toe River offer good fishing for smallmouth bass. The Nolichucky gorge, the section of the river from Poplar, North Carolina, to Erwin, Tennessee, has a reputation as one of the better naturally flowing white-water rivers in the South. This section fishes well, but it's hard to fish when you are holding on for dear life. It is best left to the white-water folks. The Toe River above and the Nolichucky below the gorge are more amenable to fishing. The Tennessee side has several riverside campgrounds, the usual boat liveries, and some river access parks. Smallmouth spawn in mid-May, and the fishing picks up in mid-June and runs through October, when water temperatures drop below 50 degrees. July is the best big-fish month.

A good guide to paddling the French Broad and other rivers in western North Carolina is Betsy Mayers's *Paddling Asheville: 28 Gently Exciting Regional River Trips.* This book identifies all the canoe floats under class 2 in the Asheville area, complete with river maps, put-ins, and take-outs.

My favorite flies include Clouser Deep Minnows in chartreuse over white or yellow, all chartreuse, olive over tan, black over white, gray over white, and olive over pink over white, and Clouser Darters in olive and purple. I tie them all on Mustad 3306 hooks in sizes 1/0 and 2. I also like Gary Lafontaine's Drop Nose Minnow in chartreuse, golden olive, black, orange, gray, olive, and purple; Kiwi Muddlers in tan and gray; and Dean Campbell's Christmas Buggers in sizes 6 and 8 in olive and brown. For top water, I prefer hair bugs such as John Likakis's Burbler in chartreuse, red, and olive; Stewart's Bassarou in chartreuse, olive, and orange; Dahlberg's Rabbit Strip Diver in white, black, and chartreuse; and Dahlberg's Dilg in chartreuse, white, and black. For foam flies, I like size 6 Hipps Foam Popping Bugs in fire tiger and size 2 Clouser Floating Minnows.

Angler: ANTHONY HIPPS

Uhwarrie River, North Carolina

The Uhwarrie River is North Carolina's easternmost smallmouth bass stream, and it is the only one in the state's piedmont region. It is located between Asheboro and Troy, about fifty miles southeast of Greensboro, in Randolph and Montgomery Counties. The smallmouth bass water flows in a winding southerly direction, from the dam that forms Asheboro City Lake to its terminus in Lake Tillery. It was stocked with smallmouths in the early 1970s and maintains a naturally reproducing fishable population.

Going north to south, the first public access for wading or canoeing is at the Highway 49 bridge crossing in Randolph County. In Montgomery County, there is access at the low-water bridge off Coggins Mine Road for a nine-mile float down to the Highway 109 bridge crossing. From the Highway 109 bridge, it is a four-mile float to the public access at the Uhwarrie National Forest recreation area. There are no more public accesses or bridge crossings until you paddle five miles to the end of the river and across Lake Tillery to Mount Morrow State Park Recreation area. You can also wade long sections from any of these access points. Other than at the bridge-crossing accesses in the national forest and state parks, the banks above the normal high-water mark are posted private property. For wade fishing, I recommend the Uhwarrie National Forest access five miles down a dirt road off Highway 109. Here you'll find three miles of wadable water in the best smallmouth habitat on the river.

The Uhwarrie River does not look like a classic smallmouth stream. It does not contain the prime smallmouth habitat of long, deep rocky riffles, moderate-flowing pools, and swift rocky runs. The flow is significantly slower than that of typical smallmouth rivers, and low-water conditions can make a canoe trip a very long, bottom-dragging endurance endeavor. The river is relatively narrow and is composed primarily of long, shallow pools and numerous narrow, ankle-deep shallow riffles. It has a silt, sand, and gravel bottom; numerous rocky shelves; undercut banks; lots of boulders; some large grass beds; and a lot of woody cover in the form of downed trees and root wads. This is a beautiful little river that has its own unique charms. It is not a river worthy of a weeklong fishing vacation, but it does produce several smallmouth in excess of twenty inches every year for skilled anglers, and if you are passing through the area, it is worth fishing for a few hours.

All of the traditional smallmouth bass flies will work on this river. My favorites are size 6 soft-bodied rubber-legged poppers in chartreuse, white, or black; crayfish-colored (rusty brown) rubber-legged marabou-tailed nymphs; and Clouser Minnows in chartreuse and white or all black. Shenk's White Minnow is another favorite fly for streamer fishing.

The typical smallmouth bass caught from this river is eight to twelve inches long. My best smallmouth from this river was a beautiful twenty-incher that annihilated a chartreuse popper, and I've caught several in the twelve to sixteen inch range. On a typical wading trip, a decent angler will catch five to ten smallmouth bass, a few largemouth bass, bluegills, yellow and white perch, and numerous redbreast sunfish. There is also the potential to catch chain pickerel, channel catfish, or white bass, especially in the lower portion of the river.

The bass in this river often use holding structures such as rocks, rocky shelves, grass beds, or logs in the middle of the river rather than holding tight to the banks. Any smallmouth-type habitat with current flow, typically in the middle of the pools, is likely to hold a few bass. Stagnant areas next to the banks should be avoided if you are primarily after smallmouth bass.

The prime times to fish this river are April and May in the spring and mid-September through October in the fall. Because this is a shallow and slow-flowing stream, it often gets too low, stagnant, and hot during the middle of the summer, and the bass become very difficult to catch.

I typically begin fishing the Uhwarrie in early spring, starting out deep and slow with a crayfish-imitating rubber-legged nymph or a Clouser Minnow on a sinking-tip line. I cast quartering across and downstream and retrieve in slow, hopping strips. When the water warms to 70 degrees, I fish more aggressively with poppers and streamers.

New River, North Carolina and Virginia

The New River starts its northward journey to the Ohio River near the sleepy mountain town of Blowing Rock, North Carolina. At its headwaters and for the first several miles, it is a fairly decent stocked trout stream. Starting at the community of Todd, North Carolina, it becomes a warmwater smallmouth bass fishery until it flows into the Gauley River in northern West Virginia, which soon empties into the Ohio River.

This is an absolutely wonderful river to wade or float in a canoe while you fish. It flows through beautiful mountain scenery for its whole course. After the North Fork and South Fork of the New River meet near

The New River in North Carolina and Virginia is a top trophy-bass destination. In the summer, it pays to get on the water early.
BOB CLOUSER

Jefferson, North Carolina, it is a large river with some pretty challenging rapids on some sections for the canoeist.

The river has an abundance of classic smallmouth bass cover, with long, deep rocky runs, rocky shelves, deep pools along steep bluffs, gravel bars, large boulders, weed beds, and downed trees.

The New River does not have as large a bass population as the James River. One of the primary reasons for this is a siltation pollution problem that has caused diminished spawning over the last few years. Road-building projects and farming practices are the primary

contributors to the siltation. New River smallmouth have a hard time reproducing in great numbers when their eggs and spawning areas are covered in sediment. As a result, the fly angler is not as likely to have the fifty-plus-fish days frequently enjoyed on the James River.

That being said, I love to fish the New River. Anglers still have some outstanding fishing days on the New, and it is worth taking a few vacation days to fish. The average size of smallmouth bass caught on the New River is larger than on other North Carolina and Virginia waters. The New River in North Carolina and Virginia provides the fly angler with the best chance to catch a true trophy smallmouth bass of over twenty inches. Every season, many fish larger than five pounds are landed by skilled anglers.

One of the best things about the New River is that it has many public fishing accesses along its length. In Virginia, the New River Bike Trail parallels the river and provides public fishing access for thirty-nine miles. The bike trail starts near Galax, Virginia, and runs north to Foster Falls. Many wade-fishing anglers use this public trail to access prime fishing spots on the river, and some actually bike to prime wade-fishing locations along the trail. The Shot Tower Park section of the trail just of I-77 has a canoe outfitter.

Prime locations to fish this river in North Carolina are at the New River State Park and public accesses near West Jefferson, Jefferson, and Sparta. Numerous canoe outfitters include the Old General Store near West Jefferson and New River Campground and Canoe near Sparta, both fine operations that will carry you upstream and let you take your time fishing back to the take-out. Not all canoe outfitters on the New cater to anglers, however, or even desire their business. Call and ask about fishing before you book a trip.

I like to start fishing the New River in midsummer, usually mid-June or later. With its larger size and higher flow volume, the New seems to take longer to heat up than other rivers. It fishes well late into November, as it also takes longer for the water to cool down. New River smallmouth respond well to Shenk's White Streamers, Clouser Minnows, and my rubber-legged nymphs and rubber-legged size 6 poppers. Clouser Crayfish fished deep and slow are very productive here, as crayfish are the primary food source.

Many lunker smallmouth hang out in the river's slow-moving deep holes. Often a sinking-tip line is needed to get the fly—a Clouser Minnow or Crayfish—down deep in these pools. The reward can be a sharply bent rod as you fight a trophy smallmouth.

James River, Virginia

The James River flows in an easterly direction across the state of Virginia, starting on the eastern front of the Blue Ridge Mountains and eventually emptying into the Chesapeake Bay below Richmond. This river is absolutely loaded with smallmouth from its headwaters near Iron Gate to the fall line at Richmond. In the summer, it's possible to catch more than fifty smallmouth a day on a float. For sheer numbers of bass, there is no finer river in the East than the James. On several occasions, this river has produced outstanding fishing days for me and my fishing partners.

Although several areas on the James River have wading access, I prefer to float this river in a canoe. This gives the angler a definite advantage, because the fishing at the public-access sites, though good, often gets crowded. In addition, using the public wading accesses is limiting, as the James flows through a lot of posted private property, which has the best fishing on the river. My favorite parts of the James to canoe and fish are the floats from Eagle Rock to Salt Petre Cave (nine miles), from Lynchburg to 6 Mile Creek (six miles), and from 6 Mile Creek to Joshua Falls (four miles). These sections are the most familiar to me, but all portions of the James River above Richmond have excellent populations of fish. In these stretches, the James contains all of the classic smallmouth cover: deep rocky runs, current eddies, ledges, weed beds, gravel bars, downed trees, undercut banks, and boulders. Practically every current break contains a population of bass.

The smallmouth fishing on the James is good from May through October. I typically start fishing here in early May. The water is still typically cool, below 65 degrees, so deeper and slower is the preferred method to catch these early-season bass. During this time of year, I fish primarily with my rubber-legged nymph, Shenk's White Minnow, and a gray over white Clouser Minnow on a sinking-tip line.

As the water temperature rises to above 70 degrees, usually in mid-June, the bass become more aggressive. At this point, I start fishing with a full-floating line and rubber-legged soft-bodied poppers. Sometimes I tie 18 inches of tippet to the bend of the popper hook and use an unweighted size 6 or 8 rubber-legged nymph as a dropper fly. If the fish show a preference for one fly over the other, I switch exclusively to either the popper or the nymph. Streamers can also be excellent flies to catch numbers of bass at this time of year.

By far the best topwater fishing on the James is during the dog days of summer, July through early September. While the reservoir waters have heated up and the lake gamefish have developed lockjaw, the James's cooler, well-oxygenated waters are having the hottest topwater bite of the year. During the heat of summer, bass are chasing damselflies, dragonflies, grasshoppers, and minnows and making their feeding presence known all over the river, often jumping clear of the water in pursuit of the large airborne insects. At this time of year, you need only a popper or slider to have an outstanding fish-filled day on the water.

On the James, many floaters fish exclusively to the banks. Though this technique is certainly effective, you should not ignore the abundant midriver structures of

Drifting the New in a boat or raft is a productive way to fish with streamers or poppers. BOB CLOUSER

current breaks, underwater ledges, rocky runs, boulders, weed beds, gravel bars, and downed trees. Practically any current break with a water depth of a foot or two may contain smallmouth bass. Some of my biggest bass from the James were taken on poppers or streamers fished around this midriver structure.

When the waters start to cool in the fall, from late September to early November, I favor casting streamers and nymphs on sinking-tip lines if the water is cool and the bass are acting lethargic, fishing them deep and slow just like in early spring. If the water is still relatively warm and the bass are energetic, this is a prime time to fish a two-fly tandem of a size 2 pencil popper with a streamer on an 18-inch dropper. I fish this tandem aggressively, much the way spin fishermen fish the Rebel Pop-R popper. On some days, this produces explosive strikes on the popper and may bag the biggest bass of the year. Sometimes, in their excitement, the bass miss the popper several times before they eat the streamer trailer—the reason why it's a good idea to have the second fly.

The James River from Iron Gate down to Glasgow is a scenic float through some beautiful forest, farmland, and mountain scenery. The floats around Lynchburg, though not as aesthetic, have tremendous smallmouth bass fishing. All of these sections are worth exploring with a canoe and fly rod.

For complete fishing and floating information on the James River, I recommend Bruce Ingram's *James River Guide,* which provides maps of the river and roads that lead you to the fishing. It also shows the public-access sites and points you to the best fishing on the river.

Northwest Alabama Creeks

The outstanding smallmouth bass fishing in Wilson Lake and Pickwick Reservoir, impoundments on the Tennessee River in northwest Alabama, is well documented in a lot of bass-fishing literature. What is not well established or written about much is the excellent smallmouth fishing in the feeder creeks to these two reservoirs.

Several wadable, canoeable creeks flow into these impoundments, and most contain large populations of smallmouth bass. The upper and middle portions of these creeks, before they become part of the reservoirs, are a smallmouth angler's heaven. Shoals Creek near St. Florian, Little Bear Creek in Franklin County near Hackleburg, and Cedar Creek near Red Bay have excellent fishing, but my favorite is the creek I grew up on, the place where I caught my first smallmouth bass, Cypress Creek near Florence.

Cypress Creek, though smaller than many of the famous smallmouth rivers, has all of the classic cover and

forage that smallmouth bass love. The current flow is nice even during drought times. The creek has numerous public accesses for canoeing or wade-fishing at bridge crossings near Florence. One of the best public-access sites is at Wildwood Park on the southwest corner of Florence. From Wildwood Park, you have more than a mile of public, wadable, smallmouth-filled water. All of the classic flies and techniques that I use on other eastern rivers work great on Cypress Creek as well. My favorite way to fish the creek is to wade upstream from Wildwood Park and cast poppers to all of the likely smallmouth-holding structures. These fish seem to love a size 6 rubber-legged popper in chartreuse or white.

Don't let the small size of Cypress Creek fool you into thinking the fish are small. It gets several lake-run smallmouth every year in addition to the resident population. Though the stream-bred fish will seldom get over twenty inches long, the lake-run fish can be more than twenty-six inches and do some serious damage to weak tippets or fly rods. In addition to smallmouth bass, on Cypress Creek you can catch spotted bass, largemouth bass, channel catfish, bluegills, rock bass, and even the occasional sauger.

When fly-fishing the creeks of northwest Alabama, you must bring most of your own flies, tippets, and gear with you. There are no fly shops within sixty miles, and most of the local tackle shops carry only a limited supply of panfish flies. For fishing these creeks, I like a 6- or 7-weight rod with a floating line and a 9-foot leader tapered down to 6-pound-test tippet.

Angler: JAMES BUICE

With thousands of miles of smallmouth water flowing through the southeastern United States, exploring all of these waters in search of bass nirvana may seem like a daunting, albeit enjoyable, task. Though numerous rivers deserve mention, three hold a special place in my angling heart. The French Broad, Little Tennessee, and Hiawassee Rivers all are productive rivers that vary in scenery, water character, and fishing.

Little Tennessee River, North Carolina

Once known for its famed trout fishery, the Little Tennessee River has seen a resurrection in angling popularity thanks to smallmouth bass. The river between Franklin, North Carolina, and Fontana Lake holds a fine population of smallmouth bass in the pound to pound-and-a-half range, with large fish being somewhat common.

So long as the pattern is buggy and has good movement underwater, it should possess the necessary mojo to elicit strikes from various members of the river's smallmouth bass population. Warmer months find the smallies looking for a floating meal with Dahlberg Divers, sliders, and various popping bugs in sizes 6 to 12. Orange, chartreuse, and "froggy" green are good bets when looking through your fly box. Larger bass, which typically feed subsurface on the Little Tennessee, can be coaxed into your net with various crayfish, Clouser Minnows in brown and white or chartreuse and white, or size 4 to 10 Woolly Buggers in black, yellow and brown, or brown.

Although Highway 28 parallels the river nearly the entire length from Franklin to Fontana Lake, wade access is limited because of private property. Launching a canoe or small pontoon boat from any of the bridge crossings along the river's route gives you several float options.

French Broad River, North Carolina

Flowing through the city of Asheville, North Carolina, the French Broad River offers nearly forty miles of pro-ductive smallmouth bass water. For the majority of its flow, the French Broad is a large river, crawling through the valleys of western North Carolina and into Tennessee. Long, slow pools are often followed by stretches of boulder-strewn shallows with sweeping gravel bars—ideal habitat for smallies.

Anglers can access the river in numerous locations, making this an ideal river for either floating or wade-fishing. Floating anglers can access the river from Johnson Brown Road off Highway 25/70 near Barnard, North Carolina, to the Stackhouse access off Lonesome Mountain Road. This stretch holds some of the best smallie fishing on the river, but watch for the rapids near Sandy Bottom, as the swift currents could mean trouble for novice boaters.

Spring and fall find anglers probing likely holding water with various crayfish and small baitfish imitations. Whitlock's Near-Nuff Crawfish in gray and brown, Clouser Minnows in brown and white or green and white, and the venerable Woolly Bugger in brown, black, and green can be found in nearly every fly box of serious French Broad devotees. During the summer months, the bass begin to crush dark green, chartreuse, and yellow dry flies, with sliders and Dahlberg Divers in sizes 8 to 12 being the favorites.

Bass on the river average one to two pounds in size, perhaps leaning more toward the two-pound class. Smallies up to five pounds are not uncommon, and larger fish are caught on the river every season.

Hiawassee River, Tennessee

Just upstream of the well-known tailwater trout fishery that put Reliance, Tennessee, on the angling map, the Hiawassee River above the powerhouse is a sleeper smallmouth fishery of the first order. Marked by huge boulders and rock outcroppings, this diminutive flow trickles southward until it meets up with the majority of the river's water, which is piped across the mountains and into the powerhouse via a massive flume system. The stretch of river above this juncture for eight miles or so holds scores of one- to two-pound smallmouth, with fish in the five-pound class possible. Though the smallmouth bass population is not as high as on some other rivers, the chances of catching a large fish pushing five pounds or more is greater.

Access is limited to foot travel, but the walk is fairly easy, thanks to a trail that parallels the river from the powerhouse to the base of the dam. Parking at the powerhouse and hiking upstream will take you through the wilds of Tennessee, complete with deer, turkey, wild boar, and the occasional rattle-headed coppermoccasin. In all seriousness, do watch for snakes. There are more copperheads here than I've seen anywhere else in the country.

Size 4 to 10 Clouser Minnows in chartreuse and white or brown and white and various crawfish patterns in sizes 8 to 12 tend to work well in the spring and fall months. From the time water begins to warm, usually in May, Dahlberg Divers in sizes 6 to 10, sliders in sizes 8 to 12, and mouse patterns catch fish until the first cold days of fall hit in late September. Damselflies, large Woolly Buggers in black and brown, and bulky baitfish imitations such as Puglisi's Baitfish in sizes 4 to 8 get the larger smallies fired up.

Angler: CHUCK KRAFT

New River and James River, Virginia

I've spent twenty-two years guiding upper and middle James River and its tributaries and the New River below Claytor Lake. Our season runs from March 1 to October 15. Up to April 1, the smallmouth are usually still in their winter holes, and we fish them with weighted minnow and crayfish patterns. Instead of covering a lot of water, we typically focus on the winter holes.

From early to mid-April, the bass are moving to their spawning areas, and we continue to fish minnow and crayfish patterns. Fishing can be a little tough, as the fish are scattered and moving. Bass begin spawning from mid-April to late May, and I discourage fishing for spawning bass. From late May to the end of the first week of June, the fish are moving from spawning to summer territory, and fishing can be tough again during this time. You'll have to make a lot of casts and cover a variety of water types. If you find fish, they will usually bite. We still fish minnow and crayfish patterns but add some insect patterns to our arsenals, hellgrammites and surface bugs.

The most consistent fishing of the year on the New and James Rivers is from the second week of June through mid-October. You will find fish just about anywhere, especially around anything that creates shade. Riffles produce a lot of small to midsize fish, and the bigger fish are usually in moderate to slower-moving current. This does not necessarily mean deep water, but moving water with overhead cover. During this period, the fish have a ton of different foods to choose from, and your fly selection should reflect this. Minnow, crayfish, hellgrammite, damselfly, dragonfly, and cicada patterns all produce big fish during this period. Mayfly and caddisfly hatches on these rivers are not as important as the larger insects.

For equipment, I recommend a good single-action reel and a medium-fast to fast-action 9-foot fly rod that casts 6- to 8-weight floating lines. Sinking lines aren't necessary on most of the water we fish. In early season, I like leaders of 8 to 10 feet made of fluorocarbon in 10- to 14-pound-test. When using weighted flies, I just use 8 feet of straight fluorocarbon. For summer fishing, I prefer tapered leaders, 9 or 10 feet long, made of good-quality mono with 18 to 22 inches of fluorocarbon for the tippet.

For surface bugs and suspending minnow patterns, I use the nonslip loop knot. In the New and James Rivers, two food items are available to the fish year-around: minnows and crayfish.

My advice for those who want to become good smallmouth bass anglers is to learn to cast and manage their line. Also learn to fish larger flies and a wide variety of flies.

Angler: BOB CLOUSER

Susquehanna River, Pennsylvania

The Susquehanna River is one of the finest smallmouth rivers in the eastern United States. It flows through New York, Pennsylvania, and Maryland. Starting in New York, the Susquehanna runs over four hundred miles, draining some of the most fertile land in the East. The main stem, sometimes called the North Branch, is joined near the town of Northumberland, Pennsylvania, by the West Branch. The now much larger river flows south to its influx into the Chesapeake Bay.

On the Susquehanna, you can find superb smallmouth angling in more than 170 miles of quality habitat in Pennsylvania. Many anglers coming to the Susquehanna in quest of smallmouth are awed by its expanse. The river can vary in width from one-half to three-quarters of a mile in many places, especially in its prime section, and its smallmouth inhabitants spend their entire lives in its excellent bottom habitat. The bottom is composed of ledges of solid rock, boulders, gravel, broken rock, and strewn rubble of all sizes and shapes. Its shallow sections boast both large and small islands, creating lees, edges, and back eddies. Grass beds are scattered among untold numbers of gravel bars. The river's mix of many speeds and depths of water provides the necessities of specialized habitat for its big smallmouth. The shorelines, meandering through many mountain ranges, are dotted with a variety of trees and brush. Many dams are located along the Susquehanna. The most important aspect of any fishing or boating outing is to put safety first. Stay away from all dams, and do not venture into any strange waters without the proper safety equipment.

The Susquehanna River has massive insect hatches, lots of crayfish and hellgrammites, and many types of baitfish. No wonder the bass grow fat. JOHN RANDOLPH

Some of the best fly fishing can be found on the approximately fifty-mile stretch from the mouth of the Juniata River south to Holtwood Dam. Here numerous grass beds and shallow gravel bars, combined with deep-water areas between many lava ledges, produce and protect more smallmouth bass than in any other section of the river. Check with the Pennsylvania Fish and Boat Commission (PFBC) about its regulations, because this area is managed as blue-ribbon smallmouth water for trophy fish. You'll find plenty of access areas on both sides of the river from north of Harrisburg downstream. Popular wading areas are in the Dauphin Narrows section north of Harrisburg, where there is access on both sides of the river in the towns of Marysville and Stoney Creek, as well as the Fort Hunter PFBC boat access. Downstream, another good spot for wade-fishing is where the Yellow Breeches flows into the Susquehanna at the town of New Cumberland.

From just south of Dock Street Dam near Harrisburg to the York Haven Dam lies another section of high-quality habitat. Although public access is limited to the southern end of this area, this is the most heavily fished section of the river. Private clubs and two large marinas are located here. The PFBC has two access facilities for this section. One is located in Dauphin County at Middletown, near the south end of Union Street. This is a good back-in ramp for shallow-draft boats such as johnboats because of the shallow water here. The west bank near the town of Goldsboro in York County has a very good access area with plenty of parking and an excellent back-in ramp. This ramp will put you on the backwaters of the York Haven Dam on Lake Frederic. On weekends, anglers should fish the north end of the pool below the Middletown riffles. Cabins fill the islands, and a lot of boaters spend their summers here. Fish close to the many islands and also around the large rocks in the north end of the pool.

The section form above the Middletown riffles to the Dock Street Dam requires a shallow-draft boat and cautious navigation. Midsummer fishing is productive around the smaller islands and numerous grass beds. Rock ledges abound in this area. Insects are plentiful in these shallow areas, providing the surface fisher with enjoyable evenings.

Many diverse fishing situations can be had from below the York Haven Dam to the Safe Harbor Dam. Conditions vary from fast-flowing water just below the dams to riffles, pools, islands, grass beds, and slack waters in the Lake Clarke Pool above the Safe Harbor Dam. Long, deep channels such as the one that forms the Accomac Pool at Accomac, York County, offer good holding water for those big bass during the hot days of August. Evening fishing gets productive around dusk near the piers of the Highway 30 bridge. The bottom end of the Columbia riffles creates enough oxygen during the hot summer months to harbor an abundance of bass. The Lake Clarke Pool above the Safe Harbor Dam is used by high-powered boats and water skiers. Good fishing exists along its rocky shoreline and also along the many islands of the upper pool. Smallmouth in this area usually travel with the abundant schools of baitfish. Locating these schools of bait and experiencing the smallmouth feeding on them will prove to be very beneficial toward your success.

Gizzard shad are abundant in this section. Smallmouth will ambush the schools of shad from the island points that dot this area. The fast-water outflow from the Safe Harbor Dam offers boating anglers excellent mid-summer angling.

Starting in mid-July, the famous whitefly hatch starts near the town of Columbia, and over a three- to four-week period, the fly emergence travels some seventy-plus miles upriver. During this time, it's possible to see flies hatching in blizzard proportions. This emergence puts the smallmouth into a feeding frenzy every evening. I've watched my clients grin in disbelief when two- to five-pound smallmouth rise and inhale a size 10 whitefly pattern.

The most productive time to wade-fish the Susquehanna River is usually governed by two important factors that can affect fly-fishing success. One of these is the water temperature. When the water is between the mid-fifties and the high eighties, you'll find prime fishing. With the water temperature above 55 degrees and rising, smallmouth will chase their prey greater distances than when it is below 55. The prime months to find these ideal temperatures are usually June through October. If you are planning a trip and can make only one outing a season, I would go sometime between mid-July and the end of September.

The second factor is the variation of the river's water levels. From late June through October, the level usually stabilizes. Fluctuation of water levels affect both the safety of the wading angler and the areas where fish can be found. A good indicator of safe and productive wading is the water stage at Harrisburg. A river stage reading at Harrisburg of four feet or less is generally suited to wading conditions in many areas of the river. As the water stage decreases, indicating that the water levels are falling, the wading angler's opportunities increase. You can obtain a report of the river's water levels by phoning 814-234-9861. The report has water-level information at many locations on the Susquehanna and a number of its major tributaries.

The many rocks, ledges, islands, and bars on the Susquehanna River provide perfect habitat and shelter for bass and the food they eat, but they also make navigating the river in low water tricky. Fortunately, there are plenty of great wade-fishing spots.
PHILIP HANYOK

At the Highway 30 bridge at Columbia, wading conditions from the bridge upstream for at least a mile exist on both sides of the river. When the water levels are low, you can find excellent smallmouth action in the center of the river. This area has ideal habitat consisting of a gravel bar strewn with bowling-ball-size rocks.

Good access areas are at the mouth of the Codorus Creek, located on the west bank of the river near York; the Haldemann riffle on the East Bank near Bainbridge; and the PFBC's Falmouth access. You can find good fly-rodding opportunities half a mile below the York Haven Dam. This area has excellent wading in low water, especially when the whitefly is hatching. The Middletown riffles are good for wading when the river stage at Harrisburg is three and a half feet or lower. This area has large boulders and ridges of rocks that harbor large smallmouth.

Shoreline wading can be found near the towns of New Cumberland, Wormleysburg, West Fairview, and Marysville along the river's west shore. You can also wade-fish the river at the mouth of the Juniata River and below.

Angler: MIKE O'BRIEN

West Branch of the Susquehanna River, Pennsylvania

Pennsylvania's West Branch of the Susquehanna River begins in Cambria County and flows some 240 miles before joining the North Branch at Northumberland. Some of the best fishing occurs in the 30-mile section from Williamsport to Lewisburg. The Hepburn Street Dam at Williamsport creates about an 11-mile pool. Although the fishing here can be good, dealing with heavy recreational boating traffic is frustrating. At Williamsport, the West Branch makes an end run around Bald Eagle Mountain and flows southeast. Anglers mainly target smallmouth bass, muskie, and catfish. Smallmouth fishing is also productive in the three main river tributaries in this region—Pine Creek, Lycoming Creek, and Loyalsock Creek. These are ideally suited for wade fishing.

When fishing the West Branch, one can't help but think of the rich history surrounding this impressive flow.

The West Branch of the Susquehanna has large bass and little fishing pressure. MIKE O'BRIEN

Coal, timber, and farming operations affected the lives of many people here, as well as the drainage itself. River sections northwest of Lock Haven still carry evidence of mine acid drainage, with very noticeable orange-stained stones. Railroads follow the river, crossing over at several locations. An archaeological dig near Montoursville revealed artifacts dating to 5,000 B.C. In 1938, the Last Raft, a vessel to commemorate the logging era, hit the bridge at Muncy and dumped its passengers into the frigid water, killing seven. Rock-filled cribs, remnants of logging booms built more than a hundred years ago, are still present in the Williamsport river section.

Pennsylvania Fish and Boat Commission (PFBC) launch sites at Loyalsock, Montoursville (township-maintained), Muncy, Montgomery, Watsontown, Milton, and Lewisburg are nicely spaced for accessing different river sections or for day float trips. Montoursville to Muncy and Muncy to Montgomery are two nice sections to float. These areas are a bit more secluded than most and offer good fishing. Float trips are best conducted in a canoe or small car-topper.

Wade fishing is available at many locations along the West Branch. The summer months offer the best flows for this style of fishing, and the water temperature is such that you can wet-wade comfortably. A few areas to get your feet wet are around Racetrack Island below the Montoursville launch, the set of riffles downriver from the Allenwood Bridge, at the pump station below Watsontown, and at Milton State Park, which is on an island. Wading is best done when the river at Williamsport is at or below the one-foot level.

A suitable water level is important for both a float and productive fishing. A reading of two and a half feet or below at Williamsport is a starting point. Fly fishers will find the water more comfortable for fishing and more conducive to catching when flows are below one and a half feet. The river level at Williamsport can be found online at the USGS streamflow website.

The West Branch is not the big, sprawling river of the main stem. Its width runs between 50 and 150 yards. Several deeper pools, including one at Montoursville reported to be over twenty feet, offer challenging fishing. The West Branch does not have the prominent ledges like the main river. It consists of riffles separated by long, flat sections flowing mostly over baseball- to basketball-size chunks of sandstone. A few sections contain ledges, and larger boulders are scattered throughout. Downed trees along the riverbanks offer sanctuaries for prey and prime fishing spots for smallmouth bass. Bass can be found at different locations depending on the time of year, water level, and water temperature. Key structure includes bridge pilings, emergent and submerged weed beds, riffles, channels and cuts, pools, bars, and islands. The mouths of tributaries are always worth investigating.

The best fishing on the West Branch has a typical spring through fall timeline. May, depending on the water volume, and then July through early October offer the most consistent fishing. Winter fishing is restricted to ice-fishing for panfish, mostly on backwater areas. If conditions permit, die-hard muskie anglers fish open flows. Spring is the time to offer smallies a mouthful. Large, bulky flies with deep profiles and lots of flash are good choices. Flies like Clouser Half and Halfs and Lefty's Deceivers work great. The effects of snowmelt and rain greatly affect water flows and fishing at this time of the year. Sinking-tip and full-sinking lines are great aids for proper presentation.

As summer develops, so does good topwater action for smallmouth. But because of the ultraclear water, fishing is anything but easy. Numerous aquatic insects add to the fish fodder, creating surface action. Beginning in July, for instance, a bright blue damselfly will be present in heavy concentrations, and a blue popping bug or a more exacting pattern will take lots of bass. However, bigger fish usually fall victim to a minnow-type offering, both surface and subsurface. Flies with lots of movement, such as Swimming Nymphs, Jailbaits, or Woolly Buggers, will take smallmouth. When using streamers or bucktails, artificial materials that offer lots of translucency produce better in the clear water. These should also be tied rather sparsely. Nymph fishing with crayfish, hellgrammite, or large stonefly imitations can be productive in the riffled areas.

Another interesting way to catch really big smallmouth is to fish for them as they follow feeding carp. When carp rout out prey from underneath rocks and silt, smallmouth bass take full advantage; look for mud streaks. Carefully presenting a nymph or crayfish imitation is the best ploy. How productive is this? In 2005, I know of seven smallmouths over four pounds—the largest four pounds, ten ounces—that were caught off the backs of carp. All were caught by sight-fishing in clear water less than two feet in depth, on bright, sunny summer afternoons. If you are up for a real test of skills, then try hooking a carp. They average fourteen to twenty pounds in the West Branch and may well be the ultimate challenge in freshwater fly fishing.

Typically in September, the smallmouth go on a topwater-feeding binge. Anglers will find good results using popping or deer-hair bugs, such as Clouser Crippled Minnows, EZ Poppers, Gaines Skipping Bugs, or Lefty's Bugs. This action may last for only several days, so timing is everything. As fall progresses and the river temperature drops, you are not fishing for numbers of bass, but size. Large streamers like Sculpin Clouser Minnows and Red and White Hackle flies usually have the most appeal. Again, a sinking-tip or intermediate line has advantages.

The West Branch of the Susquehanna River has much to offer the angler. It can be fickle, however, at times showing off its wonderful bounty, at others testing your patience and determination.

Though the West Branch is not as big as the main-stem Susquehanna, it is still big enough to float. MIKE O'BRIEN

The Juniata is a large tributary to the Susquehanna that enters the river near Duncannon, Pennsylvania. It has exceptional bass fishing and is a good alternative when the main Susquehanna River is high or muddy. BOB CLOUSER

Angler: BRIAN SHUMAKER

Juniata River, Pennsylvania

The Juniata offers everything a fly fisher could want: an excellent smallmouth fishery for most of its length, very good access, and best of all, a river that under normal conditions is safe to boat or wade if standard precautions are taken. The Juniata is the second-largest tributary of the Susquehanna, entering the main river just above Harrisburg at the town of Duncannon. It is a medium-size river, averaging from 150 to 200 feet wide. The Juniata is not much different in character from the larger Susquehanna or other smallmouth rivers in the Mid-Atlantic, such as the Potomac, Shenandoah, or James. It is shallow, with long pools, riffles, rock ledges, and grasses that grow along the edges and banks.

The Juniata offers many different ways to fly-fish for smallies, but I find that floating the river is often the best and most productive way to explore this fine river. Floating a river can put you in places that anglers on foot can't reach, giving you access to fish the deeper holes while also allowing you the opportunity to get out and fish the riffles, pockets, and grass beds.

A good outfit for the Juniata is a 7-weight, 9-foot rod with a weight-forward floating line. I like to have a second rod rigged with a full-sinking or sinking-tip line to fish the deeper holes and ledges.

You can fish the usual range of bass flies, but my top seven patterns that I always carry on the Juniata are size 4 Clouser Deep Minnows in various colors; size 4 Clouser Darters in purple, black and purple, and black and blue; crayfish; Murray's Hellgrammites; size 2 Clouser Floating Minnows in chartreuse and white, black and white; size 2 Skipping Bugs in white, chartreuse, and yellow; and dry flies to imitate the mayflies of the whitefly hatch.

Tactics for fishing the Juniata are similar to those you would use fishing any of the larger smallmouth rivers in the country; it's just done on a smaller scale. Realizing where the smallmouth live is the first step. Juniata smallmouth are found around structure, such as rocks on the bottom, and ledges crossing the river, as well as in riffles below the ledges and in the calm water of the deeper pools. They can also be found near the grass beds along the shore and in midriver. The best advice I can give on fly-fishing the Juniata is not to spend all your time fishing just one type of structure or water, because you can have rocks, ledges, grass beds, and a pool all in a one-hundred- to two-hundred-yard stretch. If you just concentrate on the first piece of structure you find, you will never get downstream by the end of the day.

In spring, bass are looking for two things: slower current and warmer water. You want to target eddies below exposed rock or along the shoreline, especially if the water is up from runoff. Use a full-sinking line or sinking-tip to present your fly near the bottom, retrieving your fly ultraslowly. One of my favorite flies at this time is the Clouser Darter in black and purple or black and blue.

The summer provides the most consistent fishing, with the smallmouth moving into their summer feeding zones. I like to target the grass beds and pools using a floating line with some type of topwater offering. Also during this time, you will see different insect hatches. On most summer days, blue damselflies hover over the water, driving the smallies nuts, and fishing a light blue popper can be very effective. A variety of subsurface patterns and presentations also work well, especially when fished on a clear intermediate line.

Early fall on the Juniata can produce very good topwater fishing. I like to target the shoreline grasses and tops of ledges with a slider-type pattern or a Clouser Floating Minnow. As the water starts to cool, use a sink-ing line with a streamer, such as a Deep Minnow or Deceiver, and fish the deeper areas below ledges and pools. An interesting hatch that comes off in September on the Juniata is flying ants, which produce some exciting topwater fishing.

One of the Juniata's attractions is that you can pick the type of water that most appeals to you. The upper stretch is smaller, with shorter and shallower pools and lots of riffles. The midsection around Mifflintown offers a mix of bridge pilings, riffles, ledges, grass beds, and deep pools. The lower section down to where it empties into the Susquehanna becomes deeper, with longer pools and big ledges.

But the best feature of the Juniata is that it offers a lot of water with a variety of structure that can be easy to fish with plenty of smallmouth bass. It is a smallmouth angler's dream on a more intimate scale than the larger smallmouth rivers.

Early fall on the Juniata offers superb topwater fishing for fourteen- to sixteen-inch bass. BOB CLOUSER

Angler: *ROGER LAPENTOR*

Flambeau River, Wisconsin

When high winds and stormy weather hit Chequamegon Bay, a not so unusual scenario, I move inland to keep my customers on the smallies. We have plenty of small and large lakes that I could fish, but the river systems of central and northern Wisconsin offer a nice change of scenery.

The Flambeau River flows right through my backyard, and with its north and south forks, it is a midsize stream. It has smallies averaging fifteen inches, with the possibility of catching twenty-inchers. Fishing begins in May and can run through October.

The stretch of the North Fork of the Flambeau from the Turtle Flambeau flowage to Holts Landing, just above Park Falls, is my favorite. It is quiet and picturesque, with little fishing pressure, though on nice days the canoes and kayaks arrive in full force. Some of this water can be fished by motorboat, but it is most effectively fished by drift boat, canoe, johnboat, or kickboat. After poling a flats boat on the lake most of the summer, rowing on the river is a welcome change for me.

You want to have your waders handy for the boat landing and for walking the boat through shallow areas during low-water periods.

Most of the river is a shoreline fishery, fishing to downed trees and rocks, but you do fish to occasional midstream boulders and logs with poppers, streamers, and sliders. My favorite poppers are Umpqua Poppers in minnow and in red and white, though I find that color doesn't always matter. These poppers are loud. A gray-ghost-colored Peck's Popper is a little more subtle, and I use Sneaky Petes in chartreuse and orange for subtle presentations. Brown over gray, brown over white, and gray over white Clouser Minnows are good for when bass are fishing on minnows.

I like an 8-weight, 9-foot rod with a Clouser taper line for turning over the more wind-resistant flies. I also bring a short sinking-tip line for fishing divers and large minnow imitations through deeper sections of the river. As the Flambeau has a healthy muskie population that ranges from twenty-five to forty-five inches, I often use light-wire tippet.

The South Fork of the Flambeau has good day floats from Lugerville to the Highway W Bridge and from Oxbo to Babbs Island. These stretches are similar to the water on the North Fork, but this water is slower and a little easier to fly-fish.

St. Croix River, Wisconsin

The St. Croix is one of the most beautiful rivers in the upper Midwest. This river is protected by the Federal Wild and Scenic Rivers Act, established in the 1970s. The upper waters, from Trego north, are too shallow to float but are excellent for wade-fishing. From July through September, anglers can catch a lot of fish that average fourteen inches.

As you head south from Trego to the Mississippi River, bass size increases to an average of sixteen to eighteen inches, with the possibility of catching a twenty-incher. This is a midsize river until it gets close to the Mississippi, and it offers lots of structure fishing on the shoreline and midstream fishing around boulders. Given the right water level, August is usually the best month on the lower end. This is an excellent topwater fishery. Fishing pressure is low until you get closer to the Mississippi River and the high-population areas.

Wisconsin River, Wisconsin

The Wisconsin River covers so much area that an entire book could be devoted to it. From Portage downstream, there are several day floats that include the usual shoreline structure, but also big bridges, man-made riprap shoreline as a result of development, and many sand islands. Fishing the eddies created by the islands can be very productive. Some stretches on the lower river around Spring Green must be fished from a canoe or jet-drive motor because of all the sandbars.

The river has excellent potential for twenty-inch fish, and the Smallmouth Alliance is seeking protection so that more fish can reach that size.

It helps to have current local information about changing water levels, as with all Wisconsin rivers. July through September are the best fishing times. For surface flies, use Peck's Poppers in gray ghost, Umpqua Minnow in red and white, and Sneaky Petes in chartreuse and orange. For subsurface fishing in the deeper stretches, use Clouser Minnows, Bay Bugs, and Diving Hair Bugs.

Angler: *TONY BUZOLICH*

Russian River, California

Almost any of the foothill lakes and streams along the west slope of the Sierra can have smallmouth in them. The Russian River north of Santa Rosa, all the way to Ukiah and beyond, probably is the best known. This is not a big river, but it has lots of gravel and brush along

Above: Most of the foothill streams along the California Sierras have good smallmouth populations in them. JOHN G. SHERMAN

Left: Though not native to California, or to many other places that now have great fishing, smallmouth bass bring enjoyment to anglers who respect this hard-fighting, adaptable fish. JOHN G. SHERMAN

its entire route. Smallmouth are numerous, although I've never taken any big ones from it. Small marabou leech patterns in olive or dark colors are popular here.

Feather River and Yuba River, California

Closer to home, the Feather and the Yuba are almost in my backyard, and both have good numbers of smallies. Being a big river, the Feather once had riverboats coming all the way to Yuba City and Marysville from San Francisco, bringing miners to the gold rush and returning with fruit and food crops for the markets. These boats would dock all along the river in this area. Though the boats are now gone, the old pilings and piers from ancient wharves remain. This river is home to a lot of nice-size smallmouth.

The Yuba River and adjoining goldfields have some very deep dredger holes in the upturned gravel from mining. The water here is quite a bit cooler than in the Feather, and the smallmouth seem to really like it that way.

As for flies, any crayfish pattern would be my first choice on either of these rivers. Clousers and Dan Blanton's Whistlers are also effective.

INDEX

Alabama, northwest creeks, 210
Aquatic insects, 69–72

Backcasting, 118
Baitfish
    behavior, 81
    color, 83
    description of, 55–68
    imitating, 79, 81, 83
    size, 81
    weight, 81, 83
Barr, John, 77
Belgium cast, 107
Bendback, 89
Bett's Foam Dragon Fly, 72
Birds, finding fish and, 52
Black–nose dace, 65, 74
Blados, Joe, 146
Blessing, Russ, 77, 93
Boat presentations
    dead drift, 135
    streamer, 141–142
Boats, selecting, 181–184
Book of the Black Bass (Henshall), 2,
    72
Bottom-bouncing techniques,
    132–133
Bridges, finding fish around, 39–40
Bright Sides Minnow (Silver), 101,
    145
Buice, James
    French Broad River, North
        Carolina, 211–212
    Hiawassee River, Tennessee, 212
    Little Tennessee River, North
        Carolina, 210–211
Buzolich, Tony
    Feather and Yuba rivers,
        California, 222
    Russian River, California, 220,
        222

Cahills, 70
California
    Feather and Yuba rivers, 222
    Russian River, 220, 222
Campbell, Arthur, 200
Casting
    back, 118
    Belgium, oval, or elliptical, 107
    distance, 116
    lift-off, 113
    line control, 113–115
    long, 105–106
    need to improve, 152
    safety tips, 117–118
    slack-line, 133
    stealth presentations, 117
    weighted flies, 107–112
Chubs, 63–65, 74
Clouser, Bob, Susquehanna River,
    Pennsylvania, 213–215
Clouser Bright Sides Minnow
    (Silver), 101
Clouser Crayfish, 93–94
Clouser Crippled Minnow, 93, 98,
    145
Clouser Deep Minnows, 74
    Baby Pike, 66
    Baby Sculpin, 83
    Baby Smallmouth Bass, 66, 83, 84
    Baby Walleye, 67, 83, 84
    Black-Nose Dace, 65
    chartreuse and white, 84
    chartreuse and yellow, 84
    colors for, 83–84
    eye size, 84
    Gizzard Shad, 67
    Olive and Tan Sculpin, 59, 84
    Orange and Brown Sculpin, 59
    red and white, 85
    Silver Shiner, 63
    Spring Chub, 64
    Susquehanna Shiner, 62

white, 84
Clouser Drake, 103–104
Clouser EZ Popper, 72, 99, 100,
    101–103
Clouser Floating Minnow, 99–101,
    144
Clouser Foxee Redd Minnow,
    86–87
Clouser Half and Half, 88–89
Clouser Hellgrammites, 72, 95
Clouser Madtom, 60
Clouser Purple Darter, 58, 86
Clouser Super Hair Deep Minnow
    (River Shiner), 84, 85
Clouser Suspender, 96–97
Clouser Swimming Nymph, 72,
    95–96
Clouser Taper, 173
Collins, Ken
    Grand River, Ontario, 202–203
    Maitland River, Ontario,
        203–204
    Saugeen River, Ontario, 204–205
Color, baitfish flies, 83
Crayfish, 68–69
    Clouser Crayfish, 93–94
Crease Flies, 146
Crimping, 170
Crippled Minnow, 93, 98, 145
Cypress Creek, Alabama, 210

Dahlberg, Larry, 77, 98, 145
Dahlberg Diver, 145
Damselflies, 72
Darters, 58, 74
    Clouser Purple Darter, 58, 86
Dead drift
    boat presentations, 135
    retrieval technique, 147, 149
    wading, 134–135
Deceiver, 89

Distance casting, tips for, 116
Divers, 144–145
Dobsonflies, 71–72
Drag, 125–127
Dragonflies, 72
Drake Dun, Clouser Green,
    103–104
Duffy, Dave
    French Broad River, North
        Carolina and Tennessee, 205
    Nolichucky and Toe rivers, North
        Carolina and Tennessee, 205

Eddies, 32–34
Elk Hair Caddis, 98
Elliptical cast, 107
Erwin, Lance, 118
Equipment
    boats, 181–184
    care of, 184, 186–189
    checklist, 189
    flies, 169–172
    leaders, 172, 174
    lines, 173, 176–177
    reels, 181
    rods, 177, 179
EZ Popper, 72, 99, 100, 101–103

Fall, fishing tips, 24–25
Fallfish, 63–65, 74
False casting, 116
Feather River, California, 222
Feed, how bass, 57
Finding fish
    birds and, 52
    bridges, 39–40
    eddies, 32–34
    flats, 47–48
    grass beds, 39
    gravel bars, 46–47
    islands, 40–41, 45–46
    mud streaks, 52
    pools, 42–44
    rocks and ledges, 34–37
    in shade, 48, 50
    sight fishing, 52, 54
    structure, 30–48
    tributaries and other inflows,
        50–52

water depth and, 30
    wood, 40
Flambeau River, Wisconsin, 220
Flats, 47–48
Flies
    See also under name of
    casting weighted, 107–112, 125
    color, 83
    for common baitfish, 74
    debarbing and sharpening, 170,
        172
    imitating baitfish, 79, 81, 83
    selecting, 169–170
    size, 81
    storing, 171, 172
    weedless, 104
    weight, 81, 83
Floating lines, 173
Floating Minnow, 99–101, 144
Fly box, basic tips, 79
Food
    aquatic insects, 69–72
    baitfish, 55–68
    crayfish, 68–69
    damselflies and dragonflies, 72
    darters, 58, 74
    dobsonflies, 71–72
    frogs, 72
    gizzard shad, 66–68
    juvenile gamefish, 66, 74
    madtoms (stonecats), 60, 74
    mice, 72, 75
    minnows, 61–65, 74
    other critters, 72, 65
    sculpins, 59, 74
Foxee Redd Minnow, 86–87
French Broad River, North Carolina
    and Tennessee, 205, 211–212
Frogs, 72
Full-sinking lines, 176
Fur Strip Clouser, 91–92

Gapen, Don, 77, 92
Gartside, Jack, 98
Gizzard shad, 66–68
Gorman, John, 5
Grand River, Ontario, 202–203
Grand River Troutfitters, 202
Grass beds, 39
Gravel bars, 46–47

Guide to Aquatic Trout Foods
    (Whitlock), 79
Gurgler, 98

Habitat, 4–5
    See also Finding fish
Half and Half, 88–89
Handling fish, 10–11
Hayes, David, 5
Hellgrammites, 71–72
    Clouser Hellgrammites, 72, 95
Henshall, James A., 1–2, 72
Henshall Bug, 72
Hiawassee River, Tennessee, 212
High-stick nymphing technique,
    134
Hipps, Anthony
    James River, Virginia, 208, 210
    New River, North Carolina and
        Virginia, 206–208
    Northwest Alabama Creeks, 210
    Uhwarrie River, North Carolina,
        206

Indicators, use of, 132
International Game Fish Association
    (IGFA), 4, 5
Islands, finding fish around, 40–41,
    45–46

James River, Virginia, 196, 208, 210,
    212
Jitterbug bass fly, 142
John Day River: Drift and Historical
    Guide (Campbell), 200
John Day River, Oregon, 199–200
Juniata River, Pennsylvania, 218–219
Juvenile gamefish, 66, 74

Kraft, Chuck, 196
    New River and James River,
        Virginia, 212
Kreh, Lefty, 52, 69, 77, 88, 97, 136,
    144
    casting tips, 105–107
    James River, Virginia, 196
    Lefty's Bug, 147

Lefty's Deceiver, 89
New River, Virginia and North
    Carolina, 196, 198
Penobscot River, Maine, 198
Potomac River, West Virginia and
    Maryland, 194–196

Lapentor, Roger, 192
    Flambeau River, Wisconsin, 220
    St. Croix River, Wisconsin, 220
    Wisconsin River, Wisconsin, 220
Leader butt
    connecting fly line to, 175
    formulas for rod weights 8 and 9,
        174
Leaders, 172
Ledges, finding fish around, 34–37
Lefty's Bug, 147
Lefty's Deceiver, 89
Leisenring, James, 134
Leisenring Lift, 134–135
Lewis, Gary, 199
Lift-off, 113
Line(s)
    care and storage, 116, 117, 184,
        186
    control, 113–115, 124–130
    floating, 173
    sinking, 173, 176–177
Line Tamer, 116
Little Tennessee River, North
    Carolina, 210–211

Madtoms (stonecats), 60, 74, 91
Maine, Penobscot River, 198
Maitland River, Ontario, 203–204
Maryland, Potomac River, 194–196
May, Steve
    Grand River, Ontario, 202–203
    Maitland River, Ontario,
        203–204
    Saugeen River, Ontario, 204–205
Mayflies, 69, 70
Mend, upstream, 127–129
Mice, 72, 75
Micropterus dolomieu, 1–2
Minnows
    behavior, 81
    black-nose dace, 65, 74

chubs and fallfish, 63–65, 74
shiners, 61–63, 74
Muddler Minnows, 92–93
Mud streaks, finding fish and, 52,
    164–168

New River, Virginia and North
    Carolina, 196, 198, 206–208,
    212
Nolichucky River, North Carolina
    and Tennessee, 205
North Carolina
    French Broad River, 205,
        211–212
    Little Tennessee River, 210–211
    New River, 196, 198, 206–208,
        212
    Nolichucky and Toe rivers, 205
    Uhwarrie River, 206
Northwest Alabama Creeks, 210

O'Brien, Mike, 140
    Susquehanna River (West
        Branch), Pennsylvania,
        215–217
Ontario, Canada
    Grand River, 202–203
    Maitland River, 203–204
    Saugeen River, 204–205
Oregon
    John Day River, 199–200
    Umpqua River, 199
Oval cast, 107

Pencil Popper, 103, 144
Pennsylvania
    Juniata River, 218–219
    Susquehanna River, 213–215
    West Branch of the Susquehanna,
        215–217
Penobscot River, Maine, 198
Pools, 42–44
Pop and drift, 147
Pop and stop, 147
Popovics, Bob, 118
Poppers
    Clouser EZ, 72, 99, 100, 101–103
    cupped face, 144

flat face, 144
Pencil, 103, 144
Potomac River, West Virginia and
    Maryland, 194–196
Presentations
    bottom-bouncing techniques,
        132–133
    changing tactics, 149
    dead drift boat, 135
    dead drift wading, 134–135
    drag, 125–127
    getting into position, 119–124
    line control, 124–130
    retrieves, 130, 146–149
    slow-drop technique, 140
    stealth, 117
    streamer, 136–142
    streamer while boating, 141
    streamer while wading, 140–141
    subsurface, 130–135
    surface, 142–143, 146
    Susquehanna Strip, 136
    upstream mend, 127–129
Purple Darter, 58, 86

Randolph, John
    John Day River, Oregon,
        199–200
    Umpqua River, Oregon, 199
    White River, Vermont, 200–201
Range, 4
Rapala lures, 146
Red and White Hackle (Seaducer),
    97–98
Reels, 181, 186–187
Retrieves, 130, 146
    dead drift, 147, 149
    pop and drift, 147
    pop and stop, 147
    skating, 149
    steady, 147
    strip and pause, 147
RIO Products, 173
Riseforms, 160
River Shiner (Clouser Super Hair
    Deep Minnow), 84, 85
Rocks, finding fish around, 34–37
Rods, 177, 179, 184, 186
Russian River, California, 220, 222

Safety, 117–118
St. Croix River, Wisconsin, 220
St. Croix Rod Co., 179
Saugeen River, Ontario, 204–205
Sculpins, 59, 74
Seaducer (Red and White Hackle), 97–98
Senses, 9, 12
Shade, finding fish in, 48, 50
Shadows, avoiding, 121–122
Shiners, 61–63, 74, 81
Shooting heads, 176
Shumaker, Brian, Juniata River, Pennsylvania, 218–219
Sight fishing, 52, 54
Sinking lines, 173, 176–177
Size
    of baitfish, 81
    of smallmouth bass, 4, 5
Skating retrieve, 149
Slack-line cast, 133
Slow-drop technique, 140
Smallmouth bass
    classification, 1–2
    features, 3–4
Sneaky Pete, 145
Spawning behavior, 5, 8–9
Spring, fishing tips, 14–17
Stimulator, 145
Stonecats, 60, 74
Streamer, 136–142
    while boating, 141–142
    while wading, 140–141
Strip and pause, 147
Stripping basket, 116, 125
Structure, 30–48
Subsurface presentation, 130–135
Sulphurs, 70
Summer, fishing tips, 18–23
Super Hair Deep Minnow (River Shiner), 84, 85

Surface presentations, 142, 146
Suspender, 96–97
Susquehanna River, Pennsylvania, 213–215
    West Branch, 215–217
Susquehanna Strip, 136
Swimming Nymph, 72, 95–96

Tackle. See Equipment
Tennessee
    French Broad River, 205, 211–212
    Hiawassee River, 212
    Nolichucky and Toe rivers, 205
Toe River, North Carolina and Tennessee, 205
Tributaries and other inflows, finding fish in, 50–52
Trophy, catching a
    casting, need to improve, 152
    flies, using the appropriate, 156–157
    locating fish, 157–159
    mud streaks, use of, 164–168
    patience, role of, 161
    planning for, 154
    riseforms, use of, 160
    stealthy, being, 161
    timing and temperature, role of, 162–163
    water rise, use of, 164
Trophy, what is a, 151
Troth, Al, 77, 93, 98

Uhwarrie River, North Carolina, 206
Umpqua River, Oregon, 199
Upstream mend, 127–129

Vermont, White River, 200–201
Vests, 187
Virginia
    James River, 196, 208, 210, 212
    New River, 196, 198, 206–208, 212

Waders, 187
Wading
    dead drift, 134–135
    streamer presentation while, 140–141
Water rise, use of, 164
Water temperature, use of, 162–163
Weedless flies, 104
Weight, baitfish flies, 81, 83
Weighted flies, casting, 107–112, 125
West Virginia, Potomac River, 194–196
Whiteflies (white miller), 69–70
White River, Vermont, 200–201
White Wulff, 104
Whitlock, Dave, 77, 79
Whitlock's Damsel, 72
Winter, fishing tips, 26–27
Wisconsin
    Flambeau River, 220
    St. Croix River, 220
    Wisconsin River, 220
Wisconsin River, Wisconsin, 220
Wood, finding fish around, 40
Woolly Buggers, 72, 93
Wulff, Lee, 177

Yuba River, California, 222

Zonkers, 92